San Francisco Sidewalk

Offline Restaurant Guide

San Francisco Sidewalk
Offline Restaurant Guide

A comprehensive guide to
Bay Area dining, presented
by the producers of
San Francisco Sidewalk

Edited by Meesha Halm

Co-published by:

sidewalk.com

SASQUATCH BOOKS
SEATTLE

ISSN 1096-2727

Editor: Meesha Halm
Associate editors: Tanya Henry and Chris Borris
Lead copy editors: Joseph Lasica, Mark Hedin, Anna Tokumoto, Dana Dubinsky
Cover design: Kristen Wurz
Interior design: Phil Kovacevich
Interior composition: Kate Basart
Cover photograph: © 1997 Richard Burbridge
Interior photographs: Michael Persson and Victor Fisher. Page ii, Andrea Russotto of Attica Trattoria (Michael Persson); page xii, Alain Rondelli of Alain Rondelli (Michael Persson); page 232, Hiroshi Tanabe of Restaurant Aya (Michael Persson); page 278, Michael Savvides (Michael Persson); page 298, wine glass (Victor Fisher).
Maps: Juliana Pennington, JXP Graphic Design. San Francisco neighborhood base source map: ©1996 Magellan Geographix, Santa Barbara, CA

San Francisco Sidewalk Offline Restaurant Guide is a print companion to the Web site http://sanfrancisco.sidewalk.com/, one of Microsoft's personalized online guides to city entertainment. Evaluations found within this book are based on reports gathered by a team of San Francisco-based writers. Reviewers always dine anonymously and never accept free meals, beverages or other services. Readers are advised that as in any region, restaurants close, relocate or change management. Therefore, all information found in this edition is subject to change. For the most up-to-date information on restaurants in the Bay Area, readers are advised to check the Web site.

Sidewalk Offline Restaurant Guides are co-published and distributed by:
Sasquatch Books
615 Second Ave.
Seattle, WA 98104
(800) 775-0817
e-mail: books@sasquatchbooks.com
Web: http://www.sasquatchbooks.com
Distributed in Canada by Raincoast Books Ltd.

Sasquatch Books publishes high-quality adult nonfiction and children's books related to the Northwest (Alaska to San Francisco). For more information about Sasquatch Books titles, write to the above address, or view the Sasquatch Books site on the World Wide Web.

Contents

Introduction

The Bay Area, birthplace of California cuisine, has long played a leading role in defining our nation's dining trends. Since the culinary revolution that emerged from Berkeley in the '70s, Northern California chefs have forged an imaginative blend of locally grown ingredients and cooking techniques with origins from around the globe. The flavors may sound exotic, but they reflect the everyday influences of the European, Asian and Latin American communities that make the Bay Area their home.

As a result, eating out in the city is usually an adventurous and exciting experience. With more than 3,000 ethnically diverse restaurants to choose from, the task of deciding where to eat often poses a bit of a quandary. That's exactly where San Francisco Sidewalk comes in: Our goal is to foster selectivity about and insight into the booming restaurant scene, to enable you to make the best decisions about where, when and how to spend your money. Our constantly growing database contains thousands of detailed restaurant reviews that are searchable in a variety of ways, including neighborhood, cuisine type, noise level and quality rating.

We at San Francisco Sidewalk realize, however, that it's not always possible to get online to check out the Bay Area's most comprehensive entertainment guide. So we selected 550 of the Bay Area's most popular restaurants from our Web site and compiled them into this handy, easy-to-use guide for those times when you can't get to a computer. (Hence the name, the **Offline Restaurant Guide**.) Within the pages of this book, you'll find the same in-the-know reviews that those who use sanfrancisco.sidewalk.com have come to trust. And just as you can search our Web site in a variety of ways, the **Offline Guide** features extensive indexes to help you find exactly what you're looking for or discover something totally new.

Whether you're looking at our reviews online or offline, we at San Francisco Sidewalk appreciate your feedback. On page xi, you'll find details on how to get in touch with us about the book or our Web site. Comments from our readers help build our strong database and inform our reviewers. We encourage readers to contact us, and we do our best to reply to everyone.

Bon Appetit.
Meesha Halm
Restaurant Producer, San Francisco Sidewalk
sf_restaurants@sanfrancisco.sidewalk.com

Acknowledgments

A book of this proportion could not have come together without the contributions of many talented and devoted people, in particular the local food writers who tirelessly ate their way through the Bay Area. Special thanks to Tanya Henry, associate restaurant producer; Chris Borris, associate producer; Don Wilcox, production coordinator; Pam Takahama, business manager; Joseph Lasica, copy chief; Mark Hedin, Anna Tokumoto, Dana Dubinsky, and Randy Alfred, copy editors; Kristen Wurz, designer; Beth Cataldo, executive producer; Kevin Wueste, general manager; and the staff at Sasquatch Books, especially Chad Haight, publisher, and Stephanie Irving, editor.

How to Use This Book

For the purposes of creating a pocket-size book, we've limited the restaurants to the best in the area (at press time). The reviews in this book represent only a portion of what is available on sanfrancisco.sidewalk. com. Our Web site offers restaurant coverage from as far south as San Mateo County to as far north as Napa and Sonoma. So if you're looking for a particular place and don't find it in the book, odds are that you'll find it there. For more on the site, see page x.

All San Francisco Sidewalk restaurant reviews are based on personal visits by our team of professional writers. Our reviewers always dine incognito and never accept free meals. We understand that above all, we're consumer reporters, telling others how to best spend their dining dollars. If our reviews or ratings sometimes seem tough, it's because we would rather err on the side of being more critical than have our readers spend their money only to be disappointed.

Star Rating System

Readers should use stars as a guide only. Star ratings are based on the quality of food, ambience, service, consistency and overall experience. All restaurants are measured against the same scale, and fewer stars do not necessarily indicate that a restaurant is not worth a visit. Half-stars are awarded in ratings where warranted.

NR	**Has not been critically rated**
No stars	**Poor**
★☆☆☆	**Fair**
★★☆☆	**Good**
★★★☆	**Excellent**
★★★★	**Outstanding, world class**

Price Range

We keep price guidelines as specific as possible, but many restaurants teeter on the edge of one category or another. Please remember that prices are subject to change, especially if a restaurant alters its menu. All prices reflect the cost of a single entree or an individual meal and don't include tax, tip or alcohol.

NR	**Has not been rated for price**
$$$$$	**$7 and under**
$$$$$	**$7-$15**
$$$$$	**$15-$20**
$$$$$	**$20-$25**
$$$$$	**$25 and over**

Key to Symbols

Some entries have been flagged with special symbols:

Good deal — Sidewalk's pick for quality and value.

Good for groups — A restaurant fit for large groups—usually with plenty of large tables or with food served family-style.

Kid friendly — A good place to take children; offers a special kid's menu.

Romantic — A good place for couples; romantically lit, nice views, quiet, intimate.

Sidewalk's choice — The Sidewalk staff's favorite restaurants, from diners to fine-dining spots.

Credit Cards and Checks

We have abbreviated the names for accepted credit cards. American Express is identified as AE, Carte Blanche as CB, Discover as D, Diners Club as DC, MasterCard as MC and Visa as V. A notation of "checks" means that a restaurant may accept a local check with proper identification.

Disclaimer

All of our reviews are based on information that was fact-checked at press time. Please note that menus may change, chefs may leave and restaurants may go out of business. The most up-to-date information can be found at sanfrancisco.sidewalk.com. We re-review restaurants regularly there, in some cases as often as every four months. Since this book is just a snapshot of a continually changing Web site, reviews and star ratings listed here may be different from those listed at sanfrancisco.sidewalk.com. We encourage you to visit the site regularly.

How to Use Our Site

The Web is a fluid medium, so the look of the sanfrancisco.sidewalk.com site may change. However, here are some basic guidelines.

Using San Francisco Sidewalk to search for a restaurant is almost as simple as flipping the pages of this book. If you have online access and a Web browser (such as Internet Explorer), simply type in the address http://sanfrancisco.sidewalk.com/ You will reach what we call the home page. From there, click on the Restaurants icon at top left. On the Restaurants page, at top right, you'll see the "Fast restaurant finder." Click on the first box and pick a cuisine, or type a restaurant name in the second box. Then hit the "Go" button. Or, click on "Find a restaurant" to get a page with a series of what we call "finders."

The finders let you search for a specific restaurant or find a list in a particular neighborhood, price range, star rating or cuisine type, or something special such as a romantic or kid-friendly place. Make your choices and then hit the "Go" button.

All of the guidelines, icons and categories in this book are the same as on the site, so if you're familiar with the book, you'll feel right at home on Sidewalk.

Send Us Feedback

Have a comment, complaint, update or suggestion? We encourage all book readers and Web site users to send feedback. Getting in touch with us is easy. You can reach us in any one of the following ways:

Mail:
San Francisco Sidewalk Restaurants
Microsoft
585 Howard St.
San Francisco, CA 94105

E-mail:
sf_restaurants@sanfrancisco.com

Fax:
(415) 547-4343
(include "Attn: Restaurants")

Want to be an armchair reviewer? Tell us about your local dining experiences and get your opinions published on our Web site. Describe the food, service and overall experience along with the date of your visit. Please be sure to include a daytime phone number with all correspondence so that we can contact you. We ask that individuals associated with food-related establishments please identify themselves as such when making comments.

sanfrancisco.sidewalk.com

Go experience something . . .

San Francisco

Reviews and neighborhood maps

Chinatown/ North Beach

Civic Center/Hayes Valley

1 Backflip
2 Bistro Clovis
3 Cafe Majestic
4 Caffe Delle Stelle
5 Caffe Trinity
6 Carta
7 Eliza's
8 Fina Estampa
9 Flipper's
10 Hayes and Vine Wine Bar

11 Hayes Street Grill
12 Indigo Restaurant
13 Jardiniere
14 La Jiao
15 Lalita
16 Max's Opera Cafe
17 Millennium
18 Moishe's Pippic
19 Powell's Place
20 Stars
21 Suppenküche
22 Thai Bar-B-Q
23 Vicolo Pizzeria
24 Vivande Ristorante
25 Zuni Cafe

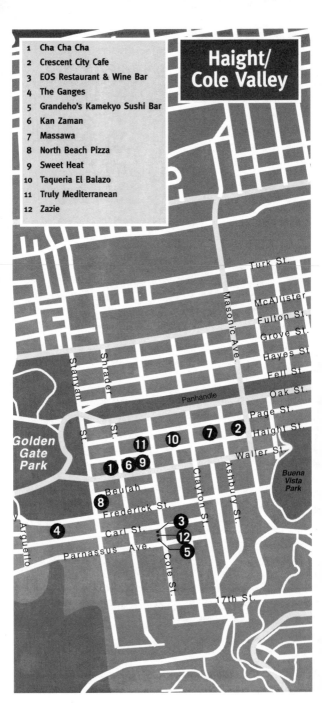

1   Cha Cha Cha
2   Crescent City Cafe
3   EOS Restaurant & Wine Bar
4   The Ganges
5   Grandeho's Kamekyo Sushi Bar
6   Kan Zaman
7   Massawa
8   North Beach Pizza
9   Sweet Heat
10 Taqueria El Balazo
11 Truly Mediterranean
12 Zazie

Haight/Cole Valley

Lower Haight/Fillmore/Japan Center

1 Brother-in-Law's Bar-B-Que
2 Gourmet Carousel
3 Kate's Kitchen
4 King Jamaican Restaurant
5 Indian Oven
6 Isuzu
7 Kushi Tsuru
8 Maki Restaurant
9 The Meetinghouse
10 Mifune
11 Now and Zen Bistro
12 Sanppo
13 Seoul Garden
14 Spaghetti Western
15 Sushi-A
16 Thep Phanom
17 Ya Halla From Nadia
18 Yoyo Bistro

Marina

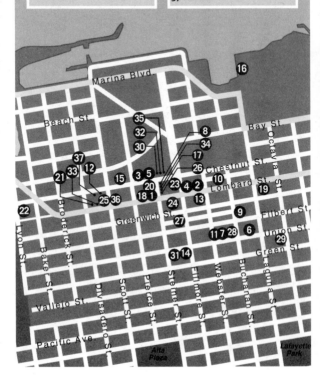

Mission/Bernal Heights

1 Angkor Borei
2 Bangkok 16
3 Bruno's
4 Chava's Mexican Restaurant
5 El Valenciano
6 Esperpento
7 Fina Estampa
8 Firecracker
9 Flying Saucer
10 Herbivore
11 Hungarian Sausage Factory & Bistro
12 La Cumbre Taqueria
13 La Taqueria
14 La Traviata
15 Liberty Cafe
16 Mangiafuoco
17 Moa Room
18 Mom Is Cooking
19 Moxie Bar & Restaurant
20 North Beach Pizza
21 Pad Thai Restaurant
22 Pancho Villa Taqueria
23 Pauline's Pizza Pie
24 Picaro
25 Rasoi
26 Red Balloon
27 Roosevelt Tamale Parlor
28 Saigon Saigon
29 Slow Club
30 Taqueria Cancun

31 Taqueria Cancun
32 Taqueria San Jose 1
33 Taqueria San Jose 2
34 Ti Couz
35 Timo's
36 Truly Mediterranean
37 Universal Cafe
38 Val 21
39 We Be Sushi
40 We Be Sushi
41 Woodward's Garden
42 Yuet Lee

approx. 2 mi. south 18
approx. 1.5 mi. south 20

Dubose Ave.
Market St.
14th St.
15th St.
16th St.
Dolores St.
Guerrero St.
Valencia St.
Mission St.
17th St.
18th St.
19th St.
20th St.
21st St.
22nd St.
23rd St.
24th St.
25th St.
26th St.
Cesar Chavez (Army) St.
Precita Ave.
Cortland Ave.

Franklin Square
Mariposa St.
Shotwell St.
South Van Ness Ave.
Folsom St.
Harrison St.
Bryant St.
Florida St.
Hampshire St.
York St.

Noe St.
Sanchez St.
Church St.
Mission Dolores Park

San Jose Ave.
Bartlett St.
Mission Street
Wool St.
Andover
Bernal Heights

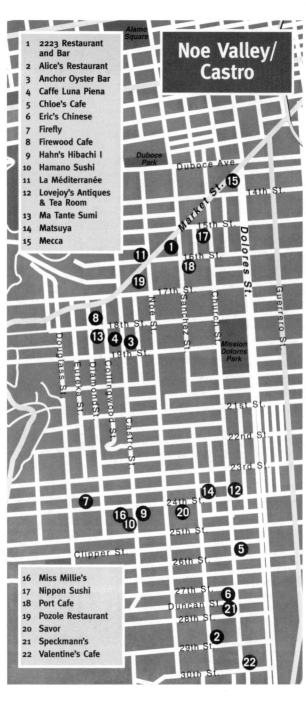

Noe Valley/ Castro

1 2223 Restaurant and Bar
2 Alice's Restaurant
3 Anchor Oyster Bar
4 Caffe Luna Piena
5 Chloe's Cafe
6 Eric's Chinese
7 Firefly
8 Firewood Cafe
9 Hahn's Hibachi I
10 Hamano Sushi
11 La Méditerranée
12 Lovejoy's Antiques & Tea Room
13 Ma Tante Sumi
14 Matsuya
15 Mecca

16 Miss Millie's
17 Nippon Sushi
18 Port Cafe
19 Pozole Restaurant
20 Savor
21 Speckmann's
22 Valentine's Cafe

Alamo Square
Duboce Park
Duboce Ave.
Market St.
14th St.
15th St.
16th St.
17th St.
Noe St.
Sanchez St.
Church St.
Dolores St.
Guerrero St.
Mission Dolores Park
18th St.
Douglass St.
Diamond St.
Collingwood St.
Eureka St.
19th St.
Castro St.
21st St.
22nd St.
23rd St.
24th St.
25th St.
Clipper St.
26th St.
27th St.
Duncan St.
28th St.
29th St.
30th St.

Pacific Heights

1 Alta Plaza Restaurant and Bar
2 Baker Street Bistro
3 Cafe Kati
4 The Elite Café
5 Ella's
6 Food Inc.
7 Garibaldi's
8 Godzila
9 Jackson Fillmore
10 La Méditerranée
11 Osome
12 Pane e Vino
13 Rassellas
14 Ten-Ichi
15 Vivande Porta Via
16 Yoshida-Ya

Chestnut St.
Lombard St.
Greenwich St.
Filbert St.
Union St.
Green St.
Broderick St.
Lyon St.
Baker St.
Scott St.
Divisadero St.
Pierce St.
Steiner St.
Fillmore St.
Webster St.
Buchanan St.
Laguna St.
Vallejo St.
Pacific Ave.
Jackson St.
Washington St.
Clay St.
Sacramento St.
California St.
Pine St.
Bush St.
Sutter St.
Post St.
O'Farrell St.
Presidio Ave.
Lyon St.
Geary Expressway

Alta Plaza

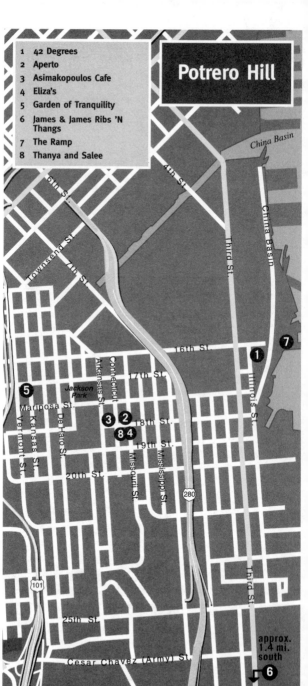

1 42 Degrees
2 Aperto
3 Asimakopoulos Cafe
4 Eliza's
5 Garden of Tranquility
6 James & James Ribs 'N Thangs
7 The Ramp
8 Thanya and Salee

Potrero Hill

China Basin

China Basin

4th St.

16th St.

6th St.

Townsend St.

7th St.

Third St.

Illinois St.

17th St.

Connecticut St.

Arkansas St.

Jackson Park

Mariposa St.

De Haro St.

Kansas St.

Vermont St.

18th St.

19th St.

20th St.

Missouri St.

Mississippi St.

280

Third St.

101

25th St.

Cesar Chavez (Army) St.

approx.
1.4 mi.
south

Russian Hill/ Nob Hill

1 Acquerello
2 Allegro
3 Antica Trattoria
4 Aromi
5 Burma's House Restaurant
6 Cafe Mozart
7 Charles Nob Hill
8 Coconut Grove Supper Club
9 Crustacean
10 The Dining Room
11 Emerald Garden
12 Fournou's Ovens
13 Frascati Restaurant
14 Golden Turtle
15 Grazie 2000
16 Hahn's Hibachi II
17 Harris'
18 House of Prime Rib
19 Hyde Street Bistro
20 Hyde Street Seafood House and Raw Bar
21 I Fratelli
22 Johnny Love's
23 La Folie
24 Maharani
25 Mario's Bohemian Cigar Store Cafe
26 Matterhorn
27 Maye's Original Oyster House
28 Nob Hill Cafe
29 Polker's Gourmet Burgers
30 Ristorante Milano
31 Rocco's Seafood Grill
32 Sushi Groove
33 Swan Oyster Depot
34 The Terrace
35 Venticello Ristorante
36 Yabbies Coastal Kitchen
37 Zarzuela

Richmond District

1 Alain Rondelli
2 Angkor Wat Cambodian Restaurant
3 Bangkok Cafe
4 Bella Trattoria
5 Blue Point
6 Brother's Restaurant
7 Cafe de Young
8 Cafe Maisonnette
9 Cafe Riggio
10 Chapeau!
11 Chiang Mai Thai
12 Coriya Hot Pot City
13 Dragon River
14 El Mansour
15 Fountain Court
16 Good Luck Dim Sum
17 Hong Kong Flower Lounge
18 Hong Kong Villa
19 Jakarta Indonesian
20 Kabuto Sushi Restaurant
21 Kasra Persian & Mediterranean Cuisine
22 Katia's
23 Khan Toke Thai House
24 Kuk Jea
25 La Bergerie
26 La Vie
27 Laghi
28 Le Soleil
29 Mandalay Restaurant
30 Mayflower Restaurant
31 Mel's Drive-In
32 Mescolanza
33 Mike's Chinese
34 Murasaki Sushi
35 Narai

Sunset District

1 Ambrosia Bakery
2 Avenue 9
3 Cafe for all Seasons
4 Casa Aguila
5 Chevy's Fresh Mex
6 Crepevine
7 Ebisu
8 Hong Kong Seafood Restaurant
9 Jeong Hyun Charcoal Barbecue House

Golden Gate Park

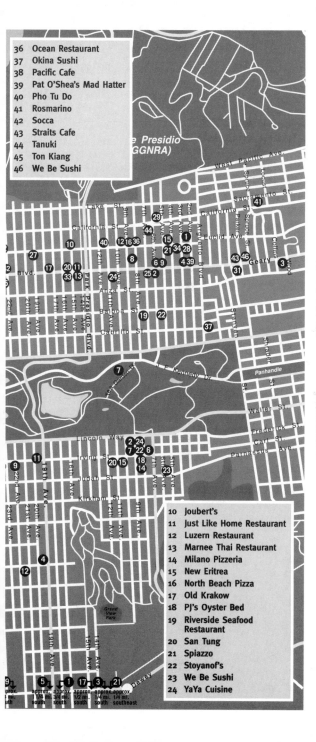

Presidio
(GGNRA)

South of Market

1. Appam
2. Basil
3. Bizou
4. Butterfield's Seafood
5. Caffe Museo
6. Cha-Am
7. Chevy's Fresh Mex
8. Delancey Street Restaurant
9. Elroy's
10. The Fly Trap
11. Fringale
12. Gordon Biersch Brewery Restaurant
13. Hamburger Mary's
14. Harry Denton's
15. Hawthorne Lane
16. Henry's Hunan Restaurant
17. Infusion
18. Jessie's
19. Kiss
20. Le Charm
21. LongLife Noodle Co. and Jook Joint
22. Manora's Thai Cuisine
23. Max's Diner
24. Max's Eatz
25. Max's Eatz
26. Palomino Euro-Bistro
27. Pazzia Ristorante e Pizzeria
28. Pier 40 Roastery & Cafe
29. Restaurant LuLu
30. Ristorante Ecco
31. Ristorante Umbria
32. South Park Cafe
33. Thirsty Bear Brewing Company
34. Town's End Restaurant & Bakery
35. Tu Lan
36. Vino e Cucina
37. Wu Kong Restaurant
38. Yank Sing

★★★☆
$$$$$

2223 Restaurant and Bar
Castro/Noe Valley: 2223 Market St.
(between Sanchez and Noe); 415-431-0692

California

 Good
for groups

Better known as the "No Name," Cypress Club owner
John Cunin's popular, often packed upscale restaurant with its brick-red painted exterior and lively hip-
ster crowd was the first in the neighborhood to offer
serious food and a happening bar scene. The terrific
American fare includes winning pizzas, fresh spinach
salad with seasonal fruit and candied walnuts for
appetizers, and generous portions of comfort food,
from roast chicken served with garlic mashed potatoes to grilled salmon with potato-chive pancakes
and Meyer lemon-caviar fondue. The long bar dominating one side of the restaurant's modern, narrow
interior serves great martinis and cosmopolitans, but
the noise level can be distracting.

Lunch/dinner daily; MC, V.

★★★☆
$$$☆☆

42 Degrees
Potrero Hill: 235 16th St. (at Illinois);
415-777-5558

Mediterranean

 Sidewalk's
choice

 Good
for groups

Tucked behind the Esprit outlet, 42 Degrees is pop-
ular with a relentlessly hip crowd of young profes-
sionals, but at night, candlelight transforms the stark,
industrial-chic space into an enchanting supper club.
Chef/owner James Moffat (partner in the Slow Club)
creates a changing menu of Mediterranean-influ-
enced food: watercress salad with duck confit, wal-
nuts and pomegranates; risotto with fava beans; or
grilled king salmon with spring onions. For dessert,
try the sublime chocolate pot de crème. Wine takes a
back seat to scotches, ports and cognacs. Live music
nightly and an inviting patio area make this a good
place to linger.

Lunch Monday-Friday, dinner Wednesday-
Sunday; outdoor seating; view; live entertain-
ment; full bar; smoke-free; free parking; MC, V.

A. Sabella's Restaurant

**North Beach: 2766 Taylor St. (at Jefferson);
415-771-6775**

Seafood

Good
for groups

Though touristy, this large, family-owned seafood restaurant on the wharf has been in business for more than 75 years, so they must be doing something right. A. Sabella's dishes out a mean clam chowder and maintains a 1,000-gallon saltwater tank harboring live Dungeness crab, abalone and Maine lobster, which appear in such standard, pricey dishes as crab cioppino and lobster thermidor. Go for the simpler preparations, and you won't be disappointed. The great views make this a prime place to watch the sunset. A piano player performs nightly, and the adjoining lounge area features a live mystery-theater dinner on Friday and Saturday.

*Lunch/dinner daily; live entertainment; full bar;
fireplace; view; valet parking; major credit cards.*

Ace Wasabi's
Rock-n-Roll Sushi

**Marina: 3339 Steiner St. (between
Lombard and Chestnut); 415-567-4903**

Sushi

Good
deal

Packed nightly with the Marina's don't-hate-me-because-I'm-beautiful crowd, Ace Wasabi's (formerly Flying Kamikazes) offers colorful twists on the standard sushi menu. Those bored with tradition will welcome the innovative combination rolls such as the rainbow Three Amigos roll (tuna, yellowtail, eel, avocado and cucumber, topped with wasabi and tobiko) and the Rock & Roll, prepared with cooked eel. The julienned vegetable salad and the calamari appetizer (thin, deliciously flavored slices of squid) are also recommended. During peak hours, service can be excruciatingly slow, but the staff is friendly and the atmosphere fun, so nobody seems to mind.

Dinner nightly; major credit cards.

Acquerello

★★★☆
$$$$$

Nob Hill: 1722 Sacramento St. (between Polk and Van Ness); 415-567-5432

Italian

Sidewalk's choice

Good for groups

Acquerello offers stellar, contemporary regional Italian cooking in a tranquil, refined setting that was formerly a chapel. The small menu changes often, but expect elegant starters such as beef carpaccio with hearts of palm and black truffles or triangular ravioli filled with swordfish in a light tomato-caper sauce. The delicate, beautifully presented entrees might include grilled quail with fresh oranges and sage, or fillet of beef topped with a vegetable red wine sauce. Try such knockout desserts as chocolate cloud cake with pralines or warm zabaglione scented with orange muscat. Though pricey, the complex selection of chic Italian and well-chosen California wines is impressive.

Dinner Tuesday-Saturday; quiet; free parking lot; major credit cards, checks.

Akiko's Sushi Bar

★★★☆
$$$$$

Downtown: 542 Mason St. (between Post and Sutter); 415-989-8218

Sushi

Good deal

Just off Union Square but worlds apart from the bustle, Akiko's Sushi Bar is tucked into a tiny space that seats four couples comfortably. A find among the pricier restaurants is the area, this unassuming, friendly spot is a good place for a cheap sushi fix. The sushi selection is standard but very fresh: yellowtail, tuna, fried eel, California roll, soft-shell crab hand roll, and uni (sea urchin) for the daring. Savory udon dishes round out the menu. The service and decor isn't much, but with prices this low, who can complain?

Dinner Monday-Saturday; MC, V.

Alain Rondelli

★★★★
$$$$$

Richmond: 126 Clement St. (between 2nd
and 3rd Aves.); 415-387-0408

French/
California

Sidewalk's choice

Romantic

Owner/Chef Rondelli's softly lit restaurant lined with
forest-green wood shutters quickly became a favorite
of the city's culinary cognoscenti. One nibble of the
foie gras and patrons start to swoon. The entrees blend
California ingredients with French technique: organic
white veal wrapped with bacon and rosemary served
with potato-caper puree; lobster drizzled with orange-
and-anise broth served with fresh fava beans. Offering
a diverse choice of wines by the glass, and two pages
of California and French selections, the understated
wine list is a study in class. Rondelli will create mul-
ticourse meals for everyone at your table for a fixed
fee per person.

*Dinner Tuesday-Sunday; prix fixe menu; full bar;
valet parking; MC, V.*

Albona Ristorante Istriano

★★★★
$$$$$

North Beach: 545 Francisco St. (between
Taylor and Mason); 415-441-1040

Italian

Sidewalk's choice

When you arrive at Albona, Northern California's only
Istrian restaurant, convivial owner Bruno Viscovi is
there to greet you as his personal guest. Istria, a
peninsula in the north Adriatic Sea, adopted both
the flavors of Italy and the Eastern spices that flowed
through its shipping ports, resulting in a uniquely
blended cuisine with memorable dishes such as
house-made ravioli stuffed with raisins and pine nuts,
and braised rabbit with juniper berries and brown
sugar. Most of the dishes, such as pan-fried gnocchi
in a flavorful sauce of chopped sirloin, are made from
his mother's recipes.

*Dinner Tuesday-Saturday; free valet parking;
major credit cards, checks.*

★★★☆
$$$$$

Alegrias Food From Spain

Marina: 2018 Lombard St. (between Webster and Fillmore); 415-929-8888

Spanish

 Sidewalk's choice

 Good deal

 Romantic

 Good for groups

Alegrias' Spanish and Argentine staff warmly welcome you to this colorful, inviting restaurant, where some two dozen varieties of hot and cold tapas are served. Chef/owner Cesar Faedi has also created an authentic main-course menu, highlighted by three versions of paella. Alegrias (Spanish for "joy") has a magical decor that enhances the dining experience: hand-painted ceramics on the wall, terra-cotta flower boxes, tiny white lights strung along a trellis, and a Moorish-style carved wood panel at the entrance. On Friday nights, patrons are serenaded with Spanish guitar music, and on Saturday, a spirited flamenco dancer performs.

Lunch Thursday-Sunday; dinner nightly; live entertainment; AE, MC, V.

★★★☆
$$$$$

Alice's Restaurant

Noe Valley: 1599 Sanchez St. (at 29th St.); 415-282-8999

Chinese

Good deal

The latest addition to the collection of upscale Chinese restaurants, Alice's joins the trend started by Eric's and Eliza's. The attentive service, open, airy space with sun pouring in, and brightly colored interior add up to a wonderfully comfortable experience. The small menu specializes in beautifully presented Hunan and Mandarin cuisine, but also boasts a few California-influenced dishes such as chicken with endive and sunflower seeds. While Alice's features lovely serving plates, an unusual glass art collection and an astonishing array of blooming orchids, the food is a bargain; lunch specials, served with soup and rice, are about $4.

Lunch/dinner daily; quiet; MC, V.

★★☆☆
**$$$**$$

Allegro
Russian Hill: 1701 Jones St. (at Broadway); 415-928-4002

Italian

Ebullient owner Angelo Quaranta runs the show at this petite Russian Hill restaurant, popular with politicos and their old-money constituents. Quaranta's secret is high-quality Italian comfort food at reasonable prices. The bruschetta is always good, followed by the house specialty, *pollo al Mattone* (a seasoned half-chicken grilled under a brick), or gnocchi. Everything, from sauces to pastas, is made fresh and cooked to order, which explains the long wait for entrees. End your meal with a piece of the fabulous tiramisu and Allegro's strong espresso zested with a twist of lemon. If possible, request the lone window table for maximum intimacy.

Dinner nightly; valet parking; full bar; AE, MC, V.

★★☆☆
**$$$**$$

Alta Plaza Restaurant and Bar
Pacific Heights: 2301 Fillmore St. (at Clay); 415-922-1444

Mediterranean

 Good for groups

This airy, split-level restaurant is popular with well-heeled locals, while after dinner the bar becomes a beacon for a mostly-gay singles crowd. Chef Amey Shaw's Mediterranean-inspired menu changes frequently, though favored items might include roasted lamb riblets with a spicy mustard sauce or braised artichokes with Italian proscuitto as starters, and a lemon chicken prepared with pine nuts, chard and wine-soaked yellow raisins for an entree. The excellent wine list is mostly California, and evocative descriptions make it fun and informative. Live jazz combos play Sunday to Thursday. When the DJ takes over on weekend nights, the bar stays busy late.

Dinner nightly; live entertainment; full bar with daily happy hour; AE, MC, V.

★★★☆
$$$$$

Ambrosia Bakery

Sunset: 2605 Ocean Ave. (between 19th Ave. and Junipero Serra Blvd.); 415-334-5305

Bakery

Good deal

Gorgeous cakes, buttery pastries, and inexpensive soups, salads and sandwiches attract a steady stream of visitors to this charming bakery and cafe. If you can make it past the dessert display, you'll find a small counter that doles out delicious sandwiches, then add a big house-baked cookie to your order (the favorite is sour cream, with a filling of brown sugar, cinnamon and walnut). Classical music wafts through the spotless, marble-trimmed dining room. Stern Grove, site of numerous free concerts and plays, is down the street; Ambrosia is the perfect place to get picnic items on the way.

Breakfast/lunch/afternoon tea daily; checks.

★★★☆
$$$$$

Anchor Oyster Bar

Castro: 579 Castro St. (between 18th and 19th Sts.); 415-431-3990

Raw bar

At this tiny, no-frills joint, regulars slip in for a half-dozen oysters on the half shell or a bowl of delicious New England clam chowder. Although the seafood is fresh, the food is pedestrian. Service is cheery and prompt; sit at the long Formica counter, and you'll often get a conversation. Several kinds of oysters are shucked daily—you can also buy a batch in the shell to go. If you do eat in, try Anchor's famous oyster shooter: an oyster tossed into a shot glass with Bloody Mary mix, Worcestershire sauce, Tabasco, and a squeeze of lemon. Bottoms up!

Lunch Monday-Saturday, dinner nightly; D, MC, V.

★★★★
$$$$$

Andale Taqueria

Marina: 2150 Chestnut St. (between Steiner and Pierce); 415-749-0506

Mexican

Good deal

A profusion of nondescript taquerias has sprung up recently, but this one heads the crowd, with its very good Cal-Mex fare and atmosphere. An adobe-style fireplace with Mexican tiles warms the inside and the outside patio. Indoors, palms sprout from a huge copper planter, and two brightly painted murals overlook the room. You might catch the lively staff singing along to the Gipsy Kings as it cooks chicken and beef on the mesquite grill. Wash down this healthy food with a thirst-quenching fresh fruit juice, or treat yourself to the house special, a margarita made with wine.

Lunch/dinner daily; outdoor seating; fireplace; full bar; cash only.

★★★★
$$$$$

Angkor Borei

Mission: 3471 Mission St. (at Cortland); 415-550-8417

Cambodian

Good deal

Despite its downtrodden location, Angkor Borei has attracted a following who brave the neighborhood for some of the finest Cambodian food in town. Start with crispy spring rolls or the excellent rendition of Cambodian crepes, filled with shrimp, pork, tofu, shredded coconut and bean sprouts and served with ground peanuts and a lemon-garlic sauce. The coveted curry dishes come in five savory variations; try the red-chicken plate of tender chicken strips in a light, spicy red-curry sauce with bamboo shoots and green beans. For dessert, order the mango slices with black sticky rice or the crispy fried banana fritters with coconut ice cream.

Lunch Monday-Saturday, dinner nightly; AE, D, MC, V.

★★★★
$$$$$

Angkor Wat Cambodian Restaurant

Richmond: 4217 Geary Blvd. (between 6th and 7th Aves.): 415-221-7887

Cambodian

Sidewalk's choice

Good for groups

For years, Angkor Wat has been winning kudos for its unique preparations of Cambodian cuisine (rumors are that Pope John Paul II asked for seconds here). Start with the Cambodian crepe, or the *samlaw kor ko* soup (diced green papaya, egglant, pumpkin and other vegetables simmered in a light lemongrass, turmeric and kaffir-lime leaf broth). For your entree, consider the pan-fried five-spice shark with ground peanuts, chiles and basil, or the lamb curry. The decor is pleasant, with antique Cambodian artwork, a glassed-in garden, and a small stage where the Cambodian Royal Ballet performs on Friday and Saturday nights.

Lunch/dinner daily; live entertainment; full bar; AE, MC, V.

★★★★
$$$$$

Anjou

Downtown: 44 Campton Place (off Stockton; between Sutter and Post); 415-392-5373

French

Good deal

Anjou's hidden location hasn't stopped *Conde Nast Traveler*, *Gourmet*, *Esquire* and *The New York Times* from singing its praises. This charming bistro, with exposed brick walls and modern-art posters, provides an attractive, somewhat cramped setting for the flavorful, well-prepared food. The menu features classic French fare but veers into more adventurous territory with dishes such as grilled chicken marinated with honey, curry and nutmeg, and galantine of Peking duck. Homemade desserts include a magnificent warm chestnut torte with pear coulis and a sinful chocolate truffle with crème de menthe sauce. The three-course lunch special is a particularly good value.

Lunch/dinner Tuesday-Saturday; full bar; major credit cards.

★★★☆
$$$$$

Antica Trattoria

**Russian Hill: 2400 Polk St. (at Union);
415-928-5797**

Italian

Sidewalk's choice

Romantic

Good
deal

When Antica Trattoria opened in 1996, the neighborhood was abuzz with talk of chef Ruggero Gadaldi's superb Italian fare. The menu changes regularly, but appetizers might include puree of potato and vegetable soup, or slices of beef carpaccio enhanced with capers, arugula, mustard and Parmesan shavings. Main dishes might include a savory monkfish wrapped in pancetta, potatoes and wild mushrooms, or a perfectly grilled pork tenderloin with gorgonzola, crispy pancetta and polenta. Service is attentive, and the restaurant offers a nice wine list, dominated by Italian wines at affordable prices. This small, simply decorated restaurant may become known as one of the city's best trattorias.

Dinner Tuesday-Sunday; MC, V.

★★★☆
$$$$$

Aperto

**Potrero Hill: 1434 18th St. (between
Connecticut and Missouri); 415-252-1625**

Italian

This neighborhood Italian restaurant serves a changing menu of wonderful pastas, superior roast chicken topped with preserved lemon, and a warm chocolate soufflé cake that's worth the splurge in calories. Try the quill-shaped pasta with cumin-roasted eggplant, tomato and chèvre, or the popular spinach and ricotta tortellini with pistachio, pancetta and sun-dried tomatoes. The dining room is a bit cramped and the wait for a table can be lengthy, but you'll forget that with a glass of good Italian wine and a basket of terrific house-made focaccia.

Lunch/dinner daily; weekend brunch; reservations not accepted; AE, DC, MC, V, checks.

Appam

★★★☆
$$$$$

South of Market: 1261 Folsom St. (between 8th and 9th Sts.); 415-626-2798

Indian

 Romantic

Among the city's top Indian restaurants, Appam offers reliably good food at fair prices. The appetizers are perfect, particularly the flaky samosas filled with spiced potatoes and peas. The specialty is *dum pukht*, curried meats and vegetables cooked in a clay pot; the tandoori dishes are also highly recommended, and be sure to order nan with your meal. The dining room features murals of Indian temple dancers and ancient landscapes, a curved mahogany bar and a blue-tiled open kitchen; best is the garden patio, with its intricately tiled fountain. Several good draft beers and a full bar are available for Appam's club-hopping SoMa clientele.

Dinner nightly; outdoor seating; full bar; major credit cards.

Aqua

★★★☆
$$$$$

Downtown: 252 California St. (between Front and Battery); 415-956-9662

French

 Sidewalk's choice

 Romantic

 Good for groups

Chef Michael Mina's exquisitely presented creations served in a sleek, opulent setting make Aqua one of the most creative seafood restaurants around. You might begin with a savory mussel soufflé or roasted spot prawns stuffed with crab, followed by Hawaiian swordfish au poivre with pancetta-wrapped shrimp dumplings or the signature seared ahi tuna with foie gras. A few nonseafood entrees are available, and a five-course vegetarian tasting menu is offered alongside the regular six-course sampler. Dessert highlights include warm lemon tartlets, blueberry brioche charlottes and soufflés. The wine list is impressive, though prices are staggering.

Lunch weekdays, dinner Monday-Saturday; pre-theater menu; valet parking; AE, D, MC, V.

Ar Roi

Nob Hill: 643 Post St. (between Taylor and Jones); 415-771-5146

Thai

Good deal

Kid friendly

With a friendly staff and competent kitchen that dishes out complex, flavorful Thai cuisine, this art deco-inspired outpost is a cut above others in the neighborhood. Start with *tom ka gai* (a velvety concoction of coconut milk, chicken, mushrooms, tomatoes, lemongrass and lime juice), golden-fried chicken wings with chili sauce and fresh basil, or the spicy chicken salad. Other good bets are tiger prawns served with peanut sauce and sautéed spinach, or eggplant sautéed with chili sauce, fresh garlic and basil. Round out your meal with an order of pan-fried sticky noodles or fragrant jasmine rice.

Lunch Monday-Saturday, dinner nightly; MC, V.

★★★★
$$$$$

Aromi

Nob Hill: 1507 Polk St. (between California and Sacramento); 415-775-5977

Italian

Romantic

Hearty, flavorful Northern Italian food has been Aromi's m.o. since it opened, drawing a young, fairly upscale clientele to its smart, casual setting with heated front patio overlooking the street. Head chef Pedro Mercado's gnocchi, bathed in a light cream sauce with wild mushrooms, is excellent. Entrees on the seasonally changing menu range from linguini and prawns in a fresh tomato sauce to roast lamb shank or roast duck in a fig sauce. Try the warm chocolate budino, a soufflé-like cake that melts in your mouth. Have it with an espresso, or paired with an aperitif in the adjacent cocktail lounge.

Lunch/dinner Sunday-Thursday, dinner only Friday-Saturday; outdoor seating; late-night bar; valet parking; major credit cards.

★★★★
$$$$$

Asimakopoulos Cafe

Potrero Hill: 288 Connecticut St. (at 18th St.); 415-552-8789

Greek

One of San Francisco's only Greek restaurants, Asimakopoulos Cafe attracts lots of loyal locals and the occasional outlander with its gallons of retsina wine and a relaxed taverna atmosphere. The food is sometimes quite good, other times barely mediocre. The spanakopita is consistently good, as is the creamy hummus with warm pita bread and the smoky mixed souvlakia grill. But some lamb dishes come out dry and sinewy when they be moist and tender. Service is as understated as the decor.

Lunch/dinner daily; loud; live entertainment; reservations not accepted; AE, MC, V.

★★★★
$$$$$

Avenue 9

Sunset: 1243 9th Ave. (between Irving and Lincoln); 415-664-6999

California

Word is spreading quickly about this sophisticated, reasonable little bistro. Exposed pipes, hand-blown light fixtures, gray tile flooring, and energetic tones of orange and yellow complement an eclectic menu that's sprinkled with proper nouns: Star Route Farms mesclun greens are mixed with Maytag Blue cheese, pears and glazed walnuts. The Petaluma duck breast comes with chile pudding and wild mushrooms; grilled lamb ribs arrive via Atkins Ranch; even the Niman Schell burger is topped with Vermont white cheddar. Desserts—such as the gingerbread cake with caramelized walnuts—get raves as well. Beer comes microbrewed, and the wine list is unorthodox: "Rhone Rangers" share space with "Italian Stallions."

Lunch/dinner daily, weekend brunch; live entertainment; major credit cards.

★★☆☆
**$$**$$

Babaloo Tapas

Marina: 2030 Lombard St. (between Fillmore and Webster); 415-346-5474

Cuban

Good deal

Kid friendly

Babaloo, with its colorful, lively dining room throbbing to the beat of thumping Latin tunes, puts a Cuban twist on tapas. The tapas menu is more adventurous and better-executed than the regular one, although it has some winning dishes as well, including an outstanding asadero cheese turnover served with sweet red pepper sauce, shrimp in garlic and roasted paprika sauce, and mashed-potato fritters filled with Spanish cheddar and cured ham. Wash down your meal with fruit-garnished sangria or one of 16 draft microbrews from the conga-shaped bar overlooking the dining room.

Dinner nightly; loud; AE, DC, MC, V.

★★☆☆
**$$**$$

Backflip

Civic Center: 601 Eddy St. (at Larkin); 415-771-3547

Eclectic

Good for groups

Drenched in a sea of blue and aqua, trendy, retro Backflip—billed as a "cocktail lounge serving cocktail cuisine"—has been attracting a fashionable crowd since it opened. Dine inside in a private cabana amid Vegas-style fountains, or outside next to the pool. The dim sum-style food (literally served off carts) is a blend of cultural influences. Popular items include the two-bite burger, star anise-crusted ahi sashimi and oven-roasted flaming mussels. Try anything smoked—the kitchen has its own cold smoker. Swank desserts (chocolate espresso mouse served in a martini glass), ports and sweet wines grace the dessert menu. Backflip sits inside the funky Phoenix Hotel, an anomaly in this seedy neighborhood.

Dinner Tuesday-Sunday; late-night dining; outdoor seating; full bar; AE, MC, V.

★★★★
$$$$$

Baker Street Bistro

Pacific Heights: 2953 Baker St. (between Lombard and Greenwich); 415-931-1475

French

Sidewalk's choice

Good for groups

Small, privately owned, unobtrusive and inexpensive enough to dine at regularly, Baker Street Bistro is the quintessential neighborhood restaurant, serving strictly French bistro fare: Sonoma rabbit in a light Dijon sauce, snails over angel hair pasta and the standard steak with lemon butter and potatoes. You can also opt for a prix fixe meal. The service is welcoming and the small selection of French and California wines, moderately priced. You'll invariably meet chef Jacques Manuera (who opened the bistro in 1991), who'll ask how everything is. You'll reply, "Everything's wonderful." And it usually is.

Lunch/dinner daily; outdoor seating; prix fixe menu; MC, V, checks.

★★★★
$$$$$

Bangkok 16

Mission: 3214 16th St. (between Guerrero and Dolores); 415-431-5838

Thai

This small, quirky restaurant sports an eclectic interior decorated with Thai art and miniature silver disco balls, gracious service and a surprisingly extensive menu, including numerous vegetarian options and an appetizer list boasting 20 choices. The *pad thai* is only average, but the grilled meats are superb and the *po-plah tod* are among the best imperial rolls available. The kitchen prepares a terrific rendition of *tom ga gai* (chicken-lemongrass soup in coconut milk) and some wonderful red curries.

Dinner nightly; quiet; AE, MC, V.

★★★★
$$$$$

Bangkok Cafe

Richmond: 2845 Geary Blvd. (between Collins and Wood); 415-346-8821

Thai

This small Thai eatery in the neighborhood just north of USF fills up with Thai-food fanatics who know about the cafe's superb dishes, including the Rice in Clay Pot—a four-course meal in a bowl, laden with barbecued pork, fish cakes, Chinese sausage, chicken, black mushrooms, sweet peas and carrots, all mixed into ginger-garlic rice and served sizzling hot—or Tofu Long Srong—grilled bean curd mixed with spinach, cabbage, string beans and carrots and topped with a heavenly peanut sauce. The lunch combo is a steal: two entrees served with jasmine rice and soup for $5.95.

Lunch/dinner daily; reservations required for large parties; AE, MC, V.

★★★★
$$$$$

Basil

South of Market: 1175 Folsom St. (between 7th and 8th Sts.); 415-552-8999

Thai

 Good for groups

Winning the award for San Francisco's most attractive Thai restaurant—a softly lit dining area with potted bamboo trees, stylish brown wicker chairs and a wall of glass blocks—Basil presents its food just as artfully, though service can be discombobulated. Some dishes, such as the crispy catfish topped with mushrooms in a spicy curry sauce, the charbroiled Atlantic salmon served over red curry-basil sauce, and the colorful spring rolls, live up to their dazzling presentations, but some of the more adventurous preparations fall flat. Stick to the standard Thai dishes and you should be justly rewarded.

Lunch/dinner daily; full bar; AE, MC, V.

Bella Trattoria

Richmond: 3854 Geary Blvd. (between 2nd and 3rd Aves.); 415-221-0305

Italian

Kid friendly

The film "Big Night" comes to life via Alessandro Iacobelli and Fabrizio Laudati, two congenial gentlemen who have taken a huge gamble by opening this small, charming Italian restaurant in the tourist-free Richmond District. Bella's regular menu offers some superb choices, such as penne al forno and made-to-order risotto, but the key is to order off chef Laudati's specials menu. Or simply take host Iacobelli's advice on whatever's best that night: anything from wild boar tenderloin to pancetta-wrapped monkfish. The addictive bread, baked daily in a wood-burning brick oven, rivals that of the best bakeries.

Dinner nightly; free parking lot; MC, V.

Bepples Pie Shop

Marina: 2142 Chestnut St. (between Pierce and Steiner); 415-931-6226
Marina: 1934 Union St. (between Laguna and Buchanan); 415-931-6225

American

Good deal

If you love pie, you'll love this quaint cafe/bakery, which has been making some of the best pies in the Bay Area since 1974. From cherry, wild boysenberry and chocolate mousse pies to a creamy chicken pie with peas and carrots or Western pie with cubed sirloin and spicy chili sauce, you can buy them by the slice or order the whole thing. A small breakfast and lunch menu is offered, with service at a counter and tables.

Breakfast/lunch/dinner daily; late-night dining; reservations not accepted; checks.

Betelnut Pejiu Wu

★★★★
$$$$$

Marina: 2030 Union St. (between Buchanan and Webster); 415-929-8855

Southeast Asian

 Sidewalk's choice

Good for groups

This sumptuously decorated Asian restaurant and "beerhouse"—styled in sensual colors of red, deep purple and gold—has the decadent feel of a 1930s Shanghai brothel and a pan-Asian menu featuring an array of authentic dishes from Vietnam, Singapore, China, Thailand, Indonesia and Japan. Some dishes get consistent raves, including the spicy coconut chicken with eggplant, lemongrass and basil, and the sun-dried anchovies with peanuts, chiles and garlic. But the green papaya salad gets mixed reviews, and Betelnut's dumplings can be downright disappointing. On weekends the place is packed, the roar of the crowd overwhelming and the competition for tables fierce.

Lunch/dinner daily; loud; outdoor seating; late-night dining; fireplace; full bar; validated parking; CB, DC, D, MC, V.

Bistro Aix

★★★☆
$$$$$

Marina: 3340 Steiner St. (between Chestnut and Lombard); 415-202-0100

California

 Good deal

Jonathan Beard bought this trendy bistro (formerly Caffe Centro), redecorated it, improved the cuisine and wine list, and lowered the prices. A stylish crowd converges for the $10.95 prix fixe menu, which offers a choice of three entrees served with soup or salad and house-made bread. Favorites include the grilled top sirloin with roasted garlic, fries and ratatouille and the fresh fettuccine with seared shrimp, leeks and tomatoes. Other items range from crackercrust pizzas to seared ahi tuna with niçoise salad. The wine list matches the food and the crowd: three-quarters California, with a European flair.

Dinner nightly; outdoor seating; prix fixe menu; AE, MC, V.

★★★☆
$$$$$

Bistro Clovis

Civic Center: 1596 Market St. (at Franklin); 415-864-0231

French

Good
deal

Besides turning out nicely prepared authentic French food, this pleasant and airy restaurant is determined to educate San Franciscans about wines and offers an ever-changing parade of "wine-tasting palettes," three small glasses of different wines from a single region in France, served with a pamphlet explaining their origins and merits. In addition to such French standards as onion soup, salade niçoise or *boeuf bourguignon*, Bistro Clovis takes an imaginative approach to its menu with more unexpected items such as curried pork with bananas and coconut, lamb salad with sun-dried tomatoes and vegetarian terrine with red bell pepper sauce.

Lunch/dinner Monday-Saturday; late-night dining; AE, DC, D, MC, V.

★★★☆
$$$$$

Bix Restaurant

Downtown: 56 Gold St (between Jackson and Pacific, Montgomery and Sansome); 415-433-6300

American

Sidewalk's
choice

Romantic

Hidden down an alleyway, Bix does a convincing impression of a 1930s art deco supper club. The menu features tasty, upscale New American cuisine, and bartenders dispense top-notch martinis and cocktails to a swanky crowd. The food is something of a letdown, but the menu includes some reliably satisfying comfort food: crispy potato pancakes with smoked salmon and caviar, pan-fried chicken cutlet with garlic mashed potatoes, and a grilled pork chop with arugula pesto. The long, adventuresome and expensive wine list concentrates on California boutique wineries. Nightly jazz enhances the milieu; if you want to fit in with the crowd come dressed nicely.

Lunch/dinner daily; loud; late-night dining; live entertainment; full bar; valet parking; all major credit cards.

Bizou

★★★☆
$$$$$

South of Market: 598 4th St. (at Brannan);
415-543-2222

French

Sidewalk's choice

At this lively bistro, chef/owner Loretta Keller (formerly of Stars) seduces even the timid with such exotica as beef cheeks, parsnip chips, salt cod ravioli and house-cured anchovies, winning diners over with her deceptively simple, flavorful, rustic French fare. For the less adventurous, there is a wonderful salad of pear, Gorgonzola, radicchio, frisée and toasted walnuts; scallops with wild mushrooms, endive and balsamic vinegar; and stuffed young chicken with celeriac, grilled apples and goat cheese. Housed in a 1906 building, the restaurant has an updated bistro feel, but the tables are packed together and service can be beastly.

Lunch/dinner Monday-Saturday; loud; full bar; AE, MC, V.

Blue Point

★★★☆
$$$$$

Richmond: 2415 Clement St. (at 25th Ave.);
415-379-9726

Seafood

Sidewalk's choice

Good deal

This sleek and sexy seafood establishment—the creation of owner/chef John Bashton—looks expensive, with its amber-stained mahogany furnishings, textured walls and polished wood floors, but isn't. Dishes such as fresh baked salmon seasoned with white wine and fresh thyme, zesty crab cioppino laden with fresh fish, and excellent rib-eye grilled with rosemary and sautéed onions range from $11 to $14. A wine list offers about three dozen choices. Wonderfully fresh oysters are always available on the half-shell.

Dinner Wednesday-Monday; validated parking; MC, V.

★★★☆
$$$$$

Boulevard

**Embarcadero: 1 Mission St. (at Steuart);
415-543-6084**

American

🏙 Sidewalk's choice

👥 Good for groups

❤ Romantic

Five years after opening her first restaurant, L'Avenue, chef Nancy Oakes teamed up with designer Pat Kuleto to open this gorgeous, bustling eatery. The interior has an art-nouveau-inspired decor, with a domed brick ceiling, pressed tin wainscoting, decorative ironwork and brightly colored mosaic tiles. Oakes' reputation was forged on her innovative New American cuisine; some great dishes on her frequently changing menu include wild mushroom risotto, spicy butternut squash soup and crab and mascarpone ravioli with truffle beurre blanc. The wine list ranks among the city's best for value, depth and sheer individuality. The sumptuous decor, professional service and celebratory atmosphere make Boulevard one of San Francisco's most exciting destination restaurants.

Lunch Sunday-Friday, dinner nightly; loud; view; full bar; valet parking; all major credit cards.

★★☆☆
$$$$$

Brandy Ho's Hunan Food

**North Beach: 217 Columbus Ave.
(at Pacific); 415-788-7527
North Beach: 450 Broadway
(at Montgomery); 415-362-6268**

Chinese

Here you'll find some of the hottest—and maybe best—Hunan food in the city. Do as the regulars do and start with fried dumplings in sweet and sour sauce or cold chicken salad, then venture to the fishball soup, house-smoked duck Hunanese or Three Delicacies—a combo of scallops, shrimp and chicken infused with onion, bell peppers and bamboo shoots. Service can be lackadaisical and the fare is pricier than at some of its competitors, but this is unquestionably one of San Francisco's most popular Chinese restaurants. The Broadway location is slightly more elaborate and sedate, while the

Columbus Avenue location is glitzier, but both feature
black-and-white granite tabletops and loads of neon.

Lunch/dinner daily; loud; AE, DC, D, MC, V.

Brazen Head Restaurant

**Marina: 3166 Buchanan St. (between
Filbert and Greenwich); 415-921-7600**

English

A perennial favorite with couples and older neighborhood folks, this dimly lit, romantic place harks back
to earlier times, with an interior reminiscent of an
English pub and a straightforward menu, featuring a
number of old standbys: roasted garlic and melted
Camembert, French onion soup, Caesar salad, melt-
in-your-mouth filet mignon topped with a Zinfandel
sauce, the Brazen Burger with sautéed onions and
cheese, and even such classics as lamb chops with
mint jelly and chicken Marsala. You'll probably have
to wait for a table, which allows a chance for a pre-
dinner cocktail at the bar.

*Dinner nightly; late-night dining; fireplace; full
bar; reservations not accepted; no credit cards,
cash or ATM cards only.*

Brother's Restaurant

**Richmond: 4128 Geary Blvd. (between 5th
and 6th Aves.); 415-387-7991
Richmond: 4014 Geary Blvd. (at 4th Ave.);
415-668-2028**

Korean

Crowds of Korean expatriates flock to this restaurant-
with-no-ambience for dishes like short ribs, chicken,
squid, beef heart and tripe and their scrumptious side
dishes, mostly marinated vegetables such as
radishes, cucumbers, spinach, bean sprouts and
kimchi—all unlike any you've tasted before. You can
cook your food on your table's grill or have the
kitchen prepare it for you. Popular dishes are the
pork or beef marinade, *jap choe*—a pile of peppery
pan-fried rice noodles mixed with beef and veggies—

and pungent grilled mackerel. There's also a less popular branch a block east on Geary.

Lunch/dinner daily; late-night dining; reservations not accepted; MC, V.

Brother-in-Law's Bar-B-Que

Fillmore/Lower Haight: 705 Divisadero St. (at Grove); 415-931-7427

Barbecue

Sidewalk's choice

When you get a hankering for a big platter of pork ribs, baked beans and corn bread, there's no better place to go than Brother-in-Law's Bar-B-Que. Half or full orders of pork ribs, pork short ends, pork slabs, beef brisket or chicken—all slathered with a rich, tangy house-made sauce—come with coleslaw, spaghetti, barbecue baked beans or a mediocre potato salad; don't pass up the outstanding 35-cent corn muffins or sweet potato pie. Although there are a few dining tables, you might want to get your order to go (dial 931-RIBS).

Lunch/dinner Tuesday-Saturday; late-night dining; reservations not accepted; free parking lot; CB, DC, MC, V.

Bruno's

Mission: 2389 Mission St. (between 19th and 20th Sts.); 415-550-7455

Mediterranean

Sidewalk's choice

Romantic

Good for groups

A former neighborhood Italian restaurant dating back to 1940, Bruno's has been refashioned into a plush supper club serving first-rate food. Chef James Ormsby (of Aqua and Lark Creek Inn) offers a marvelous, frequently changing menu featuring savory soups and salads and wonderful, engaging entrees such as tender braised oxtails served on parsnip-mashed potatoes, and seared scallops with herb gnocchi. The place is perfect for romance, with live music in the sleek main lounge or in the adjoining Cork Club. If you're looking for something unusual, see the monthly Toledo Show, a speakeasy-style cabaret.

Dinner Monday-Saturday; late-night dining; full bar; MC, V.

★★★★
$$$$$

Buca Giovanni Restaurant
North Beach: 800 Greenwich St. (at Mason); 415-776-7766

Italian

Good for groups

As you take a seat in the wine-cellar-like dining room of this strangely charming, warm restaurant, the enticing aroma of big plates of richly sauced Tuscan-style food greets you. The rabbit dishes stand out: roast rabbit with rosemary, rabbit with grappa, fettuccine with smoked rabbit. Other specialties include house-made pastas flavored with organically grown vegetables and fresh herbs, plus an array of well-executed seafood and meat dishes, including the popular roast lamb loin stuffed with mortadella and porcini mushrooms, wrapped in grape leaves. Be sure to start with the excellent calamari salad or radicchio misto.

Dinner Tuesday-Saturday; AE, DC, D, MC, V.

★★★★
$$$$$

Burma's House Restaurant
Nob Hill: 720 Post St. (between Jones and Leavenworth); 415-775-1156

Burmese

Downtown diners in the mood for something different should consider a trek to Burma's House Restaurant for their well-prepared, exotic cuisine. Best bets include an intriguing ginger salad (made with toasted shreds of ginger, fried coconut, shrimp, garlic, green peppers and sesame seeds, all mixed at the table and drizzled with lime juice), smoked duck prepared with Southeast Asian spices and tea leaves, and coconut curried chicken. Cap off your adventure with one of the unusual desserts, such as paluda ice cream (tapioca, coconut juice and paluda syrup, topped with chopped peanuts and vanilla ice cream).

Lunch/dinner daily; MC, V.

Butterfield's Seafood

**South of Market: 202 Townsend St.
(at 3rd St.); 415-281-9001**

Seafood

Romantic

Despite its unlikely location—down the street from the train terminal, sharing space with a seedy corner bar and poolroom—dining at Butterfield's is a surprisingly delightful experience. At lunchtime the room feels like a Boston seafood house, with captain's chairs and snappy waitresses. At dinner, the place turns romantic, with candles flickering gently in wall sconces. The kitchen specializes in well-prepared seafood at moderate prices; start with a plate of succulent Blue Point oysters or homemade chowder, followed by the memorable halibut served on a bed of polenta with a light marinara sauce, topped off with fresh seasonal berry sorbet.

*Lunch/dinner Monday-Saturday; loud; full bar;
free parking lot; AE, DC, MC, V.*

Byblos

**Marina: 1910 Lombard St. (between
Buchanan and Webster); 415-292-5672**

Middle
Eastern

In this unassuming, family-style Lebanese restaurant, chef Labibi Maamari (mother of the owner) prepares more than 30 of her signature mezes. Favorites are the stuffed grape leaves, baba ghanouj (a mixture of eggplant, tahini, lemon juice and garlic) and *labaneh*, a thick, mildly tart yogurt made with mint or dill. Adventurous diners should try the hard-to-find *kibbeh nayeh*, a classic Lebanese dish made of raw lamb or lean beef mixed with onions and assorted spices. If you prefer your meat thoroughly cooked, try one of the well-seasoned lamb entrees or the beef kabobs.

Dinner nightly; AE, MC, V.

Cafe Akimbo

Downtown: 116 Maiden Lane (between Stockton and Grant, Geary and Post); 415-433-2288

Asian

Good for groups

It takes some effort to find this cozy spot, but good, eclectic Asian food will be your reward: spring rolls filled with hot pâté mixed with shiitake and enoki mushrooms and topped with a mango sauce; poached calamari with miso-mustard dressing; and a cucumber salad with a soy-seaweed dressing. The lightly broiled black cod with soybeans and red bell peppers or short ribs in sherry sauce are both good choices. If you just need a quick pick-me-up (or to top off your meal), try any of the fabulous desserts.

Lunch/dinner Monday-Saturday; AE, D, MC, V.

Cafe Bastille

Downtown: 22 Belden St. (between Bush and Pine, Kearny and Montgomery); 415-986-5673

French

Romantic

Good for groups

The always bustling Bastille is like a cozy neighborhood cafe in Paris; a warm, slightly funky interior, and outdoor alleyway seating with white umbrellas and flirtatious waiters make it all the more beguiling. Crepes—both savory and sweet—are the specialty, as are a variety of mussel dishes. You won't go wrong with other typical bistro fare like the pâté with cornichons, roast chicken or the *boudin noir* with sautéed apples. The full bar has a good selection of moderately priced French and California wines. Live jazz combos play Wednesday to Saturday, attracting a boisterous nighttime crowd.

Lunch/dinner Monday-Saturday; outdoor seating; live entertainment; full bar; AE, MC, V.

Cafe Claude

★★★★
$$$$$

French

Downtown: 7 Claude Lane (between
Grant and Kearny, Bush and Sutter);
415-392-3505

At this rigorously authentic Gallic cafe—complete
with zinc bar, banquettes and old movie posters—the
cuisine is classic bistro: onion soup, *croque mon-
sieur*, salade niçoise, cassoulet. Meat lovers will
enjoy the charcuterie platter, and the specials are
always worth a try. A nice selection of reasonably
priced French and California wines is available by
the glass. The waiters are as Gallic as the furnishings, and known to sometimes dish out a little attitude along with the fare. When tables are pulled
outside on balmy evenings, the Parisian sidewalk-
cafe effect is complemented by the live jazz that
wafts through the alley four nights a week.

*Lunch/dinner Monday-Saturday; quiet; outdoor
seating; live entertainment; AE, MC, V.*

Cafe de Paris L'Entrecote

★★★★
$$$$$

French

Marina: 2032 Union St. (between
Buchanan and Webster); 415-931-5006

At this popular Union Street bistro with minimalist
decor and a glassed-in terrace area great for people
watching, a lunchtime crowd comes for the fantastic
chicken and mushroom omelet or the cafe's version
of eggs Benedict, enhanced with grilled steak medallions and green chiles. For dinner, the specialty is
tender, charbroiled New York steak with a secret 12-
ingredient sauce, along with crisp pommes frites and
a side salad. For dessert, try the semi-soufflé chocolate cake. The place livens up on weekend nights,
when an eccentric crowd dressed in Parisian clothes
starts tango dancing and singing at the piano bar.

*Lunch/dinner daily; weekend brunch; outdoor
seating; live entertainment; full bar; valet
parking; AE, MC, V.*

★★★★
$$$$$

Cafe de Young

Sunset: de Young Museum, Tea Garden Drive; 415-752-0116

American

Kid friendly

The de Young Museum's cafe has trimmed its canvas to modest lunches, with some fine results. Go for the small masterpieces: Titian-esque creamy brie and walnut pesto with tomato on a baguette, or mini-muffuletta on a kaiser roll. Main-dish salads change on a regular basis, and are richly aesthetic; a single hot pasta dish is available daily. In the morning, sample one of the cafe's house-made scones or breakfast breads. You order at the counter and lines can be long, but things move swiftly. Weather permitting, bypass the plain indoor area and retreat to the lovely outdoor patio.

Lunch Wednesday-Sunday; outdoor seating; reservations not accepted; MC, V, checks.

★★★★
$$$$$

Cafe for all Seasons

Sunset: 150 West Portal Ave. (between Vicente and 14th Ave.); 415-665-0900

California

Neither dazzling nor disappointing, this popular spot in an airy setting with a bustling open kitchen offers above-average California comfort food. The menu's heavy with salads, light pasta dishes and chicken and seafood plates with a nod to red meat: a well-prepared pork medallion entree, and a burger that's touted as one of the best in town—all reasonably priced and utterly dependable. Desserts are solid as well, and include a heavenly triple-chocolate cake. An ever-popular brunch—eggs, omelets, waffles, salads and chicken breast sandwiches—is served on weekends.

Lunch/dinner daily; weekend brunch; valet parking; AE, MC, V.

Cafe Jacqueline

North Beach: 1454 Grant Ave. (between Green and Union); 415-981-5565

French

This romantic little restaurant serves nothing but soufflés—light and luscious as they come. The changing menu may feature Gruyère cheese, vegetables, seafood, prosciutto or whatever other ingredients French-born Jacqueline Margulis has selected for the evening; if it's on the menu, consider ordering the superb (very garlicky) white-corn, ginger and garlic soufflé. The dessert soufflés, particularly the fresh peach, are truly ethereal. Many people come here just for an after-dinner sweet—a good option if you want to eat right away or don't want to spend much money: The soufflé process is slow, and prices verge on exorbitant.

Dinner Wednesday-Sunday; quiet; AE, MC, V.

Cafe Kati

Pacific Heights: 1963 Sutter St. (between Fillmore and Webster); 415-775-7313

East-West

Hidden away on a residential block, Cafe Kati gets raves for Kirk Webber's weird and wonderful polyglot cuisine, as well as his transforming culinary artistry. Dishes might include goat cheese and portobello mushrooms wrapped in filo, blackthorn cider-marinated tenderloin of pork au jus, with smoky grits and ginger apple chutney, or lobster tacos; don't miss the towering Caesar salad. The wine list is alluring, well-chosen and terrifically priced—perusing is almost as much fun as sipping, with the chef offering witty commentary on each bottle. When making a reservation, request a table in the more appealing front dining room.

Dinner Tuesday-Sunday; reservations required; valet or validated parking; AE, MC, V.

★★★★
$$$$$

Cafe Maisonnette

Richmond: 315 8th Ave. (between Geary and Clement); 415-387-7992

French

Romantic

Smaller than a UPS van, this romantic cafe is nonetheless quite popular. In a dining room that seats fewer than 10 couples, lace curtains and white linen-covered tables offer an immediate sense of intimacy. The French bistro fare usually includes owner/chef Ronald Tseng's longtime specialty, oven-roasted rack of lamb, as well as duck (roasted breast of duckling in a carrot crust), pasta (ravioli stuffed wth brie, pine nuts and roasted garlic) and seafood (fillet of salmon with a mustard-garlic crust), all expertly prepared and reasonably priced. Soups, salads and desserts round out the menu and are equally delicious.

Dinner Tuesday-Sunday; AE, MC, V.

★★★★
$$$$$

Cafe Majestic

Civic Center/Hayes Valley: 1500 Sutter St. (at Gough); 415-776-6400

California

Romantic

Good for groups

Edwardian furnishings, framed mirrors, high ceilings and candlelit tables make this one of San Francisco's most romantic locations. But like most hotel restaurants, Cafe Majestic doesn't take chances with its menu, sticking with such classics as seared ahi, roasted sea bass, grilled lamb chops and filet of beef, often incorporating an Asian accent. Everything is prepared skillfully, however, including the desserts, which might include a pistachio and cardamom crème brûlée with a cinnamon sugar cookie. A classical pianist performs, heightening the restaurant's turn-of-the-century ambience. And the bar itself dates back to mid-19th century Paris.

Breakfast/lunch/dinner daily; Sunday brunch; quiet; live entertainment Friday and Saturday evenings; full bar; reservations required; valet parking; AE, MC, V.

★★★☆
$$$$$

Cafe Marimba

Marina: 2317 Chestnut St. (between Scott and Divisadero); 415-776-1506

Mexican

Good
deal

Good
for groups

Pass through the violet velvet curtains draping the entrance of this always-packed restaurant and you'll be greeted by an explosion of color, a fiery red, 10-foot-tall papier-mache diablo towering above the room, and a dazzling array of folk art. Immediately order chips and guacamole—the best this side of Tijuana. The reasonably priced Oaxacan regional fare includes superb shrimp mojo de ajo, drenched in garlic, chiles and lime; spicy snapper tacos with pineapple salsa and grilled chicken with mild, smoky achiote seed. The one drawback besides the wait is the young and beautiful staff that sometimes doles out lousy service.

Lunch/dinner daily; weekend brunch; loud; late-night dining; full bar; AE, MC, V.

★★★☆
$$$$$

Cafe Metropol

Downtown: 168 Sutter St. (between Kearny and Montgomery); 415-732-7777

Italian

Klaus and Albert Rainer, owners of the popular Hyde Street Bistro, have brought their Austrian-inspired cuisine to this sleekly attractive downtown cafe. Lunch is quick and affordable; the dinner menu is small, but everything is well prepared and delicious. Especially recommended are the warm potato bruschetta; beef, chicken or roasted eggplant quesadillas; roasted salmon with fennel and rosemary potatoes; and the ravioli in a wild mushroom sauce. Desserts are prepared in-house daily—look for the incredibly light white-and-bittersweet-chocolate mousse, fresh-fruit cheesecakes and linzer tortes. Soup and salad combos are available for a low-budget pre-theater option.

Lunch/dinner Monday-Saturday; pre-theater menu; full bar; reservations not accepted; AE, MC, V.

★★★★
$$$$$

Cafe Mozart

Nob Hill: 708 Bush St. (at Powell);
415-391-8480

French/Asian

With its formal, old-world ambience and sumptuous menu, this utterly romantic place is a favorite destination. Asian and European flavors dominate the imaginative menu, which features free-range poultry, organic produce and fresh seafood. Start with the crepes stuffed with shredded duck and leeks in plum sauce or the grilled Polynesian tiger prawns. Both the rib-eye steak in creamy wild mushroom and sherry sauce, and the grilled medallions of beef tenderloin in béarnaise sauce, are outstanding. While the well-priced wine list has a number of French offerings, you'd do best to order a California wine. Skip the tourist-crowded lunch.

Lunch/dinner daily; quiet; fireplace; MC, V.

★★★★
$$$$$

Cafe Riggio

Richmond: 4112 Geary Blvd. (between 5th
and 6th Aves.); 415-221-2114

Italian

Located on busy Geary Boulevard, Cafe Riggio is a handsome, unpretentious restaurant serving a menu of Italian standards, prepared with a light touch at reasonable prices. Appetizers and entrees are consistently well executed. To start, order the house specialty—aged caciocavallo cheese sautéed in olive oil, fresh herbs and garlic. Move on to an oven-roasted whole sea bass with lemon and garlic. For dessert, the tiramisu is fantastic. Service is fast but friendly, and proprietor John Riggio is usually wandering around, making sure everyone is happy. Be prepared for a short wait; reservations are not accepted for small parties.

Dinner nightly; full bar; reservations required for large parties; MC, V.

★★★★
$$$$$

Caffe Delle Stelle

Hayes Valley: 395 Hayes St. (between Gough and Franklin); 415-252-1110

Italian

Good deal

Romantic

Good for groups

This perennial Civic Center favorite serves zesty Italian fare in a trattoria-like setting. Hearty and delicious, the cucina rustica features such dishes as grilled cabbage filled with mozzarella and vegetable-mushroom ragout, cheese ravioli with eggplant and tomatoes, grilled leg of lamb, roasted salmon and an intriguing pumpkin manicotti. Everyone raves about the tiramisu. Even when it gets crowded, the engaging Italian staff manages to keep smiling as it endeavors to get customers out in time for the opening curtain. The quality of the food and service, pleasant setting and proximity to the performing arts center make this one of the area's true bargains.

Lunch/dinner Monday-Saturday; AE, DC, D, MC, V.

★★★★
$$$$$

Caffe Luna Piena

Castro: 558 Castro St. (between 18th and 19th Sts.); 415-621-2566

American/
Mediterranean

Yellow brush-painted walls adorned with local artwork and a lush Japanese garden contribute to the warm, sophisticated dining environment at this restaurant specializing in contemporary American cuisine, with Italian and Mediterranean influences. Notable dishes include roasted vegetable lasagne with sweet-potato sauce and lamb shanks braised in rosemary and garlic and served with soft polenta. Expect to wait in line for the weekend brunch, the best around thanks to the oatmeal-almond French toast, yeast-raised waffles with strawberries and smoked-salmon frittata. Though the wine list lacks depth, it changes regularly and features some excellent choices.

Lunch daily, dinner Tuesday-Sunday; weekend brunch; outdoor seating; live entertainment; AE, MC, V.

Caffe Macaroni

★★★★
$$$$$

North Beach: 59 Columbus Ave. (at Jackson); 415-956-9737

Italian

This tiny, friendly, decidedly funky southern Italian restaurant serves a wide variety of antipasti and is known for its first-rate pasta dishes. The chef has a knack for blending unusual ingredients, and the pasta of the day is typically something out of the ordinary, such as squash ravioli. On the main menu, the spinach-and-cheese ravioli with wild mushroom sauce is outstanding; or consider the daily fish specials and the veal shank. Uniquely organized by texture—light-bodied whites to full-bodied reds—the wine list makes pairing the perfect wine with dinner a snap.

Lunch weekdays, dinner Monday-Saturday; cash only.

Caffe Museo

★★★★
$$$$$

South of Market: 151 3rd St. (between Mission and Howard); 415-357-4500

California

Kid friendly

Run by the folks responsible for Bix, Buckeye Roadhouse and Mustards, this sleek, attractive restaurant within the Museum of Modern Art offers imaginative Cal-Italian cafeteria food to restore museum-goers' flagging spirits. The panini are especially good—chicken with citrus marinade and onion jam or grilled vegetables with arugula and lemon dressing—as are salads, such as saffron rice with rock shrimp and tarragon. In the morning, check out the fresh-baked scones, muffins, sticky buns and homemade granola. Late afternoon, there's an assortment of gelati, sorbets and pastry to give you the energy to tackle one more photography display.

Lunch daily, dinner Thursday-Sunday; closed Wednesday; outdoor seating; reservations not accepted; AE, MC, V.

Caffe Sport

North Beach: 574 Green St. (between Grant and Columbus); 415-981-1251

Italian

Yes, the service is sometimes atrocious at this lively cafe, but in an odd way that's half the fun. But once you dig into owner/chef/artiste Antonio La Tona's huge mounds of garlic-laden pasta or tangy cioppino, most is forgiven. Sicilian folkloric paintings and icons adorn the place, along with hanging hams, fishnets, dolls, mirrors and similar bric-a-brac. You can always spot the first-time customers: They're the ones staring slack-jawed at the walls and getting intimidated by the brusque waitstaff, who won't hesitate to overrule your order with their "suggestions."

Lunch/dinner Tuesday-Saturday; loud; cash only.

Caffe Tiramisu

Downtown: 28 Belden St. (between Bush and Pine, Kearny and Montgomery); 415-421-7044

Italian

On an alleyway littered with bistros, Caffe Tiramisu is one of the best places to enjoy rustic Northern Italian fare in the area. The owners—two amiable brothers from Italy—have created an attractive, modest trattoria featuring a lineup of wonderful food. Appetizers include portobello mushrooms with zucchini and fresh goat cheese and pan-seared ahi tuna with scallops; entrees range from homemade cheese and spinach ravioli with truffle essence to roasted rack of lamb with cabernet sauce and seafood mixed grill. If you have room for dessert, the vanilla bean crème brûlée and frozen white chocolate praline mousse are dynamite choices.

Lunch/dinner Monday-Saturday; outdoor seating; MC, V.

Caffe Trinity

★★★★
$$$$$

Civic Center: 1145 Market St. (between 7th and 8th Sts.); 415-864-3333

Italian

Hidden in an office building across from United Nations Plaza, this small cafe is a surprisingly elegant spot for breakfast and lunch. Settle in behind the counter or at one of the marble-topped tables and take in the lavish mahogany decor, hand-blown-glass light fixtures and striking gilt-framed murals of animals. At breakfast, fortify yourself for the day ahead with a fresh-baked pastry, bagel or bowl of cereal washed down with a steaming bowl of caffe latte or a fruit frappé. For lunch, select from a tasty lineup of homemade soups, focaccia sandwiches and salads.

Breakfast/lunch weekdays; reservations not accepted; cash only.

Campton Place Restaurant

★★★★
$$$$$

Downtown: 340 Stockton St. (between Sutter and Post); 415-955-5555

American

 Sidewalk's choice

 Romantic

 Good for groups

Campton Place pairs a serene, elegant ambience with a kitchen that delights in innovative ideas. The food under current chef Todd Humphries is wonderful—delicious, refined and noteworthy for its subtle marriage of flavors. Starters might include tuna tartare with American caviar and lotus root, carpaccio of beef with shallots and Vietnamese herb salad or a buckwheat blini with caviar and smoked salmon. Entrees range from roasted lobster with corn risotto and truffles to sautéed squab and foie gras with French lentils. Hard-to-find California vintages pepper the extensive wine list, and desserts are decadent. The service is quietly attentive. For a more affordable indulgence, try the three-course prix fixe dinner.

Breakfast/lunch/dinner daily; weekend brunch; live entertainment; prix fixe menu; full bar; valet parking; AE, DC, D, MC, V.

★★★★
$$$$$

Capp's Corner
North Beach: 1600 Powell St. (at Green);
415-989-2589

Italian

Good deal

Good for groups

Kid friendly

One of North Beach's classic Italian restaurants,
Capp's doesn't have great food or service, but the
huge portions, low prices and feel-good atmosphere
keep the crowds coming. Prepare for a wait, and
when you do get a table, be ready to share it. The
herb-roasted leg of lamb is tops; other prix fixe
options include osso buco with polenta and veal
tortellini with sun-dried tomato sauce. Bread, soup,
salad and dessert are included with dinner. Come
with a group and bring some quarters—there's
Sinatra on the jukebox.

*Breakfast/lunch/dinner daily; prix fixe menu;
late-night dining; loud; full bar; validated
parking; major credit cards.*

★★★★
$$$$$

Carnelian Room
Downtown: 555 California St., 52nd floor
(between Kearny and Montgomery);
415-433-7500

American

Romantic

Good for groups

With its brass chandeliers, plush design and
sweeping views, the Carnelian Room can be a very
romantic place. It serves pricey contemporary American food; unless you're on an expense account,
come here strictly for cocktails and hors d'oeuvres. If
you do spring for a meal, expect a competently prepared dish such as smoked sturgeon with caviar-
whipped potatoes or rack of lamb with port wine and
rosemary sauce. Your best bet is to order the nightly,
three-course prix fixe menu. The award-winning wine
list is one of the most extensive in California. Drinks,
especially martinis, are top-notch.

*Dinner Monday-Saturday; Sunday brunch; quiet;
view; prix fixe menu; full bar; jacket and tie
required; valet parking; AE, DC, D, MC, V.*

★★★☆
$$$$$

Carta

Civic Center: 1772 Market St. (between Gough and Octavia); 415-863-3516

Eclectic

 Good for groups

This ambitious restaurant features the cuisine of a different country or culinary region each month, and chef Rob Zaborny (from the Hayes Street Grill) carries out his mission with panache, tackling such far-flung regions as Greece, Russia and India and supplementing his culinary talents with plenty of research. A New England-inspired fall menu featured butternut squash bisque, lobster Newburg, pot roast, a clambake plate and roast turkey. A large and changing selection of wines is offered. Although the dining room is nondescript, the excellent food, moderate prices and friendly service has enchanted a cadre of gastronomic tourists.

Lunch Tuesday-Friday, dinner Tuesday-Sunday; weekend brunch; pre-theater; valet parking; AE, DC, MC, V, checks.

★★★☆
$$$$$

Casa Aguila

Sunset: 1240 Noriega St. (between 19th and 20th Aves.); 415-661-5593

Mexican

 Sidewalk's choice

 Kid friendly

This colorful neighborhood hole-in-the-wall, which draws diners from all over, serves the kind of authentic, imaginative and beautifully presented dishes you'd expect to find only in Mexico. Chef/owner Luis Angeles Hoffman produces an amazingly broad range of dishes, and even the classics on his clever menu are imaginative. Hoffman's *mole poblano* sauce, for instance, includes raisins and dates, while crisp spears of jicama sweeten the fresh lime-marinated *ceviche*. While a bit more expensive than most neighborhood Mexican restaurants, it's worth it.

Lunch/dinner daily; AE, MC, V.

★★★★
$$$$$

Cassis Bistro

Marina: 2120 Greenwich St. (between Fillmore and Webster); 415-292-0770

French

Good deal

Romantic

This charming, affordable restaurant offers a good substitute for a high-priced French vacation. From the outdoor tables and the facade's colorful seacoast mural to the cheery interior with butter-colored walls, copper bar and striped banquettes, it's all reminiscent of the south of France. Once inside, you'll inevitably meet co-owner Bernard Magara, who greets guests with a sincere graciousness. For appetizers, sample the poached oysters drizzled with champagne or the *salade aixoise* tossed with olives, roasted red peppers and pesto. Heartier fare includes fresh spinach ravioli with a garlicky tomato sauce and a lovely lamb stew. If tarte Tatin is on the menu, don't pass it up.

Dinner Tuesday-Saturday; valet parking; checks.

★★★★
$$$$$

Cha Cha Cha

Haight: 1801 Haight St. (at Shrader); 415-386-5758

Caribbean

Sidewalk's choice

This perpetually packed, wildly decorated institution is widely regarded as the best Caribbean restaurant in the city. With sangria this good, hip young locals don't seem to mind the three-pitcher wait for a table on weekends. The eclectic menu has Spanish Caribbean roots, with added influences from Africa, Spain, Louisiana and Brazil. Be sure to check the specials board for the outstanding fish tapas, usually served with fresh fruit salsa. Other stellar offerings include mussels with saffron sauce or the potatoes, shrimp, plantains and calamari; but skip the steak.

Lunch/dinner daily; loud; reservations not accepted; cash only.

★★★★
$$$$$

Cha-Am

**South of Market: 701 Folsom St.
(at 3rd St.); 415-546-9710**

Thai

Following the success of his brother's restaurant in
Berkeley, chef/owner Utid (Gary) Srisawat decided to
open his own branch. Though not yet as good, it
offers innovative, fresh Thai food in a cheery,
modern, comfortable setting. Good starters are the
grilled prawns with a spicy tamarind sauce, superb
soups and terrific beef satay. For something different,
try the salmon curry or sautéed wheat gluten with
chili and garlic sauce. Other popular dishes are marinated sweet-and-sour pork chops and crispy whole
striped bass topped with spicy red curry sauce. Service is friendly and efficient, and prices are surprisingly reasonable.

> *Lunch weekdays, dinner nightly; full bar; vali-
> dated parking; AE, DC, MC, V.*

★★★★
$$$$$

Chapeau!

**Richmond: 1408 Clement St. (at 15th Ave.);
415-750-9787**

French

The decor of this small bistro is both simple and
sophisticated, as is chef Jesse Frost's upscale, well-
crafted fare. Start with the consistently good frisée
salad with lardons and poached egg, followed by flavorful breast of duck sliced over potato gratiné and
topped with wild huckleberry sauce. Other choices
include loin of lamb with roasted garlic and herb
risotto, pan-seared sturgeon with mushroom ragout
and garlic mashed potatoes, and hearty cassoulet.
Service is solicitous and friendly, and there are several prix fixe menu options. Hats off to the well-
edited, affordable wine list, which is evenly split
between France and California.

> *Dinner Tuesday-Sunday; Sunday brunch; loud;
> prix fixe menu; AE, DC, MC, V.*

Charles Nob Hill

★★★★
$$$$$

Nob Hill: 1250 Jones St. (at Clay);
415-771-5400

California

Good
for groups

Chef Ron Siegel, formerly of Yountville's French Laundry, and Aqua chef Michael Mina combine forces in this restaurant, resulting in a sumptuous California menu infused with Gallic influences. A sample tasting menu says it all: puree of wild mushroom soup with scallops, braised artichoke salad, roasted lobster with potato ravioli, thyme-scented lamb chops with risotto, chilled pear soup and warm bittersweet chocolate torte with Gianduia ice cream. The wine list is commensurate with the menu in richness and depth. Decorated with an elegant art deco style, rare woods and silk panels grace the walls, with lavish flower arrangements and discreet lighting softening the effect. This is a worthwhile splurge.

Dinner Tuesday-Sunday; pre-theater menu; prix fixe menu; full bar; valet parking; AE, DC, MC, V.

Chava's Mexican Restaurant

★★★★
$$$$$

Mission: 3248 18th St. (at Shotwell);
415-552-9387

Mexican

Good
deal

Good
for groups

A savvy working-class crowd fills this friendly Mexican restaurant brightened with sombreros, tiled tabletops and colorful paintings. Chava's dishes out superior soups, favorite entrees such as scrambled eggs with onion and tomato plus shredded beef or chorizo, and huevos rancheros. The huge $5.75 combination plates are served with rice, refried beans, homemade corn tortillas still warm from the grill and a choice of enchiladas, crispy tacos, chiles rellenos or tostadas. Two Mexican specialties are offered only on weekends: *menudo*, a spicy beef tripe and hominy soup (touted as the best cure for a hangover) and *birria*, a soupy mutton dish.

Breakfast/lunch/dinner daily; loud; reservations not accepted; cash only.

★★★★
$$$$$

Chevy's Fresh Mex

**South of Market: 150 4th St. (at Howard);
415-543-8060**
**Downtown: 2 Embarcadero Center
(between Sacramento and Clay, Front
and Davis); 415-391-2323**
**Sunset: Stonestown Galleria
Shopping Center (at 19th Ave. and
Winston); 415-665-8705**

Mexican

Good for groups

Kid friendly

Scattered throughout 11 states, Chevy's is a Mexican restaurant chain with a difference: The food is terrific, made with fresh ingredients, including the tortillas. The house specialty is fajitas, with mesquite-grilled chicken, beef, shrimp, fresh fish or vegetables, served on a sizzling iron platter and accompanied by beans, rice, sour cream, guacamole and pico de gallo. At the end of the meal, kids are treated to a complimentary scoop of vanilla ice cream in a deep-fried, sugary tortilla cone. There are numerous locations in the Bay Area, so you'll never be far away from predictably fresh Mexican-American fare.

Lunch/dinner daily; loud; outdoor seating; full bar; validated parking; AE, MC, V.

★★★★
$$$$$

Chez Michel

**Fisherman's Wharf: 804 North Point
(between Hyde and Larkin); 415-775-7036**

French

Romantic

Sophisticated without being pretentious, this sleek new incarnation of owner Michel Elkaim's namesake restaurant lures even locals into touristy Fisherman's Wharf. Elkaim produces an interesting roster of dishes on this classically contemporary French menu. In addition to the standard duck confit and

frisée salad, there's scallop ceviche, salad with crispy sweetbreads, tournedos of lamb shank, and herb ravioli in tomato broth. The extensive wine list overflows with traditional California and French classics at traditional restaurant prices; for budget-busting options, don't forget to check the "special vintages" pages.

Dinner Tuesday-Sunday; full bar; valet parking; MC, V.

★★☆☆
$$$$$

Chiang Mai Thai

Richmond: 5020 Geary Blvd. (between 14th and 15th Aves.); 415-387-1299

Thai

This Thai restaurant stands out from others in the neighborhood with its friendly service and pretty, intimate atmosphere enhanced by a profusion of colorful silk bouquets and elaborately detailed woodwork. In addition to such standard dishes as chicken lemongrass soup and deep-fried pompano, Chiang Mai serves such rarities as barbecued beef topped with chili sauce and vegetables, and skewered chicken and prawns marinated, charbroiled and served with a tangy lemon sauce. For starters, try the mushroom-and-noodle-stuffed chicken wings or the beef salad enlivened with chile and mint.

Lunch weekdays; dinner nightly; AE, MC, V.

★★☆☆
$$$$$

Chloe's Cafe

Noe Valley: 1399 Church St. (at 26th St.); 415-648-4116

Cafe

Good deal

On weekends, many local residents crawl out of bed early to stand in line for brunch at this quaint little corner cafe. Sidewalk tables are coveted, but the tiny interior is pleasant enough. Chloe's creates terrific banana-walnut pancakes, cinnamon croissant French toast and eggs scrambled with vegetables and bacon. The bread is up to Noe Valley standards, as are the home fries and gourmet sausage. Expect good coffee and a small selection of fresh-squeezed juices.

Although breakfast is the big event, Chloe's also serves a decent lunch: Grilled ham sandwiches, chef salads and artichoke lasagne are typical offerings.

Breakfast/lunch daily; loud; outdoor seating; reservations not accepted; checks.

Christophe

Downtown: 405 Mason St. (between Geary and Post); 415-771-6393

French

 Romantic

This comfortable spot, with potted palms, art deco lighting fixtures, Erte prints and large windows draws shoppers and a pre-theater crowd for its contemporary French-influenced Euro-American cuisine. Two prix fixe dinners are offered nightly, which might include seafood custard, Caesar salad, a choice of duck a l'orange, salmon Wellington with tarragon sauce or filet mignon with peppercorn sauce with a luscious profiterole for dessert. The à la carte menu includes crab and corn strudel with Chardonnay sauce, wild mushroom ragout in puffed pastry, a brochette of prawns and artichokes with basmati rice, and the popular herb-encrusted rack of lamb with garlic sauce.

Lunch Wednesday and Saturday, dinner nightly; quiet; pre-theater menu; prix fixe menu; full bar; AE, DC, MC, V.

City of Paris

Downtown: Shannon Court Hotel, 550 Geary St. (between Jones and Taylor); 415-441-4442

French

 Good for groups

Well-prepared bistro classics are the specialty at this boisterous restaurant in the Shannon Court Hotel. The dining room has wonderful art-nouveau touches, such as rod-iron lighting fixtures and lavish murals. The large open kitchen with a huge rotisserie turns out fine renditions of duck confit, lamb sirloin, bouillabaisse and herb-roasted chicken; be sure to order the acclaimed pommes frites as a side. Despite the waitstaff's snotty attitude, City of Paris is a convenient option for a quick, affordable French meal. The large attractive bar area offers a limited bar menu until midnight.

Breakfast/lunch/dinner daily; late-night dining; full bar; validated parking; AE, MC, V.

★★★★
$$$$$

Cityscape

Downtown: San Francisco Hilton, 333 O'Farrell St. (between Mason and Taylor); 415-923-5002

American

 Romantic

Perched high above the city, on the 46th floor of the downtown Hilton, Cityscape offers diners a 360-degree view of San Francisco, a comfortable bar area and a roster of nicely prepared—if predictable—American dishes. Though it attracts well-heeled business travelers, Cityscape's lack of historical cachet and generic decor hold little appeal for locals. The dinner menu emphasizes beef, tried-and-true surf and turf, grilled pork chops with garlic-mashed potatoes, and rotisserie chicken. The bar distinguishes itself with a skylight that opens up for dancing under the stars to DJ-spun pop tunes.

Dinner nightly; weekend brunch; weekday happy hour; view; live entertainment; full bar; all major credit cards.

★★★★
$$$$$

Coconut Grove Supper Club

Nob Hill: 1415 Van Ness Ave. (between Bush and Pine); 415-776-1616

California

 Romantic

 Good for groups

This swanky supper club popular with Willie Brown, Sean Connery and Sylvester Stallone boasts lower prices and a more relaxed dress code since reopening in 1996, but the California-tropical-New Orleans cuisine is as daring as ever: including prawn spring rolls with a mango-chili sauce and whole Thai snapper with sizzling ponzu sauce. However, food is

only half the allure; live bands, mostly jazz and swing, provide dynamite entertainment in this funky room with metal palm trees, white faux-leather booths and two dance floors. After 10 p.m., a different crowd arrives to dance to reggae, R&B, soul and salsa.

Dinner Tuesday-Saturday; loud; live entertainment; late-night dining; full bar; happy hour Tuesday-Thursday; men's jacket encouraged; valet/validated parking; AE, DC, MC, V.

Compass Rose

★★☆☆
$$$$$

Downtown: Westin St. Francis Hotel, 335 Powell St. (between Post and Geary); 415-774-0167

California

 Romantic

With its courtly service and sumptuous, turn-of-the-century decor (fluted columns, ornate ceilings, thick carpets and an eclectic antiques collection), this is a place where ladies wear hats, gentlemen sport ties and cocktail hour means caviar and champagne. From tea time on, the Compass Rose blossoms. The complete tea service includes homemade scones, delicate tea sandwiches, berries topped with whipped cream, petits fours and a choice of teas. An hors d'oeuvres menu designed to complement expertly prepared cocktails is served nightly until 11:30; a pianist or jazz trio is usually on hand to enhance the mood of refined elegance.

Lunch/tea/dinner daily; quiet; live entertainment; prix fixe menu; full bar; valet parking; all major credit cards.

Coriya Hot Pot City

Richmond: 852 Clement St. (between 9th and 10th Aves.); 415-387-7888

Taiwanese

Sidewalk's choice

Good for groups

Kid friendly

Taiwanese hot-pot cooking could become the next culinary rage: cheap, fun, tasty and healthy. At Coriya, you load your tray with raw seafood, beef, pork, poultry, vegetables, eggs and various sauces and condiments, then lug it all back to your table, which has a Japanese hot pot for steaming and a grill for sautéeing. The rest is up to you and your buddy (no single customers); powerful fans under the grill draw off the smoke. Modern Taiwanese music bounces off the mirrored walls, but you can barely hear it over the cacophony of laughter. Finish off your meal with a shaved-ice dessert.

Lunch/dinner daily; loud; late-night dining; MC, V.

Crepevine

Sunset: 624 Irving St. (between 7th and 8th Aves.); 415-681-5858

Creperie

Good deal

Doling out huge portions of inexpensive omelets, pancakes, salads, sandwiches and—of course— crepes of every kind, this is a popular hangout for perpetually broke UCSF students. The offerings here are better than the competition and feature a wide variety of fillings: chicken breast, peanut sauce, grilled eggplant, pine nuts, chipotle peppers, etc., accompanied by sides of potatoes and mixed greens. Best bets are the savory Florentine crepe with spinach, onions and cheddar, and the chocolate and strawberry dessert crepe topped with sweet Chantilly cream. The cafe has an industrial-looking interior with pine floors and copper chandeliers. Service is cafeteria-style.

Breakfast/lunch/dinner daily; late-night dining; reservations required for large parties; checks.

★★★★
$$$$$

Crescent City Cafe

Haight: 1418 Haight St. (between Masonic and Ashbury); 415-863-1374

Cajun/Creole

At this funky little Cajun diner, with New Orleans-style jazz bouncing off walls in dire need of fresh paint, folks come for fiery bowls of Creole gumbo and jambalaya and big plates of Southern fare: fried chicken with mashed potatoes and corn bread, po'boy sandwiches, blackened redfish, roast pork loin with mashed yams. Beginners should try the Crescent City Sampler: gumbo, crab cakes, and red beans and rice—best followed by a slice of cooling key lime pie. Breakfasts—buckwheat pancakes, house-made biscuits and gravy, Creole omelets with a side of grits—are served until 4 p.m.

Breakfast/lunch/dinner daily; loud; reservations not accepted; MC, V.

★★★★
$$$$$

Crustacean

Nob Hill: 1475 Polk St. (at California); 415-776-2722

Seafood

 Good for groups

Started by the younger generation of the family who own Thanh Long—a Vietnamese nook, famous for its giant roasted Dungeness crabs and packed since the '70s,—this vast, modern seafood fantasyland boasts three dining levels, gentle lighting from hand-blown fixtures and colorful maritime murals. Appetizers include delicious satay sticks, spring rolls, juicy grilled tiger prawns and tender calamari stuffed with prawns, mushrooms and onions. But almost everyone comes for the roasted crab and garlic noodles, a salty, finger-licking feast. Don't miss the creamy lemon sorbet served in a lemon-rind cup for dessert. The staff is knowledgeable and genuinely warm.

Lunch Thursday-Sunday, dinner nightly; outdoor seating; full bar; validated parking; AE, DC, D, MC, V.

★★★☆
$$$$$

Cypress Club

Downtown: 500 Jackson St.
(between Columbus and Montgomery);
415-296-8555

American

Good
for groups

Everything in this sumptuous eatery is over the top: bulging copper archways; light fixtures resembling huge sundaes or breasts (you choose); plump burgundy velvet booths and giant urn-like columns. But the food is not to be upstaged, crafting a bold version of New American cuisine, ranging from a "tower" of foie gras, or a sampler of various duck concoctions for starters, followed by entrees such as venison with huckleberry demi-glace or pancetta-wrapped sturgeon. Desserts are equally fabulous. The 20-page wine list is unparalleled—navigating it can be either exhilarating or intimidating (don't be afraid to consult the sommelier). If you're not up to the expensive dinner, stop in at the lively bar to start your evening.

Dinner nightly; loud; late-night dining; live
entertainment; full bar; valet parking; AE, MC, V.

★★★☆
$$$$$

Dalla Torre

North Beach: 1349 Montgomery St.
(at Union); 415-296-1111

Italian

Romantic

One of the top "view" restaurants in the city, dalla Torre is perched atop Telegraph Hill and has drawn kudos both for its elegant interior and satisfying food. Come here on a special occasion and dine in the sumptuous lower room with timbered ceiling, an Italian-style fresco and views of the bay, or the starker, attic-like upper area with sweeping bay views. The menu features dishes like grilled, almond-stuffed quail with black olive risotto and shellfish stew with fennel sausage; several pasta dishes are available as well. This is ideal for a special occasion.

Dinner daily; view; full bar; valet parking; AE,
CB, DC, D, MC, V.

★★★★
$$$$$

David's Delicatessen & Restaurant

**Downtown: 474 Geary St. (at Taylor);
415-771-1600**

Deli

David's, a theater-district institution open since 1952, offers thickly piled sandwiches, matzo ball soup, chicken livers, blintzes and other Jewish-style deli fare. Even if you're not in the mood for beef brisket or a jaw-stretching Reuben, it's hard to resist the call of more than 100 homemade European pastries, ranging from simple Russian tea cakes to a decadence made with five different kinds of chocolate. Sit at the counter, or grab a seat in one of the two dining rooms. Service is friendly and efficient.

Breakfast/lunch/dinner daily; DC, D, MC, V.

★★★★
$$$$$

de Stijl Cafe
**Downtown: 1 Union St. (at Front);
415-291-0808**

Mediterranean

Romantic

Good for groups

Taking his inspiration from the 20th century Dutch art movement, architect/owner Nilus de Matran designed this trendy spot, creating a sleek and sophisticated interior with exposed brick walls, brushstrokes of color, modern art and angular tables and chairs that are deceivingly comfortable. Excellent waffles, granola and steamed eggs with yogurt and fruit are served for breakfast, while the small Mediterranean-inspired lunch menu features spanakopita, spicy lemon chicken kabobs and penne pasta salad with broccoli raab and lemon-chili sauce. The mood is chic and easy, which makes it the darling of the architects and media types who work nearby.

*Breakfast/lunch Monday-Saturday; outdoor
seating; reservations not accepted; checks.*

★★★★
$$$$$

Delancey Street Restaurant

South of Market: 600 Embarcadero (at Brannan); 415-512-5179

American

When eating at this comfortable restaurant by the water, it's for a good cause. Run by the well-respected Delancey Street Foundation, which offers housing, vocational training and work opportunities for recovering substance abusers and ex-convicts, this multicultural restaurant features everything from matzo-ball soup to spanakopita, salmon mousse to meat loaf, plus a variety of spit-roasted meats and low-fat, low-sodium selections. Patrons tend to forgive the drab decor and occasional culinary lapses inevitable with such an ambitious menu; stick to the simpler culinary creations while enjoying the magnificent views of the bay, and you'll leave satisfied.

Lunch/high tea/dinner Tuesday-Sunday; weekend brunch; outdoor seating; view; late-night dining; valet parking; all major credit cards.

★★★★
$$$$$

Des Alpes

North Beach: 32 Broadway (between Stockton and Powell); 415-391-4249

Basque

Open since 1904, Des Alpes is one of the city's few remaining traditional Basque restaurants. Hearty, dirt-cheap seven-course dinners served family-style make this a popular spot for groups. On weekends, dozens of long tables covered with checkered cloths are crammed with boisterous patrons chowing down on platters of meats and huge bowls of soups and stews. The menu changes daily, but if you don't like the entree offered, you can always opt for the more expensive New York steak or lamb chops. Your only other choice is whether to finish dinner with the ice cream included in the tab or pay an extra $2.50 for crème caramel.

Dinner Tuesday-Saturday; prix fixe menu; full bar; MC, V.

★★★★
$$$$$

The Dining Room

Nob Hill: Ritz-Carlton Hotel, 600 Stockton St. (at California); 415-296-7465

French

Few restaurants can spoil you like The Dining Room with its tuxedoed waiters and sumptuous, regal setting of rich brocade, crystal chandeliers and live harp music. Celebrity chef Gary Danko is no longer there, and though Sylvain Portay continues the tradition of using only the finest ingredients, the loss is noticeable: Dishes such as striped bass and fillet of roast Maine lobster were good, but not four-star caliber. A few dishes, however, were outstanding, particularly the crayfish bisque and risotto with butternut squash and roasted squab. The elegantly crafted wine list has remarkably well priced selections. A final touch is the country's only "rolling" cheese cart.

Dinner Monday-Saturday; quiet; late-night dining; prix fixe menu; full bar; live entertainment; jacket and tie required; reservations required; valet parking; all major credit cards.

★★★★
$$$$$

Doidge's

Marina: 2217 Union St. (between Fillmore and Steiner); 415-921-2149

American

 Sidewalk's choice

 Good deal

 Kid friendly

Some say Doidge's serves the best American breakfast in the country—and some Sundays it seems like the whole country is trying to get in. This Union Street nook doesn't look like much: a cozy but tired country theme with cream-colored walls, matching tablecloths and bentwood chairs. But bite into Doidge's famed French toast or eggs Benedict and you're another convert. Other favorites are the eggs Florentine, breakfast casseroles, corned beef hash or any of the gourmet omelets. A special treat for kids (OK, for us, too) is the hot chocolate, which comes in its own little pot.

Breakfast/lunch daily; weekend brunch; loud; MC, V.

★★★★
$$$$$

Dottie's True Blue Cafe

Downtown: 522 Jones St. (between Geary and O'Farrell); 415-885-2767

American

Good deal

Kid friendly

This amiable '50s-style breakfast and lunch joint prides itself on making almost everything from scratch, from generous helpings of the usual diner fare to more esoteric offerings such as pancakes with blueberries and cornmeal or whole-wheat flour, ginger and cinnamon. The revamped menu includes more vegetarian items, such as the popular bean cakes-cum-sausage patties. For lunch, the hamburgers are good, but try the grilled Gruyère and caramelized-onion sandwich. Service is both brisk and friendly, and if you don't see what you want on the menu, just ask—if they have the ingredients, they'll whip it up for you.

Breakfast/lunch daily except Tuesday; reservations not accepted; AE, MC, V.

★★★★
$$$$$

Dragon River

Richmond: 5045 Geary Blvd. (at 15th Ave.); 415-387-6698

Chinese

Good for groups

A small restaurant specializing in Hakkan cuisine, Dragon River is a pleasurable discovery. It specializes in country cooking characterized by abundant servings of slow-cooked, wine-infused dishes without the piquancy associated with many regional Chinese cooking styles. The drab surroundings are soon eclipsed by the quality of the food. A large menu features seafood and fermented rice wine-flavored dishes, such as wine-flavored prawns with pickled greens and pan-fried fish balls. The star is salt-baked chicken—poached in broth, cut into small pieces, then reassembled and served with a ginger-scallion dipping sauce.

Lunch/dinner daily; loud; reservations required for large parties; MC, V.

E&O Trading Company

Downtown: 314 Sutter St. (between Grant and Stockton); 415-693-9136

Southeast
Asian

 Good
for groups

Designed to evoke a turn-of-the-century Asian trader's warehouse, this three-story Southeast Asian grill and brewery opened to great fanfare in 1997. E&O sports an open kitchen and ornate, 35-foot-long "Dragon Bar," and the menu mixes it up, with South Asian flat breads (lamb and potato-mint naan), Indonesian fried rice, Thai seafood curry and flank steak marinated in ginger, sesame and hot pepper. The craft brewery sits on the third floor and on weekends jazz and blues bands play. *Note: The restaurant was too new to review at press time.*

Lunch/dinner daily; valet parking; late-night dining; AE, MC, V.

★★★☆
$$$$$

E'Angelo

Marina: 2234 Chestnut St. (between Pierce and Scott); 415-567-6164

Italian

 Good
deal

 Good
for groups

This perpetually packed, bustling neighborhood restaurant consistently delivers "good as mom's" Italian fare in a funky, narrow dining room, featuring blue-and-white checkered vinyl tablecloths and walls lined with plywood paneling. Recommended entrees include the spinach lasagne layered with a mushroom-chicken-liver sauce (trust us, it's good), the fluffy gnocchi and the flavorful fettuccine carbonara. Side dishes such as roasted potatoes or garlicky sautéed spinach, and the thin-crusted pizzas are also outstanding. As tables for two are tightly crammed next to one another, this fun, kitschy—and noisy—restaurant is better for large parties.

Dinner Tuesday-Sunday; loud; reservations required for large parties; cash only.

Ebisu

★★★ ★
**$$**$$$

Sunset: 1283 9th Ave. (at Irving);
415-566-1770

Japanese

Voted San Francisco's best sushi by several local magazines, Ebisu has earned kudos for serving fabulously fresh fish in a festive environment. Master chefs stand behind the counter, barking out suggestions while doling out free snacks. Good choices are the melt-in-your-mouth *toro*, ruby-red *bonito nigiri* topped with flying fish roe, and *unagi nigiri*, a savory sliver of marinated eel. There's also the usual array of tempura, sukiyaki, and teriyaki entrees. The best seating is in the Japanese-style shoji-screened dining room with tatami mats; but if the wait is long, as it usually is, take whatever you can get.

Lunch/dinner daily; reservations not accepted; AE, CB, DC, MC, V.

El Mansour

★★★ ★
**$$$$**$

Richmond: 3123 Clement St. (between
32nd and 33rd Aves.); 415-751-2312

Moroccan

Decorated like a sultan's tent, with billowing fabrics, bright cushions, tarnished brass antiques and intricately woven rugs, this venerable Moroccan oasis provides a $17.75 five-course culinary adventure (including nightly music and belly dancing). After the ritual hand-washing ceremony, you start with lentil soup, followed by salad. Next comes *bastela*, a fragrant mix of chicken, cinnamon and almonds bundled in a feathery pastry shell. Choose your entree from trays of chicken, lamb, rabbit, squab, prawns and scallops—all accompanied by dishes of prunes, olives and eggplant. End with a cup of mint tea and one of the honey-sweet desserts.

Dinner Tuesday-Sunday; live entertainment; prix fixe menu; AE, DC, D, MC, V.

El Valenciano

Mission: 1153 Valencia St. (between 22nd and 23rd Sts.); 415-826-9561

Spanish

Good for groups

This first-rate Spanish restaurant ranks high among all the others in the neighborhood for its grandiose black-oak bar and huge beautiful dining room. If you want to impress your paella partner with polished wood, stained-glass ceiling lights and dancing, look no further. Seafood and meat paellas—even a delicious vegetarian version—are El Valenciano's specialties; you can see many of the ingredients for the renowned dish sizzling on the chef's grill as you walk in. Great for private parties, the ballroom-size dining room seats up to 100, and there are two smaller dining rooms in the front.

Dinner nightly; live entertainment; full bar; all major credit cards.

The Elite Café

Pacific Heights: 2049 Fillmore St. (between Pine and California); 415-346-8668

Cajun/Creole

Nicknamed "The E-Light" by locals, this busy cafe helped popularize Cajun and Creole food on the West Coast when it opened in 1981. The dark-wood interior, offset by warm peach walls, makes a handsome setting for the sumptuous portions of blackened redfish, Cajun-style filet mignon, and bowls of delicious seafood chowder and thick gumbo. The semiprivate booths are the best, but hard to come by. The small oyster bar offers a lineup of tasty appetizers ranging from shrimp rémoulade and delicately fried calamari to Louisiana crawfish and a variety of oysters.

Dinner nightly; Sunday brunch; loud; full bar; reservations not accepted; AE, DC, D, MC, V.

Eliza's

**Potrero Hill: 1457 18th St. (at Connecticut);
415-648-9999
Hayes Valley: 205 Oak St. (at Gough);
415-621-4819**

Chinese

Sidewalk's choice

Good deal

Good for groups

Kid friendly

When you step into this Chinese restaurant's Hayes Valley locale, the place settings in sunny Mediterranean colors and the Matisse-inspired mural might make you wonder if you've stumbled into a French bistro. But rest assured, chef and owner Ping Sung and his wife offer the same California-influenced Hunan and Mandarin food that made the original Eliza's, on Potrero Hill, such a hit. Start with Rangoon fried crab or unusual celery salad, tossed with carrots and cilantro. Recommended main courses include spicy chicken with fresh basil, king salmon in black bean sauce, and the great meatless mu-shu pancakes. The no-reservation policy means a wait, but that doesn't dissuade loyal patrons. Although somewhat upstaged by her newer Hayes Valley counterpart, the original Eliza's on Potrero Hill still has crowds flocking in for the excellent, innovative California-influenced Chinese food and refined, whimsically decorated atmosphere.

Lunch/dinner Monday-Saturday; Potrero branch open daily; reservations not accepted; MC, V.

Ella's

**Pacific Heights: 500 Presidio Ave.
(at California); 415-441-5669**

American

Sidewalk's choice

Even on the dreariest afternoon, you'll find a line at Ella's, a beloved, simply designed neighborhood restaurant. The secret to its success is the in-house baker, who creates all the breads and pastries. Ella's menus change every few days, but at breakfast, expect poached eggs, pancakes and the best sticky buns in the city. Lunchtime features nice salads, sandwiches on thick bread and specials like carrot soup with mint or rice casserole with rock shrimp, asparagus and lemon. Dinners are more substantial, including beef stew, pan-fried sand dabs and sautéed pork medallions. Weekend brunch is a madhouse.

Breakfast/lunch daily, dinner weekdays; weekend brunch; reservations required for large parties; AE, MC, V, checks.

★★★★
$$$$$

Elroy's

South of Market: 300 Beale St. (at Folsom); 415-882-7989

Southwestern

Good for groups

Fans of the cartoon "The Jetsons" will feel at home in the lunar-planetary decor of this multidimensional restaurant. The downstairs dining room looks like an upscale pub and caters to a Financial District crowd, serving both down-home fare—burgers, wood-fired pizza, outrageously good ribs—and nouveau cuisine, such as the Southwestern-inspired blue-corn salmon and mahi mahi. Go for the ribs. The exclusively California wine list offers stellar standards at reasonable prices. The downstairs bar area is extensive, with a custom menu that includes 13 types of martinis, nine specialty margaritas and 11 varieties of draft beer.

Lunch weekdays, dinner nightly; outdoor seating; view; full bar; valet or free parking lot; AE, DC, MC, V.

★★★★
$$$$$

Emerald Garden

Nob Hill: 1550 California St. (between Polk and Larkin); 415-673-1155

Vietnamese

Good deal

Serving wonderful French-Vietnamese food at reasonable prices, this stylish, little-known jewel of a restaurant is set under a large canvas canopy nestled in an alleyway. On the diverse menu, favorite starters are the excellent golden crepes or the asparagus and crabmeat soup. Main course highlights include the grilled Saigon-style pork chop, wonderful macadamia nut chicken, or the Evil Jungle Prince with Prawns , a provincial recipe of stir-fried prawns with mushrooms, snow peas and lemongrass in chili-coconut sauce. The tropical patio atmosphere is enhanced by live plants, silk palm trees and a scattering of Balinese paintings and Asian sculptures.

Dinner nightly; validated parking; AE, DC, D, MC, V.

★★☆☆
$$$$$

Emporio Armani Express

Downtown: 1 Grant Ave. (between O'Farrell and Market); 415-677-9010

Italian

As elegantly sleek as an Armani suit, this Euro-modern cafe is a little slice of Northern Italy plunked in the middle of the exclusive Armani boutique. Choose from a selection of pizza, panini, pasta and salads as you eye the latest designer creations. Daily specials might include such light and flavorful dishes as spaghettini with calamari in a delicate tomato sauce or broccoli in puff pastry topped with Gruyère and marinara sauce. The white-jacketed waiters don't seem to mind if you just drop in for an espresso and a little dessert (choices include tiramisu, gelato and fresh fruit with Marsala custard).

Lunch daily; loud; outdoor seating; full bar; AE, DC, D, MC, V.

★★☆☆
$$$$$

Enrico's Sidewalk Cafe

North Beach: 504 Broadway (at Kearny); 415-982-6223

California

Sidewalk's choice

This former supper club, which reopened in 1992, is equal parts restaurant, coffeehouse and jazz club, and is immediately recognizable by its Parisian-style outdoor patio, where a hodgepodge of writers, businesspeople and tourists sip well-mixed drinks or nosh on the restaurant's inventive entrees and tapas. The food is good, particularly the grilled tri-tip with fried onions and ginger chutney, and the rosemary-cured pork chop with polenta and fig chutney. The best-seller is the Niman Schell hamburger on focaccia. A solid wine list featuring obscure, high-quality European wines completes the picture. Inside, there's live jazz nightly.

Lunch/dinner daily; loud; outdoor seating; view; late-night dining; live entertainment; full bar; valet parking; AE, DC, MC, V.

★★★★
$$$$$

EOS Restaurant & Wine Bar

Cole Valley: 901 Cole St. (at Carl); 415-566-3063

East-West

 Sidewalk's choice

 Romantic

One of the most talked-about new restaurants, EOS is drawing diners to Cole Valley with chef Arnold Wong's brilliant East-meets-West fusion cuisine. Formerly of Masa's and Silks, Wong has taken the art of arrangement to a new level. Though it seems a desecration to dig in, any hesitancy will disappear with one taste of the amazing food, particularly the tender breast of Peking duck smoked in ginger peach tea leaves, the almond-encrusted soft-shell crab, or the blackened Asian catfish. For dessert, don't miss the unique bananamisu. Stark decor amplifies the nightly cacophony, so nix any idea of a quiet dinner. Afterward, adjourn to the restaurant's popular, globally stocked wine bar.

Dinner nightly; loud; AE, MC, V.

★★★★
$$$$$

Eric's Chinese

Noe Valley: 1500 Church St. (at 27th St.); 415-282-0919

Chinese

 Sidewalk's choice

 Good deal

 Kid friendly

Hunan and Mandarin cuisine is dished out in ample portions in this simple dining room that's always packed with people. Great starters include a sizzling-rice soup with tender, thick scallops and fresh snow peas, green onion cakes, or the highly seasoned stuffed chicken wings. Try Eric's Spicy Eggplant (with chicken, shrimp and basil) or the equally satisfying vegetarian version. Though some entrees suffer from an abundance of oil, most of the time Eric's offers very good fare for a very fair fee. If the wait is too long, walk around the corner to Eric's less crowded sister restaurant, Alice.

Lunch/dinner daily; D, MC, V.

★★★★
**$$**$$$

Esperpento

**Mission: 3295 22nd St. (at Valencia);
415-282-8867**

Spanish

Esperpento is Spanish for absurdity, appropriately describing the mix-and-match decor and ambience of this funky tapas restaurant, with its pink and yellow walls and flamboyant Spanish art. Boisterous patrons sit at hand-painted tables as roving bands of mariachis wander through. There are close to 40 choices of tapas, but be sure to try the creamy chicken croquettes, spicy garlic shrimp, squid cooked in its own ink or the moist and crispy potato-onion frittata. The paella is well-prepared, but you'll need to be in a group of two or more to order it. Sangria is the drink of choice.

Lunch/dinner daily; loud; cash only.

★★★★
**$$$**$$

Essex Supper Club

Downtown: 847 Montgomery St. (between Pacific and Jackson); 415-397-5969

California

Romantic

Good for groups

Located in historic Jackson Square, this elegant supper club (formerly Ernie's, the 60-year-old institution, made famous in Alfred Hitchcock's "Vertigo") draws an attractive clientele to its opulent men's-club environs, with inventive California-French cuisine: olive-coated sea bass, grilled Mission figs laced with prosciutto and seared salmon fillet with sliced potatoes and diced lobster. But flavor-wise, many dishes miss the mark and hardly seem worth the steep prices. After 9 p.m., dance to live jazz or

blues or gravitate to the wine cellar for cigars and cognac.

Dinner Tuesday-Saturday; late-night dining; live entertainment; jacket and tie required; full bar; pool; valet parking; AE, DC, D, MC, V.

Farallon

Downtown: 450 Post St. (between Mason and Powell); 415-956-6969

Seafood

Romantic

Oversize kelp-like pillars and gigantic sea-urchin chandeliers set the stage for terrific "coastal cuisine" with a decided French twist. Former Stars chef Mark Franz's menu changes daily, but you can always count on fresh and exciting combinations and show-stopping execution. Appetizers are the real draw; taste the towering mackerel tartare topped with Osetra caviar for proof. Emily Luchetti's childlike desserts (try the peppermint pattie) are pure comfort, and the wine list is both playful and impressive.

Lunch/dinner daily; late-night dining; full bar; valet parking; AE, MC, V, checks.

Faz

Downtown: 161 Sutter St. (between Montgomery and Kearny); 415-362-0404

Mediterranean

Good for groups

The rich flavors and refreshing variety of Mediterranean-Middle Eastern cooking are spotlighted at this sleek, welcoming downtown restaurant. The Mediterranean Sampler, a generous platter with dolmas, hummus, tabbouleh, baba ghanouj, tomatoes, pepperoncini and olives, is a great introduction to this cuisine. Salads and pizza are popular, but the entrees are particularly intriguing: the fettuccine Marco Polo with jumbo prawns, spinach, mushrooms and tomatoes in a light curry sauce or the clay-pot dish, packed with stuffed calamari, assorted shellfish and orzo in a lemon-saffron wine sauce. For dessert,

the black-and-white chocolate torte drenched in caramel sauce is heaven on a plate.

Lunch weekdays, dinner Monday-Saturday; loud; outdoor seating; live entertainment; valet parking; AE, MC, V.

★★★★
$$$$$

Fina Estampa

Civic Center: 1100 Van Ness Ave. (at Geary); 415-440-6343
Mission: 2374 Mission St. (between 19th and 20th Sts.); 415-824-4437

Spanish

Like its popular Mission Street parent, the Van Ness Fina Estampa has developed a loyal clientele that returns time and again for terrific tapas and spicy, robust Peruvian specialties served in a large dining room decorated with traditional paintings of angels. Sure bets for tapas are prawns sautéed in garlic, fried calamari and *anticuchos*, a national Peruvian dish of marinated beef hearts served with a mild house-made chili sauce. Recommended entrees include seafood paella and *parihuela de mariscos*, a savory dish of sautéed shellfish in a tomato-based broth. The Mission Street branch is easy to overlook, sandwiched as it is between a factory outlet and an old clothing store. But, its narrow, rather dumpy interior notwithstanding, it's worth the search.

Lunch/dinner Tuesday-Sunday; late-night dining; full bar; MC, V.

★★★★
$$$$$

Fino

Downtown: 624 Post St. (between Taylor and Jones); 415-928-2080

Italian

 Romantic

Fino may not be the best Italian restaurant in the city, but it's easily one of the most romantic. Beyond the arched windows and carved mahogany bar is a small, intimate dining room, warmed by a handsome marble fireplace. Set within the Hotel Andrew, Fino is a solid choice for downtown diners seeking a casual meal at a fair price. Besides the thin-crusted pizzas and daily

specials, recommended dishes include the mixed seafood contadina and pasta carbonara with pancetta and chile peppers. Finish the evening with chocolate raspberry crème brûlée, paired with a snifter of brandy at the bar.

Dinner nightly; quiet; fireplace; full bar; AE, DC, MC, V.

Fior d'Italia

North Beach: 601 Union St. (at Stockton); 415-986-1886

Italian

Good for groups

Billed as the oldest Italian restaurant in the United States, Fior d'Italia has occupied a prime spot overlooking Washington Square Park since 1886. Formal, tuxedoed waiters deftly serve osso buco, lasagna and veal parmigiana in the high-ceilinged dining room, where old photos on the walls echo the sense of history. While the cuisine could use a bit of a shakeup, Fior d'Italia is a safe bet for favorites like fried calamari, caprese salad or fettuccine Alfredo.

Lunch/dinner daily; view; AE, DC, D, MC, V.

Firecracker

Mission: 1007-1/2 Valencia St. (at 21st St.); 415-642-3470

Chinese

Patrons are flocking to this northern Chinese restaurant and its flamboyantly decorated dining room, covered from floor to ceiling with red-beaded lights and yards of red, flowing fabric—hence the name. Start your sizzling adventure with a pot of imported Chinese tea, ranging from the herbal chrysanthemum served with crushed sugar crystals to the sweet, tangy, dark red lychee black tea. Then move on to the uncommon chilled five-spice beef flavored with anise or the glazed baby back ribs coated with plum sauce. For your main meal, try the fiery shrimp spiced with ginger or the smoked-tea duck.

Lunch/dinner Tuesday-Sunday; reservations required for large parties; cash only.

★★★★
$$$$$

Firefly

Noe Valley: 4288 24th St. (between Douglas and Diamond); 415-821-7652

Mediterranean

Noe Valley's best restaurant is hidden in a cluster of homes, with a giant firefly sculpture above the door. Inside, two homey dining rooms are decorated with modern art. Owners Veva Edelson and Brad Levy (Levy is also the chef) have dubbed the eclectic Asian- and Mediterranean-influenced menu "home cooking with few ethnic boundaries." Specialties include bouillabaisse with monkfish, prawns, scallops and bass; vegetarian cassoulet with ground tofu, wild mushrooms, snap peas and peppers; and the signature appetizer, shrimp-and-scallop pot stickers with spicy sesame-soy dipping sauce. Don't leave without trying one of the desserts—they're as good as they look.

Dinner nightly; AE, MC, V.

★★★★
$$$$$

Firewood Cafe

Castro: 4248 18th St. (between Collingwood and Diamond); 415-252-0999

Mediterranean

This attractive cafe specializes in trendy yet familiar dishes, with a focus on creations from a wood-fired oven—from chewy-crusted pizzas to assorted roasted vegetables. Other options include six pastas, two kinds of rotisserie chicken and traditional Caesar and garden salads, both served with a choice of any three toppings (such as spiced walnuts or caramelized onions). For a real deal, order a half-chicken with roasted potatoes and a small side salad for $7.50. The interior's warm, earthy reds and yellows are inviting and soothing.

Lunch/dinner daily; MC, V.

Fleur de Lys

Downtown: 777 Sutter St. (between Jones and Taylor); 415-673-7779

French

 Sidewalk's choice

 Romantic

Good for groups

In a city crowded with noisy, industrial-chic restaurants, Fleur de Lys is a throwback to a more gracious era, with an elegant ambience, attentive staff and winning food. Chef and co-owner Hubert Keller has kept pace with the best of modern culinary trends, applying a health-conscious and inventive California spin to his refined French cuisine—along with buttery brioche and caviar, there's mushroom-crusted salmon on spinach leaves with huckleberry jus. The tasting menus are best, especially Keller's triumphant vegetarian version, which might feature a cauliflower mousseline, eggplant "caviar," handmade pasta with wild mushrooms, braised celery hearts on shallots with a tomato broth, and a selection of desserts. The wine list is on par with the sophisticated menu and astronomical prices.

Dinner Monday-Saturday; reservations required; major credit cards.

Flipper's

★★★★
$$$$$

Hayes Valley: 482 Hayes St. (at Octavia); 415-552-8880

American

 Kid friendly

An eclectic mix of styles and flavors, with classical music bouncing off textured walls lit by oxidized sheet-iron lamps, Flipper's is no ordinary burger joint (not that they serve dolphin, but still). The menu boasts an assortment of burgers, including a classic God-I-Love-America version, a hand-formed half-pound patty resting on a sesame bun. Several of the 15 other Flipper burgers come cow-free if you'd like. Among these are the Copenhagen Way, with diced beets, walnuts and a choice of ground chicken,

turkey, or tofu. Or try one of the gourmet salads or stuffed lavosh wraps.

Breakfast/lunch/dinner daily; weekend brunch; outdoor seating; reservations not accepted; cash only.

★★★★
$$$$$

The Fly Trap
South of Market: 606 Folsom St. (at 2nd St.); 415-243-0580

American

Good for groups

The name dates from the turn of the century, when customers traveled to the restaurant by horsecar, and flypaper was placed on each table to keep the insects out of the food. The Fly Trap still boasts one of the handsomest dining rooms in the city, rich and warm with brass and dark woods, and dominated by a custom-tailored bar. House specialties include celery Victor (salad of eggs, poached celery and anchovy vinaigrette) and the Hangtown Fry (oysters, bacon and eggs), along with coq au vin, creamed spinach and the best-selling Dungeness crab cake appetizer. Otherwise, diners can choose thick cuts of grilled meats, fresh seafood, pasta and a half-dozen specials.

Lunch weekdays, dinner Monday-Saturday; historic interest; full bar; valet/validated parking; AE, DC, MC, V.

★★★★
$$$$$

Flying Saucer
Mission: 1000 Guerrero St. (at 22nd St.); 415-641-9955

Eclectic

Sidewalk's choice

Romantic

This hip, pricey, always packed bistro, the interior of which is dominated by a giant Phantom of the Opera-esque mask, specializes in excellent food as well as attitude. Owner/chef Albert Tordjman's menu can be eccentric (he calls it "world beat") and it changes often, but most of his creations work rambunctiously well. Entrees are always complicated, intense in flavor and baroque in presentation: duck confit with black chanterelles on coconut-curry lentils, scallion-smothered chicken, crispy-skinned salmon topped with a tangerine-basil sauce. Desserts, such as an intricately designed mini-parade of chocolate delights, are out of this world.

Dinner Tuesday-Saturday; reservations required; AE, DC, MC, V.

★★★★
$$$$$

Fog City Diner
Downtown: 1300 Battery St. (at Lombard); 415-982-2000

American

Although recently the food and service at this flashy, upscale diner seem to have taken a turn for the worse, Pat Kuleto's sleek, chrome-and-neon design remains fun, and you still can count on many of the appetizers to be tasty and interesting. Order four or more and share them: crab cakes with sherry-cayenne mayo, sautéed Asian-style prawns with pickled ginger, spicy eggplant stir-fry with a scallion rice cake, grilled sesame chicken with mushrooms and carrots. Or you can always order a traditional cheeseburger, first-rate onion rings or fries, and cap it off with a milkshake or banana split.

Lunch/dinner daily; loud; outdoor seating; late-night dining; full bar; DC, D, MC, V.

★★★★
$$$$$

Food Inc.
Pacific Heights: 2800 California St. (at Divisadero); 415-928-3728

California

This charming sophisticated deli/cafe, packed with top-quality cooking oils, preserves, jams, wines and everything else you wish you had in your kitchen, has long been every Pacific Heighter's secret hot spot. Luscious-looking cakes, pastries, pastas and cold salads are displayed below the counter. The menu offers an array of satisfying soups, quiches, salads, appetizer platters, pizzas, pastas, sandwiches and house specials such as veggie lasagne and chicken gumbo—all made fresh daily. Seating is tight, and each made-to-order dish takes its sweet time coming. At least a half-dozen fine wines are offered by the glass.

Breakfast/lunch daily, dinner Monday-Saturday; quiet; outdoor seating; AE, MC, V.

★★★★
$$$$$

Fountain Court
Richmond: 354 Clement St. (at 5th Ave.); 415-668-1100

Chinese

Good for groups

The perpetually packed Fountain Court, one of San Francisco's best Chinese restaurants, is well-known for being able to satisfy diners who crave fresh ingredients and shun MSG, salt, oil and meat. Try the addictive vegetarian "chicken" appetizer—layers of bean curd skin rolled into loaves and braised in a brown sauce with ginger and scallions—or the excellent, crispy Shanghai duck. Steamed pork meatballs lightly fried and served on baby greens are popular, as is the fried caramel eggplant, tossed in a garlic-laden, caramelized plum sauce.

Lunch/dinner daily; AE, CB, D, MC, V.

★★★★
$$$$$

Fournou's Ovens
Nob Hill: Stanford Court Hotel, 905 California St. (at Powell); 415-989-1910

American

Romantic

Kid friendly

This grand, elegant hotel dining room has always managed to attract locals as well as hotel guests, and homey touches such as greenhouse windows, hanging braids of peppers and garlic, and a wood-burning oven lend an inviting sense of European graciousness. The menu has a California-Mediterranean bent, with such dishes as spaghetti with Maine lobster, fennel, roasted peppers and thyme; risotto with asparagus, red onions and white corn; and excellent roasted meats. Though sometimes haughty, service is attentive and professional, and extremely accommodating to children. The novel-like wine list ranks among the best in the city.

Breakfast/lunch/dinner/tea daily; outdoor seating; fireplace; full bar; valet parking; jacket required; all credit cards.

★★★★
$$$$$

Frascati
Russian Hill: 1901 Hyde St. (at Green); 415-928-1406

American

 Good for groups

Frascati features an exciting cross-cultural menu served in an Italian country-style dining room, with gallery-quality artwork and a semi-open kitchen staffed by chefs who clearly enjoy their work and seem to be on a mission to outdo themselves with every dish. A recent visit found everything from center-cut pork chops glazed with Mendocino honey-mustard to Andalusian seafood paella infused with saffron, chicken and Andouille sausage, to Thai coconut mussels and Manila clams served with sun-dried tomato bruschetta. Excellent pricing coupled with eclectic selections make the wine list enticing. Desserts such as the crème brûlée, lemon cheesecake and warm sour cherry crisp, are consistently wonderful.

Dinner Tuesday-Sunday; outdoor seating; live entertainment; valet parking; AE, MC, V.

★★★★
$$$$$

The French Room
Downtown: Clift Hotel, 495 Geary St. (at Taylor); 415-775-4700

French

 Romantic

 Good for groups

 Kid friendly

High ceilings, immense chandeliers and Louis XV furnishings provide a grand hotel setting for fine French-California food—but for the money, more exciting dining experiences could be had elsewhere. Starters include an iced seafood sampler and truffled risotto with roasted portobello mushrooms, asparagus, prosciutto and goat cheese. Cedar-plank salmon with sautéed spinach and white bean cassoulet, lobster cioppino and seasonal wild game are some of the tempting entrees. Desserts are rich enough to make you swoon. Service is as polished as you'd expect, and no place in town puts on a more elegant Sunday brunch.

Breakfast/lunch/dinner daily; weekend brunch; quiet; prix fixe menu; theater menu; full bar; live entertainment; valet parking; AE, DC, D, MC, V, checks.

★★★☆
$$$$$

Fringale

South of Market: 570 4th St. (between Bryant and Brannan); 415-543-0573

French

 Sidewalk's choice

 Good deal

Chef/co-owner Gerald Hirigoyen, named one of the 10 best chefs in the nation by Food & Wine magazine, draws crowds to his charming, lively French bistro with its casual blond-wood-trimmed interior, friendly, largely French waitstaff and surprisingly agreeable prices. French-born Hirigoyen draws upon his Basque origins to produce his gutsy, flavor-packed fare, such as the outstanding steamed mussels sprinkled with garlic and parsley, Roquefort ravioli with pine nuts and basil, and meltingly tender pork tenderloin. He also showcases his pastry chef's talents with a lineup of tempting desserts, including an incredible vanilla-bean crème brûlée.

Lunch weekdays, dinner Monday-Saturday; full bar; AE, MC, V.

★★☆☆
$$$$$

The Ganges

Cole Valley: 775 Frederick St. (between Arguello and Stanyan); 415-661-7290

Indian

 Sidewalk's choice

There's no safer place for cows to linger than near this vegetarian/vegan Indian restaurant featuring a choice of 10 to 15 very spicy vegetarian curries each night, including asparagus in yogurt sauce, bananas stuffed with ginger, coconut and chiles, and spinach in coconut sauce. Order them combination-style, and they come with many Indian sides: roasted lentil wafers, dal, chapati, raita, spicy batter-fried vegetables and chutney. Plus, you get Indian sweet tea on the side. The food is absolutely fresh, and is cooked to order as you sit on cushions at knee-high tables, listening to live Indian music.

Dinner Tuesday-Sunday; live entertainment; senior discount; MC, V.

 ★★★☆
$$$$$

Garden Court
Downtown: 2 New Montgomery St. (at Market); 415-512-1111

California

 Romantic

 Good for groups

For more than a century, the afternoon tea and Sunday brunch at the Sheraton Palace's ornate Garden Court has been a city tradition, and its lavish setting (now an official landmark) transports diners to a bygone, more luxurious age. Tea time brings a selection of tasty sandwiches, scones and rose-petal marmalade, all served on bone china with live harp and chamber music playing in the background. Dinner hasn't always lived up to the regal surroundings, but the new chefs present an interesting California menu with European and Asian flourishes, such as gingered quail with cranberry vinaigrette and roasted squab with shiitake mushrooms. The vast, somewhat pricey wine list is a "who's who" of impressive producers.

Breakfast/lunch daily, dinner Monday-Saturday; quiet; full bar; jacket and tie required; validated parking; AE, DC, D, MC, V.

★★★☆
$$$$$

Garden of Tranquility
Potrero Hill: 2001 17th St. (at Kansas); 415-861-8610

Chinese

 Good for groups

In this pleasantly tranquil dining room, with a thatched-roof canopy, potted bamboo trees and white lantern-shaped lights, Mandarin fare dominates. There are the standard appetizer choices—garlic eggplant, onion pancakes, crab puffs—and very good entrees such as sesame scallops, prawns with pecans, sizzling basil beef and Monk Comes Over, a clay-pot dish bubbling with chicken, beef, pork, scallops, shrimp, tofu and vegetables seasoned with garlic and pepper. Service is attentive and efficient, and the chefs are willing to alter an order to your specifications.

Lunch/dinner daily; AE, DC, MC, V.

★★★★
$$$$$

California

Garibaldi's

Pacific Heights: 347 Presidio Ave. (between Sacramento and Clay); 415-563-8841

This sleeper restaurant with an elegant, unstuffy ambience presents a wide-ranging California-Mediterranean menu at reasonable prices. The pleasant room is simply fashioned with white-clothed rows of tables, framed art and a pretty wood and gilded-metal bar. For starters, try the asparagus appetizer, sautéed with pancetta, garlic, chili oil and oyster sauce, or the grilled black Mission figs stuffed with Stilton and wrapped in prosciutto. Move on to the lamb tenderloin or the excellent paella. Desserts include a wild huckleberry parfait with white chocolate mousse and house-made sorbets and gelatos. Weekend brunch is particularly good.

Lunch/dinner daily; weekend brunch; full bar; AE, MC, V.

★★★★
$$$$$

Indian

Gaylord India Restaurant

Fisherman's Wharf: 900 North Point (between Polk and Larkin); 415-771-8822

Although it's pricey and part of a chain, Gaylord deserves respect for serving delicious Indian food in a comfortable, tony Ghirardelli Square setting. Crisp table linens, a collection of Indian art and a sweeping bay view lend the restaurant an elegant air, mirrored by the (sometimes overly) formal service. The elaborate menu offers almost all classical Northern Indian dishes, including savory garlic and onion breads, excellent tandoori meats and a variety of interesting curries. Five special prix fixe dinners that include

delightful combinations of the many tandoori items and delicious breads are available nightly.

Lunch/dinner daily; weekend brunch; view; prix fixe menu; full bar; AE, DC, D, MC, V.

$$$$$

Gira Polli
North Beach: 659 Union St. (between Powell and Stockton); 415-434-4472

Italian

Gira Polli's chicken, bronzed slowly over a wood fire, is unmatched anywhere in town for flavor and price. Although there's a selection of salads and pastas, the specialty is "turning chicken," flavored with rosemary and lemon and served with a side of browned Palermo potatoes. Then there's the G.P. Special, a meal that feeds two: half a chicken, potatoes, salad, veggies and a roll for $9.95. Seating in this tiny cafe is a joke during the mealtime rush; instead, order your food to go (including a slice of the exquisite lemon cheesecake) and have a picnic in Washington Square.

Dinner nightly; loud; AE, MC.

★★★☆
$$$$$

Globe
Downtown: 290 Pacific Ave. (between Front and Battery); 415-391-4132

American

A sure sign of success for this new eatery: It's become a hangout for a who's-who in the local food world. Owner and executive chef Joseph Manzare (formerly at Spago) decided to start small and do it right, opening a simple, chic 44-seat restaurant that uses seasonal ingredients supplied by local farmers. The American/California menu changes weekly, but might include a grilled sardine appetizer served on frisée greens, followed by wood-fire-roasted lamb on artichoke puree or pork chops with cherry-pepper ragout and green-olive tapenade; the wine list consists mainly of California vintages. Another boon: Globe is open until 1 a.m.

Lunch weekdays, dinner Monday-Saturday; loud; late-night dining; full bar; AE, MC, V.

Godzila

★★★★
$$$$$

**Pacific Heights: 1800 Divisadero St.
(at Bush); 415-931-1773**

Sushi

Good deal

Every night this Pacific Heights fish factory is packed with a mostly young, boisterous crowd hip to the fact that it serves some of the lowest-priced high-quality sushi around. You can get two sushi rolls, miso soup, a side of rice and a big Sapporo draft for about $10. One of the best selections is the Rock-n-Roll, a heavenly slice of barbecued eel wrapped with avocado in a roll of seaweed and rice. There's usually a wait after 7 p.m., though the line moves quickly and the staff keeps you supplied with beer.

Dinner nightly; AE, DC, MC, V.

Gold Mountain

★★★★
$$$$$

**Chinatown: 644 Broadway (between
Columbus and Stockton); 415-296-7733**

Chinese

Good for groups

This triple-decker Chinese restaurant is the quintessential dim sum parlor, especially at lunchtime, when dozens of stainless-steel carts laden with exotic treats are wheeled across the elaborately decorated room. Huge, powerful fans do little to disperse the savory smells of chicken and pork. This is one of the most popular dim sum spots in the city, and the room is so immense you could seat a party of 1,000 here without a hitch. Evenings are more subdued, and are an opportune time to sample house specials like crispy chicken, spicy salted prawns or any of the excellent noodle dishes.

Lunch/dinner daily; AE, MC, V.

Golden Boy Pizza

★★★☆
$$$$$

North Beach: 542 Green St. (between Grant and Stockton); 415-982-9738

Pizza

Good deal

The freshly baked pizza squares prominently displayed in the front window exert a magnetic pull on any pizza lover who happens to walk by. The pizza squares at Golden Boy are so thick, soft and loaded with toppings that they're served with a knife and fork. The pierced and tattooed staff will wrap your slice to go, but it's far more entertaining to sit down at the counter with a beer as punk rock fills the air, and check out the hundreds of far-out photos, stickers and oddments that cover the walls.

Lunch/dinner daily; cash only.

Golden Flower Vietnamese Restaurant

★★★☆
$$$$$

Chinatown: 667 Jackson St. (at Grant); 415-433-6469

Vietnamese

Good for groups

Perpetually packed, this small, homey Vietnamese restaurant does a brisk business ladling out steaming bowls of *pho* to a multiracial crowd of Chinatown locals. There's usually a wait during lunch, but the line moves quickly. The most popular item is *tai pho* (No. 5), a rice noodle soup brimming with sliced rare steak and vegetables. Other good choices include the seafood soup and the shrimp and pork salad roll, which comes wrapped in rice paper. For dessert, try a cool glass of *cha sua da*, an amazingly strong, sweet iced coffee.

Lunch/dinner daily; cash only.

★★★☆
$$$$$

Golden Turtle
Russian Hill: 2211 Van Ness Ave. (between Broadway and Vallejo); 415-441-4419

Vietnamese

The Golden Turtle is a quantum leap above the Vietnamese soup houses that have recently sprung up, with an elaborate wood-paneled interior and a soothing, romantic ambience. Recommended dishes include imperial rolls made with minced pork, prawns and crab; barbecued quail flambéed with rum; five-spice roasted chicken; or any of the seasonal crab dishes. Although not on the menu, one of the best offerings is a chicken dish flavored with black mushrooms, bamboo shoots and chili sauce. Service is polite and professional here, but it sometimes proceeds at a turtle's pace.

Dinner Tuesday-Sunday; AE, DC, MC, V.

★★★☆
$$$$$

Good Luck Dim Sum
Richmond: 736 Clement St. (between 8th and 9th Aves.); 415-386-3388

Chinese

Good deal

Go to Good Luck Dim Sum, stand in line with the locals who already know how good this place is, then point to the "three for $1" menu and say, "One of everything." You'll end up with 45 pieces of the best dim sum you'll ever taste: shark fin dumplings, pork *siu mai*, fried puffs, turnip cake, pot stickers, sugar cake, egg rolls and the most fantastic—and least expensive—shrimp dumplings around. Service is brusque but fast, and within minutes you'll be out the door. There are some Formica-topped tables in the back, but most order to go.

Breakfast/lunch/dinner daily; checks.

★★★★
$$$$$

Gordon Biersch Brewery Restaurant

South of Market: 2 Harrison St. (at Embarcadero); 415-243-8246

California

Good for groups

Most folks come for the beer at this industrial, brick, steel and concrete microbrewery and restaurant, where they can choose from a mix of pilsners, marzens, bocks, ales and seasonal beers. To complement the selection of libations, Gordon Biersch's kitchen dishes out highly spiced, eclectic fare ranging from hearty burgers and garlic fries to hoisin-glazed baby back ribs, salt-baked mussels, Thai chile-marinated seafood with shiitake mushrooms and layered tuna sashimi with wasabi sauce. For dessert, try the Florentine ice-cream sandwich, made with peanut brittle and exquisitely presented. The kitchen can't always pull off the more ambitious creations, but when it does, the result is some very interesting pub grub. This place gets so packed (it can hold up to 5,000 people) and so noisy that many take refuge outside.

Lunch/dinner daily; loud; view; late-night dining; full bar; valet and validated parking; MC, V.

★★★★
$$$$$

Gourmet Carousel

Fillmore: 1559 Franklin St. (at Pine); 415-771-2044

Chinese

Good for groups

It's easy to miss this little family-run Chinese restaurant on the corner of a busy intersection, but locals know it well. The food is good, portions are generous and prices are low. The delicious pot stickers are crisp on the outside and moist on the inside, while prawns stir-fried with vegetables are a consistent favorite. Adventurous souls might try crab meat and fish-stomach soup or pork bellies in a clay pot—cuisine definitely not for the squeamish. Friendly waiters whisk about the small, simply decorated room, which sports several large tables equipped with Lazy Susans that are perfect for groups.

Lunch Tuesday-Saturday, dinner Tuesday-Sunday; MC, V.

Grandeho's Kamekyo Sushi Bar

Cole Valley: 943 Cole St. (at Parnassus); 415-759-5693

Japanese

Good for groups

Spotless, sedate and serious about sushi, Grandeho's eschews the latest sushi-bar trend of pounding rock music, and its gleaming blond-wood furnishings, a lavender-hued ceiling and mustard-colored walls create a soothing environment. Chef Yoko Yama prepares orders from a menu of mostly standard Japanese fare such as *unagi* (eel), *tamago* (egg) and the ubiquitous California roll. A full menu of entrees is also available: tempura, teriyaki, udon/soba and a surprisingly good chicken katsu. Vegetarians haven't been overlooked either; several dishes, such as the house-made pot stickers, are clearly marked as meat-free.

Lunch/dinner daily; loud; AE, MC, V.

Grazie 2000

North Beach: 515 Columbus Ave. (between Union and Green); 415-982-7400

Italian

Romantic

Though its much-smaller-but-widely-praised neighbor L'Osteria del Forno seems to have overshadowed it, Grazie 2000's busy open kitchen turns out reliably good renditions of southern Italian dishes in an inviting atmosphere with amiable, efficient service. Veal dishes—including many sautés and a hefty chop stuffed with spinach, prosciutto and Gorgonzola with port wine sauce—are excellent. The pastas are quite good, as is any daily special featuring fresh seafood. Appetizers are fairly standard. Although the menu contains few surprises, Grazie 2000 prepares contemporary favorites with a bit more style than many of the older restaurants in North Beach.

Dinner nightly; AE, MC, V.

 ★★★★
$$$$$

Great Eastern

Chinatown: 649 Jackson St. (between Kearny and Grant); 415-986-2500

Chinese

 Good for groups

Steelhead, sea bass, abalone and other hard-to-find denizens of the deep are housed in huge fish tanks at this Hong Kong-style dinner house. Diners sit at large round tables and share the seafood specialties along with a dizzying array of exotic dishes, including boiled goose chitterlings and soft-shell turtle. It's best to opt for a set dinner, particularly the one that comes with crab and scallop soup, sautéed sea conch and scallops, a whole steamed Dungeness crab, squab, bean sprouts rolled with vegetables, an entire steamed rock cod and dessert. Both dining rooms are sleek and lit by crystal chandeliers.

Lunch/dinner daily; late-night dining; AE, MC, V.

★★★★
$$$$$

Greens

Marina: Fort Mason, Bldg. A (between Buchanan and Beach); 415-771-6222

Vegetarian

 Sidewalk's choice

 Romantic

 Good for groups

 Kid friendly

Although the food is not as innovative as it was at first, Greens still produces gourmet vegetarian food that is often so good, even carnivores succumb. Located in converted barracks, with spectacular views and a giant, petrified tree as a centerpiece, Greens is owned and operated by the Zen Center, and much of the produce comes from the center's Green Gulch farm. Chef Annie Sommerville's menu changes regularly, but dishes may include mesquite-grilled polenta, phyllo turnovers filled with mushrooms, spinach and Parmesan cheese, and fettuccine topped with mushrooms, peas, goat cheese and crème fraîche. Soups, salads and the restaurant's famous breads (from Tassajara Bakery), are also available to go.

Lunch/dinner daily; weekend brunch; view; free parking lot; D, MC, V, checks.

★★★★
$$$$$

Hahn's Hibachi

Castro: 1305 Castro St. (at 24th St.);
415-642-8151 (Hahn's Hibachi I)
Nob Hill/Russian Hill: 1710 Polk St.
(between Clay and Washington);
415-776-1095 (Hahn's Hibachi II)
Marina: 3318 Steiner St.
(between Lombard and Chestnut);
415-931-6284 (Hahn's Hibachi III)

Korean

 Good deal

Plates piled high with sweet-hot Korean barbecue, quick service and low prices characterize all three Hahn's Hibachi locations. Barbecued chicken is the big draw, but you can get the same sauce slathered onto beefy short ribs, spare ribs, flank steak or pork. Shrimp, scallops and oysters are also available. There are many vegetarian options on the extensive menu, which includes vegetable kabobs, pot stickers, tempura, udon and several satays served over rice with sprout salad and kimchee. Also check out the weekday lunch specials and daily dinner combination plates.

Lunch/dinner daily; Castro branch has free parking lot; MC, V on Castro, cash only on Polk and Steiner.

★★★★
$$$$$

Hamano Sushi

Noe Valley: 332 Castro St. (at 24th St.);
415-826-0825

Japanese

 Sidewalk's choice

This inviting Japanese restaurant provides a sleek environment for sampling impeccably fresh sushi. The raw shrimp rolls and barbecued eel are excellent, and the vegetarian sushi is very inventive. Regulars give kudos to the appetizers such as lightly

fried tofu in soy-ginger sauce with scallions and shrimp flakes, braised cod in miso sauce, and spinach cooked in spicy peanut sauce. For entrees, there's everything from tempura to teriyaki. While the generally attentive service can get frenetic on weekends, the owners make up for it with their genuine warmth, and the personable chefs keep a running commentary as they work.

Dinner nightly; loud; reservations not accepted; AE, MC, V, checks.

★★★☆
$$$$$

Hamburger Mary's
South of Market: 1582 Folsom St. (at 12th St.); 415-626-5767

American

A longtime hangout for the alternative crowd has reached institution status as much for its groovy scene as for its burgers—a little greasy, but big, juicy and served on nine-grain bread. Go with the spicy home fries as an accompaniment. Fresh fish is also on the menu, as are sandwiches, soups, salads and vegetarian entrees, and breakfast is served all day. The place can be extremely loud. Instead of conversing, you can ogle fellow patrons and the hundreds of garage-sale items that Hamburger Mary's justifies as decorative choices.

Breakfast/lunch/dinner daily; weekend brunch; weekday happy hour; loud; late-night dining; full bar; AE, DC, D, MC, V.

★★★☆
$$$$$

Harbor Village Restaurant
Downtown: 4 Embarcadero Center (between Sacramento and Clay at Drumm); 415-781-8833

Chinese

Good for groups

This giant Hong Kong-style seafood and dim sum restaurant serves standout food in an upscale environment, but misses top honors because of minor inconsistencies in cooking and major flaws in service. Lunch is a dim sum extravaganza, with master chefs from Hong Kong turning out plates of sublime morsels of vast, interesting variety. At dinner, choose from an enormous Cantonese menu that includes rare items, among them prized varieties of shellfish kept alive until the moment they're ordered, served with exquisite simplicity (if exorbitantly priced). Try to stagger your order so that it arrives a few dishes at a time.

Lunch/dinner daily; view; full bar; valet parking; all major credit cards.

★★★★
$$$$$

Harris'

Russian Hill: 2100 Van Ness Ave. (at Pacific); 415-673-1888

American

 Romantic

 Good for groups

Not just another steak house, Harris' hushed, formal club setting is a living monument to guiltless beef eating. Harris' choice Midwestern beef, aged for three weeks and grilled to order, can be chosen by cut and by size; larger cuts have the finest flavor, but the pepper steak and the rare prime rib are great. You'll also find lobster, lamb chops, pasta dishes and one vegetarian option. Harris' lists its exemplary martini as a starter, but you might also want some oysters, French onion soup or excellent Caesar salad. An extensive wine list predictably carries many reds; Scotch drinkers have nearly a dozen choices.

Dinner nightly; quiet; live entertainment; fireplace; full bar; valet parking; jackets encouraged; all major credit cards.

★★★★
$$$$$

Harry Denton's

South of Market: Harbor Court Hotel, 161 Steuart St. (between Mission and Howard); 415-882-1333

American

 Good for groups

Presided over by veteran bartender Harry Denton, this restaurant in the Harbor Court Hotel owes its considerable success more to the popularity of its bon-vivant owner, terrific bayside location and uptown party atmosphere catering to a singles crowd than to any brilliant creations emerging from the kitchen.

Expect comfort fare such as pot roast with buttermilk mashed potatoes and pappardelle with smoked chicken served in generous portions by agreeable waiters. Lunchtime offers a more sedate experience; after 10 p.m., the rugs are rolled up to create a waterside dance floor, with live bands playing every night except Sunday.

Breakfast/lunch/dinner daily; weekend brunch; loud; view; late-night dining; live entertainment; full bar; valet parking; all major credit cards.

Harry Denton's Starlight Room

Downtown: Sir Francis Drake Hotel, 450 Powell St. (at Sutter); 415-395-8595

Supper Club

Glamour practically oozes from the woodwork at this fabulous supper club perched on the 21st floor of the Sir Francis Drake Hotel. Luxurious furnishings, silk draperies, a stand-up Biedermeier-style bar and a 360-degree view of downtown makes the Starlight Room one of the superlative cocktail experiences going. The menu features about a dozen light entrees and appetizers, ranging from butternut squash tortellini to pan-roasted crab-and-corn cakes to the "raw bar" platter. The clientele tends to be over-25 and on the dressy side. It's all very chic and romantic and surprisingly affordable.

Dinner nightly; daily happy hour; loud; view; late-night dining; full bar; live entertainment; valet parking; all major credit cards, checks.

★★★★
$$$$$

Hawthorne Lane

**South of Market: 22 Hawthorne St.
(between Howard and Folsom);
415-777-9779**

California

Sidewalk's choice

Good for groups

Since opening in 1995, Hawthorne Lane has become one of the city's hottest destinations, fueled by its sophisticated, appealing interior and the culinary pedigrees of owners/chefs Anne and David Gingrass (formerly of Spago and Postrio). The Asian- and Mediterranean-influenced American menu includes the Gingrass' signature pizzas and homemade duck sausage, plus notable new items such as Chinese-style roasted duck with fresh apricot chutney, and seared pepper-and-ginger-coated tuna and rice nori with Asian barbecue sauce. The wine list delivers California favorites and selections from France, Italy and Chile. Renowned pastry chef Nicole Plue's desserts are wonderful, and the personable staff is utterly without attitude.

Lunch weekdays, dinner nightly; full bar; live entertainment; valet parking; CB, DC, D, MC, V.

★★★★
$$$$$

Hayes and Vine Wine Bar

**Hayes Valley: 377 Hayes St. (between
Franklin and Gough); 415-626-5301**

California

This hip yet comfortable little wine bar is a marvelous place for libations and light eats before or after a Civic Center performance. Hayes and Vine stocks hundreds of wines from around the globe, and more than 30 are available for imbibing by the taste, glass, or even better, the tasting trio. The simple but cosmopolitan fare consists mainly of French nibbles designed to enhance your wine-drinking pleasure: pâté, cheeses, smoked trout, oysters and caviar. Pricing is reasonable considering the depth of choice, and the knowledgeable staff is passionate about wine, without being pretentious.

Light dinner Monday-Saturday; late-night dining; MC, V.

★★★★
$$$$$

Hayes Street Grill

Hayes Valley: 320 Hayes St. (at Franklin); 415-863-5545

Seafood

If you're looking for one of the best fish dinners in San Francisco, visit serene, elegant Hayes Street Grill (partly owned by food critic Patricia Unterman), which does only a few things, but does them extremely well. The menu emphasizes fresh Pacific seafood that's perfectly mesquite-grilled or delicately sautéed. Expect snapper, swordfish and tuna among the seasonally changing selections, along with succulent raw oysters, savory soups, salads, french fries (a house specialty) and superb calamari fritto misto. An ideal little wine list sports fabulous prices and selections. The polite, efficient staff will move mountains to get you out the door in time for the opera or symphony.

Lunch weekdays, dinner nightly; full bar; AE, CB, MC, V.

★★★★
$$$$$

Helmand

North Beach: 430 Broadway (between Kearny and Montgomery); 415-362-0641

Afghan

Sidewalk's choice

Romantic

An oasis of good taste on Broadway's garish strip, Helmand serves delicious renditions of distinctive Afghan cuisine in a pretty room lit by brass chandeliers and small table lanterns. The light and variously spiced house-made yogurts, an Afghan staple, dress several favorite appetizers, including dumplings filled with onions and beef and topped with carrot sauce, and deep-fried then baked sweet baby pumpkin tempered with a piquant yogurt-garlic sauce. Try the tender marinated rack of lamb or meatballs with cinnamon-spiced tomato sauce. Service is personable, if scattered, and the short wine list is well chosen and priced.

Dinner nightly; valet and validated parking; MC, V.

★★★★
$$$$$

Henry's Hunan Restaurant

South of Market: 110 Natoma St.
(between New Montgomery and 2nd St.);
415-546-4999
Downtown: 924 Sansome St.
(at Broadway); 415-956-7727

Chinese

 Good
for groups

Hunan Restaurant's cavernous interior, neatly furnished in tones of black and red, is a definite cut
above that at most Chinatown eateries, and the
quality of this sinus-clearing cuisine is better too.
Standout dishes such as the Hunan chicken salad,
harvest pork, *kung pao* chicken and house-smoked
duck are all reasonably priced and served with verve.
If you're sensitive to spicy dishes, request that the
kitchen go easy on the peppers. Weekday lunch specials are accompanied by a slice of delicious deep-
fried pie filled with onions, cheese, and pork. After
dinner, have a margarita in the dimly lit cocktail
lounge.

Lunch/dinner weekdays; AE, MC, V, debit card.

★★★★
$$$$$

Herbivore

Mission: 983 Valencia St. (between 20th
and 21st Sts.); 415-826-5657

Vegetarian

 Sidewalk's
choice

 Good
deal

A recent addition to the neighborhood, this chic and
airy self-serve restaurant with a true reverence for
fresh, organic produce has clearly landed in the right
spot—just ask its appreciative, casually dressed
crowd. Herbivore takes vegan cooking to a higher
level, with a menu boasting crisp green salads and
charbroiled vegetable sandwiches, as well as heartier
offerings such as tofu-ricotta and mushroom lasagne,
seasonal veggie shish kebabs and grilled seitan
steaks marinated in lemon-garlic sauce. Presentation
is simple but artful, the food uniformly fresh and

tasty. Sidewalk seating makes this a nice choice on sunny afternoons.

Lunch/dinner daily; outdoor seating; reservations not accepted; cash only.

★★★★
$$$$$

Hing Lung

Chinatown: 674 Broadway (at Stockton); 415-398-8838

Chinese

Though hanging roast ducks and chickens adorn its front windows, this estimable combination roast house/*juk* joint/noodle mecca is entirely plain inside, a large room with tinted mirrors, tiled floors and Formica tables. Most people come for the *juk*—a hearty, delicious porridge made by slow-cooking white rice with meat, fish or other goodies. It's best enjoyed with a side of Chinese fry bread tossed into the steaming concoction. *Juk* comes in nearly 20 versions here, and if you've wanted to break out of the Chinese food rut, now's the time to do it—and here's the place.

Breakfast/lunch/dinner daily; late-night dining; MC, V.

★★★★
$$$$$

Home Plate

Marina: 2274 Lombard St. (between Pierce and Steiner); 415-922-4663

American

A bright neighborhood brunch spot known for its buttermilk pancakes, waffles smothered with fresh fruit, fat omelets stuffed with everything from spinach to applewood-smoked ham, scones and homemade granola. The place is tiny; if you want to slide in at prime time, call ahead to put your name on the waiting list. Breakfast is served all day, but you can also get salads, sandwiches and hot lunches in the afternoon.

Breakfast/lunch daily; weekend brunch; loud; MC, V.

★★★★
$$$$$

Hong Kong Flower Lounge

**Richmond: 5322 Geary Blvd.
(at 16th Ave.); 415-668-8998**

Chinese

Good for groups

Kid friendly

Part of a Hong Kong empire, the glimmering green, gold and red decor of the gilded Hong Kong Flower Lounge is pure Kowloon glitz, but the food hasn't suffered from the move to California, thanks largely to the Hong Kong chefs, who adhere to the high standards of their homeland cuisine. Among the best dishes on the vast menu are exquisite minced squab in lettuce cups, delicate crystal scallops in shrimp sauce, fried prawns with walnuts and any fresh fish from the tanks. There's an excellent, moderately priced version of Peking duck. Dim sum is also served.

Brunch/lunch/dinner daily; loud; AE, MC, V, DC.

★★★★
$$$$$

Hong Kong Seafood Restaurant

**Sunset: 2588 Noriega St. (at 33rd Ave.);
415-665-8338**

Chinese

While nowhere near the caliber of San Francisco's legendary Hong Kong Flower Lounge, this very popular multiroom dim sum restaurant draws dozens of Chinese families on weekends. Sure bets are the shrimp and pork dumplings; the more adventurous should sample the crispy taro croquette or turnip pudding. The regular menu offers a dizzying array of choices, though a number of the specials are posted in Chinese only. Through a second entrance, they sell dim sum to go from a small bakery counter. Expect a formidable line on Sunday mornings for both the dining room and the takeout counter.

Lunch/dinner daily; cash only.

Hong Kong Villa

Richmond: 2332 Clement St. (between 24th and 25th Aves.); 415-752-8833

Chinese

One of the more popular Cantonese restaurants on Clement, this clean, bright spot specializes in fresh-from-the-tank seafood, which you'll spot the moment you walk through the door. Prawns, pan-fried in the shell with spicy salt, are pricey and messy, but exceptionally sweet and flavorful. Rock cod, steamed whole and served with black bean sauce, is a feast for the eyes and taste buds. Don't overlook the delicious clay-pot dishes, roasted half-chicken with bean curd, dim sum or—if you're with a party of four—the house-special dinner.

Lunch/dinner daily; loud; MC, V.

The House

North Beach: 1230 Grant Ave. (at Columbus); 415-986-8612

Asian

Passing hands seamlessly from founding chef Larry Tse to his brother-in-law Mike Mak, this small, spare restaurant specializes in classic Western dishes with Eastern flavors. For starters, try the grilled Chinese chicken salad with sesame-soy vinaigrette, Caesar salad with wok-seared scallops, or taro-pork spring rolls. The menu is heavy on daily specials, but may include a veal chop with shiitake-oyster sauce, or grilled Chilean sea bass topped with ginger-soy sauce. For dessert, the apple crumb pie à la mode and crème brûlée are both superb. Though the list is tiny, the wines are perfectly chosen and priced barely above retail.

Lunch/dinner Tuesday-Saturday; AE, MC, V.

House of Nanking

★★☆☆
$$$$$

Chinatown: 919 Kearny St. (at Jackson);
415-421-1429

Chinese

At this tiny, greasy, wildly popular hole in the wall, expect horrendous lines for a cramped table with a plastic menu listing only half the best dishes. Owner/chef/head waiter Fang is famous for his inventive revisions of traditional dishes: succulent duck dumplings, sesame-battered scallops in spicy garlic sauce, dizzyingly delicious hot prawn and green onion pancakes with peanut sauce, and Nanking chicken. (Check out what other diners are eating and point.) The prices for this outstanding food are some of the most reasonable around, but the service is terrible, which is why this restaurant doesn't earn three stars.

Lunch Monday-Saturday, dinner nightly; loud; cash only.

House of Prime Rib

★★★☆
$$$$$

Nob Hill: 1906 Van Ness Ave.
(at Washington); 415-885-4605

American

With wingback chairs, thick carpets, wood paneling and fireplaces, this San Francisco institution looks like a British country manor. You'll be served Eastern corn-fed roast beef, sliced at your table, accompanied by side orders such as baked potatoes and creamed spinach. You'll also be treated to the famous spinning salad: a salad bowl rotated on ice, drizzled with dressing then scooped onto chilled plates. A few seafood dishes are also offered. Attentive, old-fashioned service, the handsome and cozy setting and truly excellent roast beef make this an exceptional value (you can even request seconds!).

Dinner nightly; full bar; valet parking; AE, DC, D, MC, V.

★★★★ $$$$$ Hunan Homes

Chinatown: 622 Jackson St. (between Kearny and Grant); 415-982-2844

Chinese

Sidewalk's choice

Good for groups

This far-from-fancy eatery (mirrored walls, fish tanks, tacky chandeliers) is regarded as one of Chinatown's best Hunan restaurants. Be sure to start with the excellent hot and sour soup, followed by a platter of scallops sautéed with snow peas, baby corn, celery and mushrooms, prawns with bean curd and straw mushrooms, or the wonton soup chock-full of shrimp, chicken, barbecued pork, squid and vegetables. For those who've tried everything, order the Succulent Bread appetizer. Photographs of the more popular dishes are posted, but it's what you can't see—fiery spices—that make all the difference.

Lunch/dinner daily; AE, MC, V.

★★★★ $$$$$ Hungarian Sausage Factory & Bistro

Bernal Heights (see Mission map): 419 Cortland Ave. (between Wool and Bennington); 415-648-2847

Eastern European

Sidewalk's choice

A neighborhood crowd fills the quaint, small dining room at this family-run bistro, which serves home-cooked Hungarian meals. Sausages—mild, hot and smoked—are the house specialty. They're crafted from old family recipes. To start, try the savory mushroom crepe or the chunky chicken-liver pâté. Entrees include spicy chicken fricassee with tomato, green pepper and onion ladled over spaetzle or breaded pork cutlets served with red cabbage and parsley potatoes, but the signature sausage dishes are your best bet. The waitstaff is very friendly, but the food can be slow in coming. Most nights, a traditionally dressed musician plays.

Lunch/dinner Tuesday-Sunday; outdoor seating; live entertainment; MC, V, checks.

Hyde Street Bistro

★★★☆
$$$$$

Austrian

Romantic

Russian Hill: 1521 Hyde St. (between Jackson and Pacific); 415-441-7778

In the quest for the perfect sophisticated-yet-unpretentious neighborhood restaurant, serving good food at reasonable prices in an intimate ambience, Hyde Street Bistro delivers, and then some. Patrons are treated like longtime friends in this inviting spot specializing in hearty Austrian/Italian fare, such as Viennese spinach gnocchi with pancetta and Gorgonzola cream sauce, grilled halibut with Chardonnay cream sauce or Wienerschnitzel with potato pancakes and lingonberry compote. Specials are listed on a small chalkboard near the entrance, where those who didn't make reservations should expect to wait. The wine list isn't notable, but includes a number of reasonably priced varietals.

Dinner nightly; valet parking; AE, MC, V.

Hyde Street Seafood House and Raw Bar

★★★☆
$$$$$

Seafood

Russian Hill: 1509 Hyde St. (at Jackson); 415-931-3474

A perfect mixture of elegance and earthiness, this well-kept San Francisco secret is almost exclusively a locals' spot. As you sit in this quaint, moderately priced restaurant filled with nautical memorabilia, enjoying fantastic fresh seafood while the cable cars clang past, take comfort that most tourists haven't discovered this gem. The house specialty is fish cooked in papillote, best accompanied by the excellent Caesar salad. But first, sample the divine lobster bisque or superb crab cakes, or graze on the riches of the raw bar: prawn and crab cocktail, smoked salmon, clams and several types of raw oysters.

Dinner nightly; AE, DC, D, MC, V.

★★☆☆
$$\$\$

I Fratelli

**Russian Hill: 1896 Hyde St. (at Green);
415-474-8420**

Italian

Upscale Italian comfort food is the draw at this venerable restaurant. It attracts a mostly older neighborhood clientele in a homey trattoria setting, complete with blue-checkered tablecloths and wicker lamps. There are no surprises here, just high-quality, satisfying house-made pasta dishes. Top choices include smoked chicken tortellini in a light cream sauce with prosciutto, broccoli and artichoke hearts, and freshly made fettuccine flavored with smoked trout, cream and capers. Chicken, fish and steak dishes are also popular, though lacking in originality, and desserts are solid, if unsurprising. At I Fratelli, it's consistency that counts.

Dinner nightly; valet parking; AE, MC, V.

★★☆☆
$$\$\$

Il Fornaio

**Downtown: 1265 Battery St.
(at Greenwich); 415-986-0100**

Italian

What started as a baker's school in Milan then became a chain of restaurants and bakeries in California. This Il Fornaio serves reliable—occasionally outstanding—Northern Italian food and fantastic baked goods in an airy, stylish setting. The antipasti are generally well prepared, and crisp pizzas and calzones from the wood-burning oven are particularly delightful. Interesting pasta choices include spinach and egg linguine tossed with shrimp, garlic and parsley; and ravioli stuffed with spinach, Swiss chard and basil in a rich pine nut and tomato sauce. The meats from the rotisserie are consistently well prepared. Dessert tortes, cakes and cookies offer further proof of the bakers' skills.

*Breakfast/lunch/dinner daily; outdoor seating;
full bar; valet parking; AE, DC, MC, V.*

★★★★
$$$$$

Imperial Palace

Chinatown: 919 Grant Ave. (between Jackson and Washington); 415-982-8889

Chinese

Good for groups

Though not as popular as it once was, this luxurious setting with marble tables and rare antiques still offers high-quality dim sum and Cantonese fare. Dim sum is served on small trays laden with circular bamboo baskets which allow for fewer choices, but with prodding the waitresses will make a special trip. Beg for the eggplant or shrimp-and-scallop dim sum, or the shrimp pancakes and barbecued pork rolls. For dinner, entrees such as crispy chicken in lemon sauce or stir-fried rock cod in black-bean chili sauce are recommended. As many of the best dishes aren't on the English menu, ask for suggestions.

Lunch/dinner daily; full bar; free parking lot; AE, CB, DC, MC, V.

★★★★
$$$$$

Indian Oven

Fillmore: 233 Fillmore St. (between Waller and Haight); 415-626-1628

Indian

One of San Francisco's best northern Indian restaurants, this classy, modern establishment, with track lighting, an open kitchen and fresh flowers offers fantastic food at reasonable prices. Be sure to start with an order of samosas (crisp spiced vegetable puffs) or, better yet, order the assorted appetizers plate. Most popular are the tandoori dishes (chicken or lamb prepared in the restaurant's wood-burning clay oven) or the prawns with tomatoes and spices. Don't forget to order the melt-in-your-mouth garlic nan, an Indian flat bread. Bear in mind, service can be excruciatingly slow and the kitchen inconsistent.

Dinner nightly; AE, D, MC, V.

★★★★
$$$$$

Indigo Restaurant

Hayes Valley: 687 McAllister St. (between Gough and Franklin); 415-673-9353

California

Romantic

This Hayes Valley restaurant, with its spacious white dining room, blue-tiled bar and plush velour banquettes, quickly became a favorite of theatergoers when it opened in spring 1997. The inventive cuisine changes daily, but you can always expect a salmon, a vegetarian and a pork chop special. The flat breads are always wonderful (look for one with fava bean puree and assorted wild mushrooms), and you'd do well to heed the house's suggested wine pairings listed alongside most dishes. End with the "chocodero" mousse cake or the unusual lavender crème brûlée.

Dinner Tuesday-Sunday; prix fixe menu; full bar; valet parking; AE, CB, DC, D, MC, V.

★★★★
$$$$$

Infusion

South of Market: 555 2nd St. (between Bryant and Brannan); 415-543-2282

American

Good deal

Though it's trendy, noisy and specializes in fruit-infused vodka drinks, this sleek, stylish gem is also serious about food. Its spare, modern furnishings stand in dramatic contrast to the intense, spicy complexity of the rustic American cuisine, which blends European, Asian and Caribbean influences. Entrees range from guava empanadas with brie to salmon in a crisp walnut crust with strawberry, papaya and ginger vinaigrette to roasted honey-cider brined chicken. Save room for dessert, especially the strawberry shortcake and the chocolate brownie torte. Live jazz, blues, or folk groups perform on a perch above the bar Thursdays through Saturdays.

Lunch/dinner Tuesday-Sunday; loud; live entertainment; full bar; AE, DC, MC, V.

★★★★
$$$$$

Irrawaddy

Marina: 1769 Lombard St. (between Octavia and Laguna); 415-931-2830

Burmese

Hidden on a busy stretch of Lombard Street, this authentic Burmese eatery is worth a visit. Inside is a comfortable dining room with sunken booths and huge pillows. Crispy Golden Triangles, pastry puffs filled with spiced potatoes and ground beef, are good starters, as are the onion fritters, superb green-tea leaf salad and sweet-and-sour daikon radish soup. The Mandalay noodle dish, tossed with braised chicken and roasted split-pea powder, is superb, as is the house-special sea bass steamed in a banana leaf. Diners go shoeless at the table, so be sure to wear clean socks.

Dinner nightly; AE, MC, V.

★★★★
$$$$$

Isuzu

Fillmore: 1581 Webster St. (at Post); 415-922-2290

Japanese

 Good for groups

Popular with Japanese families, this is a good place for groups, particularly for family-style ordering. Though the high-ceilinged dining room could use a face lift, the cuisine is always impeccable and surprisingly inexpensive. The fried calamari, lobster thermidor and teriyaki eel are all excellent choices, but the real treats here are the fresh-fish specials. Deep-fried flounder served whole, for example, always elicits raves. Isuzu also serves above-average sushi and clay-pot dishes, and unlike most restaurants in Japantown, has a full bar. After dinner, take in a movie at the Kabuki 8 cinemas.

Lunch Monday-Saturday, dinner nightly; closed Tuesday; full bar; validated parking; MC, V.

★☆☆☆
$$$$$

It's Tops Coffee Shop

Castro: 1801 Market St. (at McCoppin); 415-864-9352

American

Owned and operated by the same family since 1952, It's Tops is a true slice of nostalgia, serving up pancakes, omelets, deep-fried sides and grilled sandwiches in a tiny space dominated by a soda counter. Burgers and ice cream sundaes are on the menu too, of course. Expect a wait on weekend mornings and remember to read Bruce and Sheila's house rules printed on the menu: No Hate, Love Only Food; Please Don't Feed the Pigeons; No Cheapskates Allowed, and so on. Diners cram their quarters in the old time jukeboxes while they wait for their food.

Breakfast/lunch daily; late-night dining; loud; MC, V.

★★☆☆
$$$$$

Izzy's Steak & Chop House

Marina: 3345 Steiner St. (between Lombard and Chestnut); 415-563-0487

American

 Good deal

 Good for groups

 Kid friendly

Izzy's dark-wood interior, inviting full bar and stone fireplace hark back to the Rat Pack era, when a fine steak was de rigueur. Two of the most popular choices at this boisterous, charming spot are the juicy 8-ounce fillet medallions coated with cracked pepper and brandy, and the New York sirloin aged 21 days and served with potatoes au gratin and creamed spinach. There are also pork chops with cinnamon and apples, loin lamb chops, shrimp with beer and spices, and peppered swordfish with lime-chive sauce. A slice of key lime pie is a refreshing end.

Dinner nightly; fireplace; full bar; validated parking; AE, DC, MC, V.

★★★☆ $$\$\$$

Jackson Fillmore

Pacific Heights: 2506 Fillmore St.
(at Jackson); 415-346-5288

Italian

If you manage to snag a table or a seat at the bar, feasting at this friendly, cozy yet boisterous neighborhood trattoria is a great way to gear up for a movie down the street. Best is the complimentary warm bruschetta appetizer, drenched in olive oil and aromatic garlic with a tangy tomato-and-basil topping. Also try the portobello mushrooms, grilled with olive oil and garlic and served over arugula. The entrees, while generally excellent, can be uninspired: while you'll dream about the ricotta ravioli with pesto and mozzarella, the roasted chicken is decidedly unmemorable.

Dinner nightly; all major credit cards.

★★★☆ $$\$\$$

Jakarta Indonesian

Sunset: 615 Balboa St. (at 7th Ave.);
415-387-5225

Indonesian

 Good for groups

Prices here are low enough to allow for family-style experimentation, choosing from dozens of grilled, fried, sauced and spiced dishes served among the native masks, sculptures and shadow puppets of Jakarta's dining room. Start with the triangles of spiced ground beef wrapped in phyllo dough or shrimp cakes with sweet corn, or a light, flavorful soup of lemongrass, mushrooms and coconut milk. For two people, the *rijsttafel* (rice table)—a $35 feast that includes 10 Indonesian dishes ranging from braised oxtail to Javanese fried chicken—is the way to go.

Dinner Tuesday-Sunday; valet parking; AE, D, MC, V.

★★★★
$$$$$

James & James Ribs 'N Thangs

Potrero Hill: 5130 3rd St. (at Shafter Ave.);
415-671-0269

Barbecue

 Sidewalk's choice

 Good deal

Good for groups

This unassuming storefront barbecue operation serves the best ribs in the city, as well as moist barbecued chicken, fine beef links and tasty sides (especially the yams and baked beans). As rib joints go, this is a pretty classy one, with several nice wood tables and framed photos of local celebrities on the walls. Come early for the sweet potato pie, and bring your own if you require a brew with your ribs. Besides being an excellent chef, owner Wedrell James is a well-respected actor, director and producer.

Lunch/dinner Tuesday-Saturday; late-night dining; no liquor license; reservations not accepted; cash only.

NR
$$$$$

Jardiniere

Civic Center: 300 Grove St. (at Franklin);
415-861-5555

California

 Sidewalk's choice

 Good for groups

With award-winning chef Traci des Jardins at the helm and an interior by celebrity designer Pat Kuleto, Jardiniere had immediate status when it opened in fall 1997. The theatrical silver and black interior rises two stories, with a dramatically lit circular silver railing and a domed gold ceiling studded with tiny lights. Food ranges from earthy (lamb loin) to chi-chi (lobster strudel, foie gras); a unique element is the cheese aging room downstairs, visible to diners. *Note: The restaurant was too new to review at press time.*

Dinner daily; full bar; live entertainment; valet parking; AE, MC, V.

★★★★
$$$$$

Jeong Hyun Charcoal Barbecue House

Sunset: 2123 Irving St. (between 22nd and 23rd Aves.); 415-665-0966

Korean

Built for comfort, not for looks, each of the booths at this humble Korean restaurant has a huge vent that whisks away smoke from the tabletop hibachi you use to grill various meats. The menu is heavy on beef, the most popular dish being *kalbi*—thinly sliced, sweet-tasting marinated short ribs that cook in mere seconds—accompanied by more than a dozen small plates of delicacies, ranging from cold marinated vegetables to glass noodles and rice. In addition to short ribs, you can get pork, chicken and salmon barbecue. Eating here makes for an adventurous feast that never gets tiresome.

Lunch Monday-Saturday; dinner nightly; MC, V.

★★★☆
$$$$$

Jessie's

South of Market: 1256 Folsom St. (between 8th and 9th Sts.); 415-437-2481

Cajun

Haitian-born owner Jessie Leonard-Corcia is determined to let the good times roll at this festive Creole and Cajun restaurant. To capture that New Orleans spirit, the dining area is splashed with bold shades of burgundy, eggplant and terra-cotta. The back windows overlook a tropical garden, and the generous portions of food are authentic and well-executed— spicy and creative favorites such as smoked chicken and seafood jambalaya, gumbo, crayfish étouffée and red beans and rice. The adventurous might try the spicy alligator sausage or Creole ratatouille pillows. Top off your meal with the wonderful bread pudding.

Lunch Tuesday-Friday, dinner Tuesday-Sunday; outdoor seating; live entertainment; AE, DC, D, MC, V.

★★★★
$$$$$

Johnny Love's

Russian Hill: 1500 Broadway (at Polk);
415-931-6053

California

Though this is more of a singles bar than a restaurant, the menu does go beyond ordinary pub fare to offer dishes like pan-roasted chicken with pumpkin seeds, goat cheese and black beans and thick-cut New York steak. Dine at cocktail tables or cozy booths lining the club's perimeter, or at the U-shaped oak bar. Dinner is served until 10 p.m.; diners who stay for the entertainment get their cover charge waived.

> *Dinner daily; loud; live entertainment; full bar;*
> *valet parking or free lot; AE, DC, D, MC, V.*

★★★★
$$$$$

Joubert's

Sunset: 4115 Judah St. (between 46th and
47th Aves.); 415-753-5448

African

Sidewalk's
choice

At this South African vegetarian restaurant, chef/owner Patrick Conlon uses many of his grandfather's recipes, blending flavors of India, Asia and Africa to create dishes such as seasoned soya patties served with mashed potatoes and crimini mushroom gravy, or *isipingo samp*, which is made from curried hominy, black-eyed peas and rice infused with nuts, raisins and curry. Newcomers should try the three-course prix fixe menu. The wine list has a large selection of South African, organic and kosher wines.

> *Dinner Wednesday-Sunday; quiet; AE, MC, V.*

★★★★
$$$$$

Just Like Home Restaurant

Sunset: 1924 Irving St. (at 20th Ave.);
415-681-3337

Middle
Eastern

Sidewalk's
choice

Good
deal

Beyond the arched doorways of this Lebanese cafe with a deli counter in front lies a casual dining room featuring delicious food fresh from the oven. Along with the standard Middle Eastern tidbits, all richly seasoned, you'll find unusual appetizers such as *tohalat* (sliced lamb spleen stuffed with fiery walnut pesto) and the herbed-bread snack, *mana-eesh zater.* Baba ghanouj exhibits both smokiness and a touch of fire; heavenly *kufta kabobs* (with flavorful, top-quality beef) are spiced with an earthy touch of green chile. For dessert, indulge in buttery house-baked *baklava*, or pistachio-studded sesame *halvah.*

Lunch/dinner daily; quiet; beer only; AE, MC, V, checks.

★★★★
$$$$$

Kabuto Sushi Restaurant

Richmond: 5116 Geary Blvd. (between 15th and 16th Aves.); 415-752-5652

Japanese

Sidewalk's
choice

Kabuto has probably the finest sushi bar in the city. Celebrated owner Sachio Kojima performs magic in a blur of bamboo rollers and blades, proving definitively that fresh, raw fish can be one of the most perfect foods. Expect all the classic nigiri and makimono rolls (clam, tuna, herring, daikon) as well as some unusual treats if you allow the charismatic Kojima to surprise you. Besides teriyaki, tempura and sashimi entrees, the kitchen also prepares grilled shellfish, soups and tofu dishes. If you like your wasabi nuclear-hot, ask for the good stuff that Kojima hides behind the counter.

Dinner Tuesday-Saturday; AE, MC, V.

Kan Zaman

★★★★
$$$$$

Haight: 1793 Haight St. (between Shrader and Cole); 415-751-9656

Middle
Eastern

 Good
deal

This dirt-cheap Middle Eastern oasis—a mini-replica of a 14th century Moorish palace—inspires guests to shed their shoes and indulge in fantasy by gathering around knee-high tables under a canopy tent, lounging on pillows while sampling an array of appetizers. The menu focuses on traditional staples: hummus, baba ghanouj, well-spiced kabobs done to perfection. Bar-side, guests rent *hookahs* (huge water pipes) for smoking one of the house's fruity Egyptian tobacco blends. On weekends, belly dancers jiggle through the crowd. This place is always packed, as it's hard to find such good food and festivity for less than 10 bucks.

Lunch Tuesday-Sunday, dinner nightly; live entertainment; cash only.

Kasra Persian and Mediterranean Cuisine

★★★★
$$$$$

Richmond: 349 Clement St. (at 5th Ave.); 415-752-1101

Middle
Eastern

 Good
for groups

A grand Persian restaurant with a giant fireplace and wood bar, Kasra concentrates on one main dish: Persian-style grilled kabobs, available in more than a dozen versions. Side dishes, such as the Shirazi salad (a minty version of the classic herbed-tomato-and-cucumber mixture) or the smoky grilled eggplant mixed with tomatoes and chopped egg, are interesting and tasty. For dessert, try the dreamy rose-water-pistachio ice cream. On weekends, Kasra features traditional belly dancing, as well as Russian folk music.

Lunch Friday, dinner nightly; live entertainment; fireplace; AE, MC, V.

★★★★
$$$$$

Kate's Kitchen

Lower Haight: 471 Haight St. (between Fillmore and Webster); 415-626-3984

Southern

Despite its sketchy location, Kate's is an amazingly good restaurant, offering food made from scratch every morning with recipes taken from a sacred southern cookbook: thick slabs of orange-spiced French toast with maple syrup, buttermilk-cornmeal pancakes, scallion-cheese biscuits, hushpuppies, and huge plates of hash loaded with chunks of corned beef, carrots, onions and potatoes. Even the waitresses have down-home drawls. Lunch is worth the trip for the meatloaf sandwich, roast chicken or Smiling Cow (steamed veggies over brown rice). Thumping hip-hop music bounces off the country-themed decor, and tattooed locals mingle with the occasional Gap-clad outsider.

Breakfast/lunch daily; weekend brunch; loud; reservations not accepted; cash only.

★★★★
$$$$$

Katia's

Sunset: 600 5th Ave. (at Balboa); 415-668-9292

Russian

Easily the most attractive and romantic Russian restaurant in the city. Large, tinted windows slide open to let sunlight bathe the tiny dining room, while a guitarist plays Russian music in the background. Owner/chef Katia Troosh prepares all the traditional Russian dishes. For appetizers, try the mildly spiced beef dumplings or piroshki filled with beef, mushroom or cabbage. Beef Stroganoff, usually a heavy dish, is surprisingly light and tender. All entrees come with fresh vegetables, nicely balancing the meat-heavy menu. For dessert, the chocolate meringue is a must.

Lunch/dinner Tuesday-Sunday; weekend brunch; live entertainment; AE, D, MC, V, checks.

★★☆☆
$$$$

Kelly's on Trinity

Downtown: 333 Bush St. (between Kearny and Montgomery); 415-362-4454

American

 Kid friendly

 Good for groups

With pastel colors, high ceilings and views of Trinity Plaza, this deluxe cafeteria opened by Kelly Mills (formerly of the Clift Hotel) is a pleasant place to grab a quick lunch: sandwiches made with first-rate ingredients, including freshly baked breads, gourmet deli meats and fresh local produce; salad samplers (from a choice of more than 20 different salads); and fresh-fruit smoothies made at the new juice bar. Note that service can get a little snarly at times.

Breakfast/lunch weekdays; outdoor seating; view; reservations required for large parties; cash only.

★★★☆
$$$$

Khan Toke Thai House

Richmond: 5937 Geary Blvd. (between 23rd and 24th Aves.); 415-668-6654

Thai

 Sidewalk's choice

 Good deal

 Romantic

 Good for groups

 Kid friendly

One of San Francisco's first Thai restaurants still ranks among its best. Surrounded by lavishly carved teak, exotic Thai statues and intricately woven tapestries, you'll feel you've left the city behind. Start with a bowl of the mild *tom ka gai* soup, followed by tiny squid mixed with fresh greens, hot chiles, lemongrass and mint leaves and deep-fried pompano topped with sautéed ginger, onions, pickled garlic and yellow bean sauce. Other good bets are *pad thai* and beef with spinach and peanut sauce. There's also a quite decent wine list.

Dinner nightly; outdoor seating; live entertainment; AE, DC, D, MC, V.

★★★★
$$$$$

King Jamaican Restaurant

Fillmore: 1279 Fulton St. (between Fulton and Divisadero); 415-567-1294

Jamaican

Sidewalk's
choice

Set in a table-free storefront cluttered with Jamaican crafts and dance hall tapes, in the spot formerly occupied by Prince Neville's, this restaurant is now strictly takeout and delivery. And deliver it does, providing authentic, exciting Jamaican specialties. The salmon (big, fresh and meltingly moist) is deliciously prepared with a curry sauce or stuffed with crab; curried goat is tender in a rich, spicy coconut sauce; fried plantains are ripe and succulent. Vegetarians do well here, with curried mixed vegetable dishes and a spicy five-bean soup.

Lunch/dinner Tuesday-Sunday; cash only.

★★★★
$$$$$

Kiss

South of Market: 680 8th St. (between Brannan and Townsend); 415-552-8757

Asian/French

Romantic

Basing their decor on Gustav Klimt's "The Kiss," co-owners Morgan and Unni Song transformed this cavernous, high-ceilinged room into a pleasantly dramatic and romantic place to dine, with attentive service and substantial Asian-French fare. Chef Morgan Song's specialties include juicy roasted rack of lamb, chicken breast stuffed with rice in orange Pernod sauce, and grilled whole red trout stuffed with spinach. The wine list, primarily composed of French and California selections, is reasonably priced and includes several by the glass. For dessert, if Song's soufflé (made with Grand Marnier) is on the menu, don't pass it up.

Lunch Monday-Saturday; quiet; AE, DC, MC, V.

Korea House

Japan Center/Fillmore: 1620 Post St. (at Laguna); 415-931-7834

Korean

Good for groups

Popular with Korean expatriates, this country-style restaurant offers Korean barbecue, but the real draws are the skillfully prepared dishes featuring chicken, beef, pork and seafood entrees, as well as the less common tripe and beef tongue. Main dishes arrive with a half-dozen flavorful side dishes, so a twosome can fill up on one entree. The restaurant's most outstanding feature may be its hours: If you can't stomach the usual greasy-spoon food after a night on the town, head to Korea House, open until 3 a.m. on weekends.

Lunch/dinner daily; late-night dining; MC, V.

Kowloon Vegetarian Restaurant

Chinatown: 909 Grant Ave. (between Washington and Jackson); 415-362-9888

Chinese/
Vegetarian

Good deal

This unassuming vegetarian Chinese restaurant pulls in locals, who come for the cheap, satisfying, meat-free fare. There's nothing fancy about the bamboo-wallpapered interior or the Formica tables, but richly flavored dishes like thousand-layer tofu crisp with vegetarian ham, peas, corn and carrots make up for the lack of ambience. The kitchen works wonders with tofu and wheat gluten: Kowloon chow mein, featuring vegetarian chicken and pork and a variety of vegetables, mushroom-vegetable egg rolls and a mind-boggling assortment of sweet and savory dim sum.

Lunch/dinner daily; no liquor license; reservations not accepted; MC, V.

★★★★
$$$$$

Kuk Jea

Richmond: 4611 Geary Blvd. (between 10th and 11th Aves.); 415-751-6336

Korean

 Good deal

Good for groups

Dreary and devoid of ornamentation, this San Francisco transplant of a traditional Korean meat house, also known as Wooden Charcoal BBQ, exists for functionality, not fashion, serving excellent food to a mostly Korean crowd. The meat is grilled at your table, having marinated in a complex bath of sesame, soy, ginger, scallions, garlic and black pepper. The outstanding lunch special consists of an enormous platter of charcoal-grilled beef, pork, ribs or chicken, rice, pickled cucumbers, tangy salad, bean sprouts, kimchee, fried radish, soup and tea for $4.95.

Lunch/dinner daily; reservations not accepted; MC, V.

★★★★
$$$$$

Kuleto's Restaurant

Downtown: 221 Powell St. (between Geary and O'Farrell); 415-397-7720

Italian

 Kid friendly

 Good for groups

 Romantic

Garlands of garlic and whole prosciuttos dangle over the 40-foot-long mahogany bar in a handsome, cozy interior created by designer Pat Kuleto. Kuleto's delivers satisfying California-Italian fare at reasonable prices. The antipasti are excellent, and though the rest of the menu can be inconsistent, memorable main courses include the simple but savory angel hair pasta with tomatoes, basil and garlic; saffron risotto dotted with shrimp, scallops and sun-dried tomatoes; and roast duck with grappa-soaked cherries and black-pepper polenta. An extensive wine list includes several selections available by the glass.

Breakfast/lunch/dinner daily; live entertainment; full bar; AE, DC, D, MC, V.

★★☆☆
$$$$$

Kushi Tsuru

Japan Center/Fillmore: 1737 Post St. (between Buchanan and Webster); 415-922-9902

Japanese

Hidden deep in the Kintetsu Mall, this modest restaurant serves superior Japanese food at moderate prices. Unless you're craving noodles, it's a much better choice overall than the popular Mifune next door—cleaner, quieter and more attractive, with friendlier service and better food. Sushi is top grade, including melt-in-your-mouth eel, and the tempura udon is a veritable three-course meal in one: soup, salad and a side plate of tasty tempura. The bento box overflows with sushi rolls, tempura, sashimi, vegetables and Kushi Tsuru's wonderful crispy, broiled fish.

Lunch/dinner daily; MC, V.

★★★☆
$$$$$

Kyo-Ya

Downtown: Sheraton Palace Hotel, 2 New Montgomery St. (between Market and Mission, 2nd and 3rd); 415-512-1111

Japanese

A branch of a Japanese chain, the elegantly austere Kyo-Ya in the Sheraton Palace Hotel caters to visiting businessmen, serving some of the best sushi and sashimi in town. Order a decanter of *sake* (there are about a dozen varieties) and some *toro* (tuna belly), *ebi* (shrimp), *hotate* (scallops) or any of the items on the extensive list of sushi offerings. They're sure to be some of the finest you've ever had.

Lunch Tuesday-Friday, dinner Tuesday-Saturday; quiet; full bar; valet parking; AE, DC, D, MC, V.

★★★★
$$$$$

La Bergerie

Richmond: 4221 Geary Blvd. (between 6th and 7th Aves.); 415-387-3573

French

Good deal

Good for groups

Romantic

A dinosaur of a restaurant, La Bergerie features classic French food and decor so hopelessly out of date, it's almost back in fashion. So why bother? Because the restaurant has established a solid reputation for consistently well-prepared dishes at bargain prices. The escargot appetizer is about half of what you'd pay at any other French restaurant, and the delicious garlic-encrusted rack of lamb is only $16.75, including soup, salad, coffee and sorbet. There's a good selection of inexpensive French wines to complement your meal.

Dinner nightly; AE, D, MC, V.

★☆★★
$$$$$

La Cumbre Taqueria

Mission: 515 Valencia St. (between 16th and 17th Sts.); 415-863-8205

Mexican

Good deal

Though it's no longer the most popular taqueria in the Mission, die-hard fans still stand in line for a quick, cheap fix of Mexican fast food. The menu offers only tacos and burritos, with the filling of your choice. The carne asada burrito is a top seller; the tacos de carnitos deluxe are delicious, too. Pair your bundle of spicy joy with Mexican beer or *horchata*, a cool, sweet, grain-based drink found at most taquerias.

Lunch/dinner daily; loud; reservations not accepted; checks.

★★★★
$$$$$

La Felce

North Beach: 1570 Stockton St. (at Union); 415-392-8321

Italian

Boisterous patrons with hearty appetites come to La Felce, king of traditional Italian restaurants, which hasn't changed a bit since opening in 1976. Dig into huge plates of classic northern Italian food, served in a dimly lit dining room at tables set with white cloths and single red carnations. Start with a hefty platter of sliced tomatoes draped with anchovies, shredded onion and a tangy vinaigrette, then move on to fettuccine Alfredo or carbonara, chicken cacciatore or the house specialty, *saltimbocca* (veal rolled with prosciutto, then sautéed in white wine and mushrooms). Finish with the house specialty, a fried cream custard.

Lunch weekdays, dinner nightly; closed Tuesday; full bar; validated parking; AE, CB, MC, V.

La Folie

★★★★
$$$$$

Russian Hill: 2316 Polk St. (between Green and Union); 415-776-5577

French

Sidewalk's choice

Romantic

In a charming, family-run restaurant with cotton clouds painted on sky-blue walls, Chef Roland Passot serves generous portions of astoundingly good food. Passot's exuberant but disciplined menu changes often. Memorable starters range from wonderful foie-gras plates to salad of crab, lobster and smoked salmon tossed with avocado, crème fraîche, caviar and tomato vinaigrette. Perfect entrees have included free-range Sonoma duck breast drizzled with Oregon wild huckleberry sauce, and roast rack of lamb with persillade crust and cranberry timbale. The owner's roots surface in the pricey, decidedly Franco-California wine list. Passot has thoughtfully included a separate Vegetable Lover's Menu.

Dinner Monday-Saturday; prix fixe menu; full bar; valet parking; AE, DC, D, MC, V.

★★★★
$$$$$

La Jiao

Civic Center: 536 Golden Gate Ave. (between Van Ness and Polk); 415-771-1997

Asian

Good for groups

This large, attractive restaurant features an interesting Chinese-focused menu with Thai and Singaporean influences. La Jiao is busiest during lunch, when the kitchen offers the most Thai dishes, but that is also when the food is weakest. At dinner, expect intriguing fare such as thin-sliced pork with Peking sauce, Szechuan eggplant with pork and spicy ginger-garlic sauce, and deep-fried tofu nuggets; or choose from several pan-Pacific noodle dishes, including Korean-style egg noodles with fresh seafood and vegetables in a piquant broth, and Singapore rice noodles with barbecued pork.

Lunch weekdays, dinner Monday-Thursday, Saturday; late-night dining; full bar; MC, V.

★★★★
$$$$$

La Méditerranée

Castro: 288 Noe St. (at Market);
415-431-7210
Pacific Heights: 2210 Fillmore St.
(at Sacramento); 415-921-2956

Mediterranean

Good deal

Kid friendly

A local chain popular with Bay Area diners, La Méditerranée skillfully blends the sun-splashed cuisines of Greece and North Africa. Savory sandwiches of *lahvosh* bread are layered with cream cheese, herbs, cucumbers, lettuce, feta cheese and tomato. Traditional Greek phyllo pie gets a twist with chunks of tender chicken, almonds, chickpeas, currants and cinnamon, or with lean ground beef seasoned with pine nuts, onions and spices. Everything is reasonably priced, but one of the best deals is the Mediterranean *meza*, an assortment of 10 house specialties for two or more that runs $10.50 per person.

Lunch/dinner Tuesday-Sunday on Noe, Monday-Saturday on Fillmore; outdoor seating at Noe; reservations not accepted; AE, MC, V, checks.

★★☆☆
$$$$$

La Scene

Downtown: 490 Geary St. (at Taylor);
415-292-6430

California

Good for groups

Romantic

A cozy candlelit restaurant that makes the most of its theater district proximity, La Scene has been retooled as a California bistro. Starters feature a tasty onion-confit tart, gravlax with cucumbers and beets, and hummus with mint pesto and lentil chips. Salads include a sesame-carrot-cabbage concoction topped by grilled shrimp, while crispy duck-leg confit and braised lamb shank are popular entrees. The wine list showcases a small but well-priced selection of California favorites. A $21 three-course prix fixe dinner is offered nightly.

Dinner nightly; live entertainment; theater menu; prix fixe menu; full bar; valet parking; AE, DC, D, MC, V.

★★★☆
$$$$$

La Taqueria

Mission: 2889 Mission St. (between 24th and 25th Sts.); 415-285-7117

Mexican

Good deal

Kid friendly

Don't expect a wide variety of Mexican fare from the folks at this nondescript restaurant, but their burritos, tacos and quesadillas are some of the best in town: fresh, cheap, delicious and guaranteed to fill you up for little more than pocket change. The moist, meaty fillings include grilled beef, pork, sausage and chicken, and besides the usual beer and soda there are great *aguas frescas* (try the cantaloupe) and *horchata* (a sweet rice drink).

Lunch/dinner daily; loud; outdoor seating; reservations not accepted; checks.

La Traviata

Mission: 2854 Mission St. (between 24th and 25th Sts.); 415-282-0500

Italian

 Romantic

This hidden gem of a restaurant, which boasts a loyal clientele despite its dicey location, has dedicated every square inch of the narrow dining room to opera. But even with arias sounding overhead, the place manages to be quiet and intimate. The service is old-world gracious, and the owners win over guests with their outstanding house-made gnocchi and limited list of consistently well-prepared pastas. Try the alla Carreras (a powerful toss of prosciutto, sausage, mushrooms and tomatoes) or the robust puttanesca (a spicy red sauce with capers, black olives and anchovies). The most appropriate finale is the coveted tiramisu.

Dinner Tuesday-Sunday; AE, DC, D, MC, V.

La Vie

Richmond: 5830 Geary Blvd. (between 22nd and 23rd Aves.); 415-668-8080

Vietnamese

 Sidewalk's choice

Good deal

Hidden among the dozens of ethnic restaurants that line Geary, relaxing, stylish, refreshingly spartan La Vie is one of the best Vietnamese restaurants in San Francisco. For a good dinner, start with deep-fried sticky rice balls stuffed with minced pork, shrimp, carrot and mushroom, followed by the wonderful crab and asparagus soup and stir-fried clams with mint leaves and black bean sauce. Then select your entree: Flaming Beef and Prawn is delicious and cooked at your table with elaborate flair. The perfect place for a fun, low-budget evening.

Lunch/dinner daily; MC, V.

Laghi

★★★☆
$$$$$

**Richmond: 1801 Clement St. (at 19th Ave.);
415-386-6266**

Italian

Fans crave the top-notch Italian food at this tiny corner
trattoria, despite cramped quarters and high prices.
Chef/owner Gino Laghi's pragmatic menu changes
nightly, and preparations are kept simple, letting the
quality of the fresh ingredients shine. Breads and
pastas are house-made to match Gino's sauces, which
are often laden with exotic fungi. Try his legendary
risotto with red wine and black truffles. Whether it's
grilled sea bass or free-range chicken baked
between two bricks, be assured that Gino has put
heart and soul into each dish. And don't be surprised
if he checks in on you to make sure you're satisfied.

Dinner Tuesday-Sunday; AE, CB, DC, MC, V.

Lalita

★★☆☆
$$$$$

**Civic Center: 96 McAllister St.
(at Leavenworth); 415-552-5744**

Thai

Ensconced in a rather unsavory neighborhood, this
utterly modern Thai restaurant stands out from others
with a staff outfitted in stiff-collared shirts and ties,
and a separate cocktail lounge and full bar that
serves microbrewed beers on tap. Some of the more
unusual offerings include salmon steamed in banana
leaves and stuffed with ground chicken, coconut milk
and mild red chiles, and marinated lamb simmered in
masamum curry and served with tamarind sauce. For
dessert, consider Lalita's Special—warm, sticky rice
laced with tropical fruits and coconut milk.

Lunch/dinner daily; full bar; DC, D, MC, V.

Le Central

Downtown: 453 Bush St. (between Grant and Kearny); 415-391-2233

French

 Good for groups

In business for more than two decades, Le Central still reigns as San Francisco's premier power brasserie, drawing the likes of Mayor Willie Brown and Wilkes Bashford. Newcomers grouse about indifferent service and some say the food—classics such as cassoulet, steak with pommes frites, crab cakes beurre blanc and warm garlic sausage with potato vinaigrette—has slipped a bit in recent years. Brick walls dotted with art posters, bentwood-and-cane bistro chairs, a zinc bar and a row of mirrors hand-lettered with daily specials all add to the casually sophisticated Parisian ambience.

Lunch/dinner Monday-Saturday; full bar; valet parking; AE, DC, MC, V.

Le Charm

South of Market: 315 5th St. (between Howard and Folsom); 415-546-6128

French

 Sidewalk's choice

Good deal

Romantic

This traditional-looking bistro on a charmless industrial street is prized by culinary cognoscenti for its good French food at bargain prices. Talented husband-and-wife team (Alain Delangle, formerly a chef at the Sherman House, and Lina Yew, formerly the pastry chef at Fleur de Lys) turn out classic rustic bistro fare such as onion soup, boeuf bourguignon and tarte Tatin with caramel sauce on the prix fixe menu, and à la carte items that include sautéed escargot, duck confit and an interesting salad of chicken livers. The wine list offers a nice choice of domestic and French vintages.

Lunch weekdays, dinner Tuesday-Saturday; outdoor seating; prix fixe menu; AE, MC, V.

★★★ ☆
**$**$$$$

Le Soleil

Richmond: 133 Clement St. (between 2nd
and 3rd Aves.); 415-668-4848

Vietnamese

With its pleasing decor and a bounteous array of
well-prepared French-influenced Vietnamese fare
presented in more than 70 menu items, Le Soleil is
widely considered the best Vietnamese restaurant in
San Francisco. Start with well-prepared crisp spring
rolls; a classic Vietnamese crepe, rolled at the table
with mint leaves, raw vegetables and a tangy dipping
sauce; or the excellent minced shrimp wrapped in
sugarcane, barbecued porks balls, and tangy crab
and corn soup. The best entrees are the five-spice
chicken, Saigon-style barbecued pork chop and
jumbo shrimp still in their shells.

Lunch/dinner daily; AE, MC, V.

★★★ ☆
**$$**$$$

Lhasa Moon

Marina: 2420 Lombard St. (at Scott);
415-674-9898

Tibetan

Good
deal

Good
for groups

Introducing San Francisco's only Tibetan restaurant,
a charming and relaxed place offering simple, satis-
fying regional Indian-influenced food. Some items
are out of the ordinary—boldly flavored cheese soup
floating with bits of chopped beef, green pepper and
onion, or earthy daikon radish sautéed in ginger and
cilantro—but many dishes will taste familiar to those
acquainted with Chinese and Indian food: thin-
shelled dumplings filled with meat, vegetables and
spices, deep-fried curried chicken, shaptak, or
sautéed bean thread strings, potatoes and celery. The
restaurant closes occasionally, when the manage-
ment goes yak trekking in the Himalayas.

*Lunch Thursday-Friday, dinner Tuesday-Sunday;
AE, MC, V.*

Liberty Cafe

Bernal Heights: 410 Cortland Ave. (between Bennington and Andover); 415-695-8777

American

Sidewalk's choice

Bernal Heights' best restaurant has garnered quite a following for its seasonally changing menu, which includes permanent favorites such as chicken pot pie and traditional Caesar salad. In winter, expect dishes like boeuf bourguignonne with buttered noodles and persillade; in summer, vegetarian tamales might appear. The divine fruit pies are rightly praised as well. This plain-Jane cafe holds only a dozen tables, so expect a wait outside most nights, but once you're seated, a well-briefed staff treats you to quick and professional service.

Lunch Tuesday-Sunday, dinner Tuesday-Saturday; weekend brunch; reservations not accepted; AE, MC, V.

Lichee Garden

Chinatown: 1416 Powell St. (between Powell and Broadway); 415-397-2290

Chinese

Good deal

Kid friendly

For more than a decade, Lichee Garden has been a favorite spot for superb (and surprisingly inexpensive) Cantonese cuisine. Though the quality of most dishes is above average, stick to the house specialties: spicy salted prawns, whole Dungeness crab, minced squab with pine nuts, crispy-skinned half chicken, pork spareribs, and excellent and unusual wild-game clay-pot dishes (not on the menu). The decor is pleasingly austere, and though the harried waiters in clipped gold jackets and black bow ties sometimes provide uneven service, all things considered, this is one of Chinatown's best Cantonese restaurants.

Breakfast/lunch/dinner daily; MC, V.

Little City Antipasti Bar

★☆☆☆
$$$$$

North Beach: 673 Union St. (between Powell and Stockton); 415-434-2900

Italian

 Good for groups

One of the first places in San Francisco to cash in on the grazing trend, this tiny brick-walled corner restaurant offers a wide selection of antipasti plates served tapas-style. Most diners skip the entrees and share a bunch of small plates, starting with the perennial favorite—roasted garlic and baked brie. Other popular choices are sliced garlic sausage with mashed potatoes; linguine with clams, wine and arbor chilis in roasted tomato sauce; and Japanese eggplant with ricotta cheese and spicy tomato sauce. Try to snag a seat in the front room, dominated by a large and perpetually packed bar.

Lunch/dinner daily; loud; AE, MC, V.

Liverpool Lil's

★☆☆☆
$$$$$

Marina: 2942 Lyon St. (between Lombard and Chestnut); 415-921-6664

English

 Kid friendly

 Good for groups

This warm, friendly neighborhood pub does a lively business serving steak-and-kidney pies and pints of Bass Ale to a mostly older crowd of locals. Along with beef Wellington, Bedford ribs and shepherd's pie, the well-rounded menu lists pasta dishes, seafood, salads and a bloody good burger. On warm nights, find a seat at one of the sidewalk tables festooned with twinkling lights. Inside, if you want intimacy, go early and stake out the small table in the front alcove.

Lunch/dinner daily; weekend brunch; outdoor seating; full bar; MC, V.

★★☆☆
$$$$$

Lo Coco's

North Beach: 510 Union St. (between Grant and Stockton); 415-296-9151

Italian

Warm and lively Lo Coco's is widely regarded as one of the best Sicilian restaurants in the city. Chef/owner Giovanni Lo Coco, a native of Sicily, has put together a menu showcasing the region's traditional cuisine—the saffron-infused fennel- and anchovy-spiked pasta, for example, is based on a recipe more than a thousand years old. For a well-rounded meal, start with the salad studded with pecans, blue cheese, currants and olives, then move on to pappardelle with fresh porcini mushrooms, or a light, crispy-crusted pizza. Finish Sicilian style, with Lo Coco's superb cannoli.

Dinner Tuesday-Saturday; MC, V.

★★★☆
$$$$$

L'Olivier

Downtown: 465 Davis St. (between Washington and Jackson); 415-981-7824

French

 Good
deal

 Good
for groups

 Romantic

Classic French fare served in a charming country-house dining room with brass chandeliers, patterned wallpaper and a large greenhouse window distinguishes this longtime downtown favorite. The kitchen concentrates on lovingly prepared traditional dishes: bouillabaisse, tripe Normandy, roast duckling a l'orange, seafood sausage, rabbit casserole and homemade desserts, such as crème brûlée. A prix fixe lunch menu with dessert costs $16, and at $25 for four courses, the nightly prix fixe menu is a great deal. Professional service rounds out this elegant, if predictable, dining experience, making it a great place to take your less adventurous companions.

Lunch weekdays, dinner Monday-Saturday; prix fixe menu; full bar; valet parking; AE, DC, D, MC, V.

London Wine Bar

**Downtown: 415 Sansome St.
(at Sacramento); 415-788-4811**

Cafe

The London Wine Bar, established in 1974, claims to be the first establishment in the country dedicated to wine. Happy hour is especially lively, and the downtown crowd doesn't seem to mind the limited menu; they come to experience the wine in an old-world environment of brick walls, mahogany paneling and stacked boxes of wine. Lunch is a bustling affair with standards such as pork chops, pasta marinara, quesadillas, focaccia sandwiches and salads. The 42-page wine list sports sizzling bargains on California and international bottles, and a rotating selection of quirky producers offered by the glass is exhilarating.

Open daily; loud; all major credit cards, checks.

LongLife Noodle Company & Jook Joint

Embarcadero: 139 Steuart St. (between Mission and Howard); 415-281-3818

Asian

A modern, stylish dining room sets the stage for one of the newer dining trends to hit the Bay Area: Asian noodles. LongLife serves a spectrum of Asian noodles, ranging from Japanese udon to Vietnamese rice sticks and Chinese egg noodles; they're paired with an interesting mix of ingredients and given whimsical names like Laksa Luck and Buddha's Bliss. Also on the menu are pan-Asian buns, wraps, rice and jook (savory Chinese rice porridge) dishes. Be prepared for a wait during lunchtime.

Lunch/dinner daily; loud; MC, V.

★★★☆
**$$**$$$

L'Osteria del Forno

North Beach: 519 Columbus Ave. (between Union and Green); 415-982-1124

Italian

Sidewalk's choice

Step inside this tiny jewel of a restaurant and you could be entering a cafe in Siena, complete with small tables, wine served in water glasses and a food-savvy staff. The restaurant puts its brick-lined oven to use making superb thin-crust pizzas, lightly covered with fresh mozzarella, and the house-made pastas are brimming with complex flavors. Try the ravioli filled with pumpkin, butter and sage sauce, as well as the outstanding focaccia sandwiches or meat dishes. Even the coffee is top-notch. Baskets of warm focaccia tide you over while you browse the list of Italian wines.

Lunch/dinner daily; full bar; reservations not accepted; cash only.

★★☆☆
$$$$

Lovejoy's Antiques & Tea Room

Noe Valley: 1195 Church St. (at 24th St.); 415-648-5895

Tea Room

Sidewalk's choice

Good deal

Romantic

Everything, from the china you're eating off to the chair you're sitting in, is for sale at this bright, cozy English tearoom. It's best to choose the High Tea option: Two people can split four types of sandwiches and two salads, and sample a selection of flaky, hot scones, complete with thick preserves and double Devon cream. The crustless sandwiches range from cucumber to a lightly smoked finan haddock. Tea choices include a smoky house blend, Earl Grey, Ceylon and, in a nod to California sensibilities, a few herbal varieties.

Lunch/high tea Tuesday-Sunday; outdoor seating; no liquor license; cash only.

Luzern Restaurant

Sunset: 1427-29 Noriega St. (between 21st and 22nd Aves.); 415-664-2353

Swiss

Romantic

For nearly two decades, this little Swiss hideaway has doled out generous—though pricey—portions of Wienerschnitzel, veal cordon bleu, cheese fondue and all those other caloric, dairy-laden dishes that taste so good (and stay so long). You'll find better prices at lunch for items like filet of sole or veal goulash. The single-room restaurant is furnished with little more than a small wood bar, a dozen or so tables, and cowbells and postcards from the owners' homeland. Nothing fancy, just undeniably quaint.

Lunch Thursday, dinner Wednesday-Sunday; MC, V.

★★★★
$$$$$

Ma Tante Sumi

Castro: 4243 18th St. (between Diamond and Douglass); 415-626-7864

Japanese/
French

Romantic

Maybe it's the tables set with Japanese pottery and linen cloths, or the complimentary blue cheese-caramelized onion mini-quiches, but it's hard not to get into a festive mood at this small restaurant serving creative yet understated Japanese-French cuisine. The imaginative menu changes seasonally, with starters such as warm coconut-milk crepes with vegetables in curry-and-lime-leaf sauce, served with mint-cilantro dip, and entrees like grilled tuna with wasabi and fish roe or succulent skewers of bay scallops and shrimp, served on a small salad with avocado and mango and dressed with tarragon-ginger vinaigrette.

Dinner nightly; AE, D, MC, V.

MacArthur Park

Downtown: 607 Front St. (at Jackson);
415-398-5700

American

Good for groups

Kid friendly

Since 1972, MacArthur Park has been a fixture in lively, historic Jackson Square, providing good American regional cooking and an upscale after-work watering hole. Ensconced in a former warehouse, the dining room has an airy feel, with brick walls, potted plants and trees, and greenhouse windows overlooking the wooded square. Barbecued meats (especially baby back ribs), great onion strings and skinny fries, Cobb salads, grilled fish and juicy burgers are the culinary highlights. Desserts are huge versions of American classics such as fruit pies, fudge-brownie sundaes and butterscotch banana cream tartlets. The waitstaff is particularly good with kids.

Lunch weekdays/dinner nightly; view; outdoor seating; full bar; valet parking; AE, DC, D, MC, V.

★★★★
$$$$$

Maharani

Nob Hill/Russian Hill: 1122 Post St.
(between Van Ness and Polk);
415-775-1988

Indian

Good for groups

Romantic

Maharani doesn't get much press attention but it's one of San Francisco's better Indian restaurants, known for excellent vegetarian specialties, and serving highly spiced food that is low in salt and oil. In addition to a pretty main dining room, there are private dining tents, swathed in fabrics and beaded curtains, with low tables, lots of throw pillows and a buzzer to summon the waiter. Popular choices include the Maharani Special—a spiced half-chicken roasted in the tandoori oven and served with addictive nan bread, salad and potatoes—as well as the tandoori chicken wings appetizer and fiery lamb vindaloo.

Lunch/dinner daily; full bar; validated parking; AE, DC, D, MC, V.

★★☆☆
$$$$$

Maki Restaurant

**Japan Center/Fillmore: 1825 Post St.
(between Webster and Fillmore);
415-921-5215**

Japanese

One of the best of the Japantown restaurant scene is a tiny place ensconced in the Kinokuniya Mall that serves incredibly fresh and flawless preparations of Japanese standards such as udon, soba, sushi and donburi. Maki's house specialty is *wappa meshi*, a dish from northern Japan that combines seasoned fish, chicken and vegetables with steamed rice in a wooden basket, but the real treats here are Chef Makiguchi's marvelous daily *tsumami* (appetizer) dishes. The elegant, kimono-clad waitstaff glides through the spotless, calming dining room distinguished by blond wood furnishings, orchid arrangements and rows of sake bottles.

Lunch/dinner Tuesday-Sunday; AE, MC, V.

★★★☆
$$$$$

Mama's Girl

**North Beach: 1701 Stockton St. (at Filbert);
415-362-6421**

American

 Good deal

Since before the dawning of the Nixon administration, tourists and locals alike have lined up for Mama's legendary 11-egg "momelets," cinnamon French toast, and pan dore—slices of sour baguette and sautéed apples topped with a tangy lemon-butter sauce. Lunch is more pedestrian: hot dogs, burgers, sandwiches and the like. The Italian country decor is cute as all get-out—floral tablecloths, country furnishings, big windows overlooking Washington Square Park—though the noise level can be overwhelming.

*Breakfast/lunch Tuesday-Sunday; loud; view;
no liquor license; reservations not accepted;
cash only.*

**$$**$$$

Mandalay Restaurant
Richmond: 4348 California St. (between
5th and 6th Aves.); 415-386-3896

Burmese

Stick with Mandalay's traditionally Burmese dishes,
avoiding the mediocre Mandarin offerings. Recommended appetizers include deep-fried dumplings
filled with minced-meat curry and meat satays.
Equally flavorful are the Burmese soups, especially
the richly spiced chicken curry and noodle number.
For an entree, try the Mandalay squid or the minty-
sour Burmese greens grown by the owner and served
with prawns in a hot-sour sauce. Unfortunately, Mandalay's food can be uneven. The storefront room is
pleasant enough, with hanging lanterns, traditional
artwork and blond wood adding detail to an otherwise
spare setting. Service is overly rushed.

Lunch/dinner daily; MC, V.

**$$**$$$

Mandarin
Fisherman's Wharf: 900 North Point St.
(between Polk and Larkin); 415-673-8812

Chinese

Good
for groups

Perched on the fourth floor of Ghirardelli Square, the
Mandarin wows the tourist-studded crowd with
sweeping views of the bay, opulent Asian furnishings
plus a large and varied menu. For more than 25 years
it was considered San Francisco's finest Chinese
restaurant, but a recent change in ownership has
brought a slight erosion in quality. These days, everything from Mongolian fire pots to Peking duck to
Mandarin minced squab to wild rice with sesame-
infused jellyfish finds a place on the menu. Still, you
can count on reliable standbys such as tea-smoked
duck, glazed walnut prawns and beggar's chicken.

Lunch/dinner daily; loud; view; full bar;
validated parking; AE, DC, MC, V.

★★★★
$$$$$

Mangiafuoco

Mission: 1001 Guerrero St. (at 22nd St.); 415-206-9881

Italian

 Romantic

Mangiafuoco has a solid reputation for serving flaw-less house-made pastas and hearty meat dishes cooked on a wood-burning grill at below-average prices. Must-order dishes from chef/proprietor Gian-carlo Bortolotti's kitchen include the carpaccio appe-tizer with artichokes, capers and mustard, Sonoma lamb chops with mustard and huckleberry sauce, the gnocchi and risotto of the day and anything cooked in parchment paper, especially the mangiafuoco. The funky little dining room is decorated with eccentrici-ties such as dusty Italian scooters, mismatched fur-nishings, abused wood flooring. And the clientele reflects the staff—hip, nonchalant, but perfectionists when it comes to food.

Dinner nightly; MC, V.

★★★★
$$$$$

Manora's Thai Cuisine

South of Market: 1600 Folsom St. (at 12th St.); 415-861-6224

Thai

 Kid friendly

 Good for groups

A popular stop for lively crowds of club-hoppers, Manora's consistently turns out one good Thai meal after another, despite its vast 60-entree menu. Hap-pily, the dining room has retained its old-world ele-gance, with ornate wooden room dividers and a shimmering gold-trimmed facade. Start with fried fish cakes with minced green beans and Thai spices, or fresh mint rolls stuffed with fresh vegetables, mint, noodles and shrimp, and served with peanut dipping sauce. Rich, well-prepared curries and fresh seafood dishes are the favored entrees. Don't bother with the wine list; go straight for the Singha beer.

Lunch weekdays, dinner nightly; full bar; MC, V.

★★★★
$$$$$

Marina Central

**Marina: 2001 Chestnut St. (at Fillmore);
415-673-2222**

California

Good
for groups

**In the former home of a 60-year-old institution called
Marina Joe's, Marina Central has quite a reputation to
live up to. The eclectic menu emphasizes seafood.
Appetizers range from shrimp-and-pork wontons with
spicy ginger dipping sauce to stone-fruit and butter
lettuce salad tossed with nectarine vinaigrette and
pecorino cheese. Entrees are equally far-ranging:
pepperoni pizza, spit-roasted half-chicken with truffled potatoes, pastas and an oak-grilled steak, but
the execution often falls short. The large, windowed
dining room is noisy, and erratic service is a weak-
ness.**

*Lunch/dinner daily; weekend brunch; loud; late-
night dining; full bar; happy hour Thursday-Sat-
urday; AE, DC, MC, V.*

NR
$$$$$

Mario's Bohemian Cigar Store Cafe

**North Beach: 566 Columbus Ave.
(between Green and Union); 415-362-0536
Russian Hill: 2209 Polk St. (between Green
and Vallejo); 415-776-8226**

Coffeehouse

Good
deal

**Nearly a century ago, this historic, charmingly
threadbare corner cafe was a card club for gentlemen. Today it's a hip cafe, but the oak bar and old
photos are pleasant reminders of the past. The small
menu includes huge hot sandwiches, including eggplant and the popular meatball, both dressed with
grilled onions and melted Swiss cheese, and served
on focaccia. Numerous Italian and California wines
are served by the glass at refreshingly affordable
prices, and the cappuccino has won several awards.**

Lunch/dinner daily; view; cash only.

Marnee Thai Restaurant

★★★☆
$$$$$

Sunset: 2225 Irving St. (between 23rd and 24th Aves.); 415-665-9500

Thai

Sidewalk's
choice

Good
deal

Cleverly designed to create the illusion of dining in a small village hut in Thailand—with palm-frond mats, bamboo and hanging plants—Marnee Thai is one of San Francisco's best Thai restaurants. Be sure to start with the crispy chicken wings sautéed with fresh chiles, garlic and crispy sweet basil and the fried corn cakes. Popular entrees are the chicken sautéed with fresh ginger, onions and dried mushrooms, spicy crab noodles, and whole deep-fried pompano fish. But most diners take advice on what to order from the owner—she is, after all, also adept at fortune-telling.

Lunch/dinner Wednesday-Monday; AE, MC, V.

Masa's

★★★★
$$$$$

Downtown: 648 Bush St. (between Powell and Stockton); 415-989-7154

French/
California

Romantic

Masa's has enjoyed a decades-long reign as the city's most exalted—and expensive—culinary destination. But the vertigo-inducing prices reflect the precious ingredients, stunning presentations, flawless service and labor-intensive nature of the delicious French-California cuisine produced by Julian Serrano. Four- and five-course tasting menus are offered nightly. One, for example included sautéed snapper with red wine sauce, foie gras with Madeira truffle sauce, medallions of fallow deer with caramelized apples and Zinfandel sauce and chocolate-cappuccino trifle with orange sorbet. As you'd expect, the wine list is an impressive tome, with more than 20 vintages by the glass. The dining room was recently refurbished with modern art and walls

covered in red Italian silk, making it more conducive
to a special-occasion splurge.

*Breakfast/lunch/dinner Tuesday-Saturday; quiet;
prix fixe menu; full bar; reservations required;
jacket and tie required; valet parking; all major
credit cards.*

Masons

**Downtown: The Fairmont Hotel,
950 California St. (between Mason
and California); 415-772-5233**

California/
Fusion

The Fairmont Hotel recently embarked on an Asian-
influenced menu for its flagship restaurant; and while
some of chef Katsuo Sugiura's dishes work beautifully, others are flawed. The more successful East-
meets-West fare includes Dungeness crab and rock
shrimp ravioli in white truffle sauce, and seared
salmon and ginger-lime confit in a Sauternes-curry
sauce; but there are always the standard oak-grilled
steaks and chicken dishes. The sophisticated 42-page
wine list is one of the best around, with a vast selection of surprisingly well-priced bottles. The dining
room retains its old-world elegance, and accom-
plished pianists add to the regal surroundings. Service is elegant, and helpful with the complex menu.

*Dinner nightly; live entertainment; prix fixe
menu; full bar; all major credit cards.*

Massawa

**Haight/Cole Valley: 1538 Haight St.
(between Ashbury and Clayton);
415-621-4129**

Ethiopian

A funky, midsize restaurant where good, inexpensive,
filling food makes up for the graceless decor. House
specialties include spiced beef, chicken, lamb and
fish stews, as well as a medley of spiced vegetable
options, such as chickpeas, lentils, zucchini and
spinach. They're served on *injera* (a sour, spongy
bread), with little piles of tossed salad to refresh the

palate, all eaten with your hands. It's best to order entrees family-style, presented on a huge platter. Newcomers should order the meat and/or vegetable combo. Have liquids on hand to counteract the heat.

Lunch/dinner Tuesday-Sunday; AE, DC, MC, V.

★★★☆
$$$$$

Matsuya

Noe Valley: 3856 24th St. (between Church and Sanchez); 415-282-7989

Japanese

Loyal patrons fill up this hole-in-the-wall Japanese restaurant—the oldest sushi bar in the city—night after night to get a taste of owner Fusae Ponne's witty, charismatic presence as well as her first-rate sushi. Everything is impeccably fresh, and the well prepared nightly specials reflect what's in season. In addition to his reliable sushi standards, longtime chef Yoshitomi Takechi also makes terrific teriyaki and *donburi* (bowls of steaming rice with assorted toppings).

Dinner Monday-Saturday; reservations not accepted; MC, V.

★★★☆
$$$$$

Matterhorn

Russian Hill: 2323 Van Ness Ave. (between Vallejo and Green); 415-885-6116

French

Fondues galore and rich, substantial entrees are the main attractions at this remarkable recreation of a Swiss chalet. The furnishings and architectural details were created in Switzerland, then shipped here in pieces and put back together—you'd have to go to the Alps to find anything more authentic. Cheese fondue comes in nine different versions, all served with salad and a baguette. Cream of sweet corn soup filled with chicken dumplings is also a favorite, followed by bacon-wrapped pork tenderloin Zermatt, or Wienerschnitzel. For dessert, there's chocolate fondue or a slice of fresh apple strudel.

Dinner Tuesday-Sunday; prix fixe menu; full bar; valet parking; DC, D, MC, V.

Maxfield's

★★★★
$$$$$

Downtown: Sheraton Palace Hotel, 2 New Montgomery St. (between Market, 2nd and 3rd Sts.); 415-392-8600/ 415-546-5089 (for reservations)

American

A handsome, traditional, decidedly masculine-looking restaurant in the Sheraton Palace Hotel, Maxfield's caters to the power-lunch crowd and is perhaps best known for the magnificent Maxfield Parrish painting dominating the bar area. But it also serves a modest lineup of American grill items, such as beef medallions with sautéed chanterelles and scalloped potatoes, grilled swordfish and shrimp with pineapple salsa, and a whopping burger draped with avocado, smoked bacon, grilled mushrooms and cheddar cheese. A vegetarian menu is also available.

Lunch weekdays, dinner nightly; happy hour Thursday-Friday; full bar; valet/validated parking; all major credit cards.

Max's Diner

★★★★
$$$$$

South of Market: 311 3rd St. (at Folsom); 415-546-6297

American

 Good deal

 Kid friendly

 Good for groups

The SoMa outpost of Dennis Berkowitz's New York-style diner-and-bakery empire serves up folksy pronouncements that reveal the owner's eagerness to please along with gargantuan portions of big-calorie items like meatloaf and mashed potatoes, fried chicken doused in country gravy, jaw-breaking deli sandwiches and the biggest desserts you'll ever attack with a fork. Once you cast your dietary worries to the wind, you'll enjoy Max's upscale-diner ambience, friendly and efficient service, and good-quality food.

Lunch/dinner daily; full bar; AE, DC, D, MC, V.

Max's Eatz

★★☆☆
**$**$$$

**Downtown: 595 Market St. (between 2nd
St. and Stevenson); 415-896-6297
South of Market: 30 Fremont St. (between
Market and Mission); 415-543-8777**

Deli

Max's Eatz (part of the chain that includes Max's
Diner, Max's Opera Cafe and Sweet Max's) is every-
thing you'd expect from a New York-inspired deli. The
owners roast their own meats, bake their own breads
and pastries, and serve it up to the business-lunch
crowd, who come for their trademark sandwiches—
no one makes them taller, thicker, drippier or more
delicious. In addition to the standards, such as pas-
trami, roast beef, and turkey, Max's provides vege-
tarian and low-fat dining options, offering salads and
daily specials, such as tandoori chicken or black-
ened snapper with tomato relish. Sinful dessert
selections include strawberry shortcake, chocolate
mousse, cheesecake and brownies.

> *Breakfast/lunch weekdays; outdoor seating at
> downtown branch; full bar in SoMa, no liquor
> license downtown; reservations not accepted;
> AE, DC, D, MC, V.*

Max's Opera Cafe

★★☆☆
**$$**$$

**Civic Center: 601 Van Ness Ave. (at Golden
Gate); 415-771-7301**

American

Like Max's Diner (see above), the Opera Cafe appeals
to hearty appetites with generous portions of comfort
food like meatloaf and mashed potatoes, tall deli
sandwiches and enormous desserts. But here the
well-prepared food and friendly service come with a
bonus at dinnertime: singing waiters.

> *Lunch/dinner daily; loud; outdoor seating; late-
> night dining; live entertainment; full bar; reser-
> vations not accepted; AE, DC, D, MC, V.*

★★★★
$$$$$

Maye's Original Oyster House

Nob Hill: 1233 Polk St. (between Sutter and Bush); 415-474-7674

Seafood

Established by Yugoslavian immigrants in 1867 as a chop house, Maye's built its reputation on serving steaks and fresh seafood to politicos, artists and boomtown rowdies. It's now primarily an old-world seafood restaurant, serving unsurprising dishes to a mixed crowd. Expect oysters, crab, calamari, grilled fish and so forth, plus pasta, steaks and chops. The specialty is a pan-fried sand dab; the fish has a rich nutty flavor and the waiter deftly debones it at the table. You'd do best to stick with simple seafood dishes and, of course, fresh oysters.

Lunch/dinner Monday-Saturday; full bar; reservations required; validated parking; AE, MC, V.

★★★★
$$$$$

Mayflower Restaurant

Richmond: 6255 Geary Blvd. (between 26th and 27th Aves.); 415-387-8338

Chinese

Diners will want to linger over their meals at the Mayflower's bright, spotless, semiopulent dining room, complete with crystal chandeliers, where generally flawless Cantonese fare is served. Seafood dishes are popular, particularly the dried scallop soup with bamboo shoots, fresh prawns baked in the shell, sautéed squab fillet with fungus and tender greens, and sautéed prawns with cubes of wonderful crispy fried milk. Excellent dim sum is featured daily, but solo diners should choose Lunch Special A, a huge platter of fresh sautéed seafood in black bean sauce. It comes with barbecued ribs, soup, fried rice and dessert, all for $6.50.

Lunch/dinner daily; full bar; MC, V.

★★★☆
$$$$$

Maykadeh
**North Beach: 470 Green St. (at Grant);
415-362-8286**

Middle
Eastern

Romantic

Every meal at this cheerful, comfortable Middle
Eastern restaurant begins with a complimentary *sabzi*
plate—a refreshing snack of feta cheese, onions,
fresh basil and mint tucked into warm pita bread. The
most venturesome appetizers are the tender lamb
tongue in a creamy sauce and the succulent
mesquite-grilled calf brains with saffron-scented
lemon butter. Main-course choices include stews and
kebabs, well-marinated and tender, served with basmati rice and a ramekin of tart crimson *sumac*
powder made from a Middle Eastern berry for seasoning your dishes. End the adventure with lush,
rose-perfumed ice cream.

Lunch/dinner daily; valet parking; MC, V.

★★★☆
$$$$$

McCormick & Kuleto's
**Ghirardelli Square: 900 North Point St.
(between Polk and Larkin); 415-929-1730**

Seafood

Good
for groups

Unfortunately, the food at this large, multilevel Ghirardelli Square restaurant often fails to live up to the
stupendous bay views or handsome interior designed
by Pat Kuleto. In the formal dining room, you'll find
lots of fish on the menu, along with salads, vegetarian dishes, and poultry and beef preparations, but
the seafood tends to be lackluster and overcooked.
Patrons report better luck in the upstairs Crab Cake
Lounge, with its oyster bar and selection of burgers,
pizza and, of course, crab cakes.

*Lunch/dinner daily; weekend brunch; view; full
bar; validated parking; AE, DC, D, MC, V.*

Mecca

★★★☆
$$$$$

Castro: 2029 Market St. (between Duboce and 14th St.); 415-621-7000

American

Sidewalk's choice

Stepping inside this supper club feels like entering a secret enclave: Velvet curtains sway dramatically, copper heating ducts line the ceilings and banquettes ring the zinc bar, where glamorous trendsetters smoke cigars and watch the nightly entertainment. Hearty American bistro fare is served in several dining rooms. Chef Lynn Sheehan creates wonderful appetizers—including herbed flat bread with hummus and pickled spring onions, and grape leaf-wrapped goat cheese with beets—while some entrees are more successful than others. The fish dishes are delicious, especially the grilled tuna on a ragout of artichokes and sun-dried tomatoes. Mecca's wood-burning oven also turns out great pizzas.

Dinner nightly; live entertainment; late-night dining; full bar; smoke-free; AE, DC, MC, V.

The Meetinghouse

★★★☆
$$$$$

Fillmore: 1701 Octavia St. (at Bush); 415-922-6733

American

Sidewalk's choice

Good deal

Romantic

Good for groups

Owners/chefs John Bryant Snell and Joanna Karlinsky, veterans of Tra Vigne, took an old apothecary space and converted it into a warm neighborhood restaurant, which has won raves for its pleasing design, New American cuisine and professional service. Memorable meals on the tiny seasonal menu include rock shrimp and scallion johnnycakes, with sweet pepper relish and watercress; lamb and goat-cheese turnovers garnished with sun-dried tomato relish; and very tender braised pork flavored with pepper, juniper and clove. The reasonably priced all-American wine list perfectly matches the food. And toques off to the divine desserts.

Dinner Wednesday-Sunday; AE, MC, V.

★★★★
$$$$$

Mel's Drive-In

**Marina: 2165 Lombard St. (between Steiner and Fillmore); 415-921-3039
Richmond: 3355 Geary Blvd. (at Parker); 415-387-2244**

American

Good for groups

Kid friendly

Revisit America's halcyon days at a perpetually packed shiny, happy replica of a 1950s diner. With a few modern twists, the menu is true to the '50s theme: juicy burgers, grilled cheese sandwiches, cholesterol-be-damned chocolate shakes and blue-plate specials, such as a house-made turkey dinner complete with lumpy mashed potatoes and stuffing. Breakfast is served all day. Nineties touches include several relatively healthy salads, espresso, yogurt shakes, beer and wine. Kids get crayons for doodling plus junior meals served in cardboard cars. Too bad the prices are up to date.

Breakfast/lunch/dinner daily; weekend brunch; late-night dining; reservations not accepted; free parking lot; cash only.

★★★★
$$$$$

Mescolanza

Richmond: 2140 Clement St. (at 23rd Ave.); 415-387-8040

Italian

Mescolanza is the perfect neighborhood trattoria—consistently good, reasonably priced, friendly, small and cute. Jeff and Toni Piccinini have won over diners by offering big plates of well-prepared northern Italian dishes, such as tender house-made gnocchi bathed in a sweet meat sauce, linguine carbonara, scampi and veal Marsala. Calorie-counters can choose the Tuscan pizzettas made with light, simple toppings. There are several nice wines to complement your meal. The pretty place features blue-and-white-checked tablecloths that match the tiled floor, walls adorned with copper pans and painted plates, and an antique hutch filled with Italian cookbooks.

Lunch/dinner daily; full bar; all major credit cards.

★★★★
$$ $$$

Mifune

Japan Center/Fillmore: 1737 Post St. (at Buchanan); 415-922-0337

Japanese

Sidewalk's choice

Good deal

Kid friendly

Arguably San Francisco's most revered noodle house, Mifune's stark red and black dining room is a veritable beacon for noodle lovers. You really only need to make two choices from the exhaustive menu. First, decide whether you want udon or soba noodles. Then, choose from 55 versions of soothing broths, ranging from beef to chicken, tempura and miso—comfort food, Japanese-style. In addition to noodles, Mifune offers a limited sushi and tempura menu, as well as sake and beer. The lunch special is also a deal: niku or tori noodles with sushi, salad and tea for $6.25.

Lunch/dinner daily; reservations not accepted; AE, DC, D, MC, V.

★★★★
$$ $$$

Mike's Chinese

Richmond: 5145 Geary Blvd. (between 15th and 16th Aves.); 415-752-0120

Chinese

Good for groups

Though Mike's was considered one of the finest Cantonese restaurants in its early-1970s heyday, it's now mostly frequented by neighborhood folks. Kee Lum Won (aka Mike) runs the show, welcoming customers to his sleek, soothing, ever-so-classy restaurant. For starters, try the fabulous pot stickers, barbecued chicken salad, mustard greens soup, boiled wontons and noodles. Then move on to legendary main dishes like succulent crispy chicken and Peking duck. Though Mike's may look like Fort Knox from the sidewalk—those brick walls and thick wooden doors would repulse a tank—it's as quiet as a cathedral inside.

Dinner Wednesday-Monday; quiet; full bar; MC, V.

Milano Pizzeria

★★★★
$$$$$

Pizza

Sunset: 1330 9th Ave. (between Judah and Irving Sts.); 415-665-3773

Yes, there is a pizzeria in San Francisco that comes pretty close to baking real New York-style pie. With the perfect thin-but-crunchy crust to start, Milano's finishing touches include super-fresh vegetables, piles of real cheese that ooze off the edges, and a sauce that is not too spicy, not too wimpy. Most regulars order their pies to go, the most popular being the Ultimate Vegetarian. Pasta dishes are also available. Decor is pizza-house basic: padded vinyl booths, ceiling fans, old pictures of San Francisco.

Lunch/dinner daily; loud; late-night dining; reservations not accepted; cash only.

Millennium

★★★★
$$$$$

Vegetarian

 Romantic

Civic Center: Abigail Hotel, 246 McAllister St. (between Larkin and Hyde); 415-487-9800

This attractive vegetarian restaurant in the Abigail Hotel offers "optimal health cuisine" with panache, thanks to the skillful cooking of Eric Tucker. The weekly-changing menu reflects the season's bounty, encompassing vegetarian and vegan dishes, but includes some cunning meat substitutes, such as a grilled seitan that's a dead ringer for beef. The portobello mushrooms glazed with a sweet Moroccan dressing and rosemary polenta layered with basil tofu ricotta, duxelles and spicy tomato sauce are also good. Romantics might want to investigate the Full Moon Aphrodisiac Night package, which includes a room for two in the funky, 1920s-style Abigail Hotel.

Dinner nightly; prix fixe menu; MC, V.

★★★★
$$$$$

Miss Millie's

Noe Valley: 4123 24th St. (between Castro and Diamond); 415-285-5598

Vegetarian

Kid
friendly

Weekend breakfast and brunch are the draw at Miss Millie's, a cute, retro restaurant with ivy-covered hand-painted booths, shelves lined with colorful old dishes, and the sweet aroma of cinnamon buns baking in the kitchen. Topping the list of breakfast favorites are lemon-ricotta pancakes and French toast layered with bananas and maple syrup. Lunch features onion soup topped with Gruyère and grilled New York sharp cheddar and goat cheeses on sourdough topped with roasted tomatoes. At dinnertime, try the roasted-beet and orange salad, followed by artichoke and broccoli gratin with white beans, cauliflower and arugula.

Breakfast/lunch daily, dinner Monday-Saturday; weekend brunch; outdoor seating; MC, V.

★★★★
$$$$$

The Moa Room

Mission: 1007 Guerrero St. (at 22nd St.); 415-282-1007

Eclectic

Just off the Valencia corridor, this sleek and stylish spot (opened in mid-1997) joins a slew of other trendy but generally excellent restaurants popping up in the Mission's new bohemian enclave. Decorated in electric shades of orange and green and crammed with tables and banquettes, the Moa serves what it calls "borderless cuisine" reaching into Asia, New Zealand and the Americas. All the produced is grown and picked weekly from the owner's organic farm in Napa so the menu changes weekly and truly reflects the seasons. Complementary bottled Evian is poured freely and the small wine list offers some great little known wines from Zealand.

Dinner Monday-Saturday; AE, CB, DC, D, MC, V.

★☆★★
$$$$$

Moishe's Pippic

Hayes Valley: 425-A Hayes St. (between Franklin and Gough); 415-431-2440

Deli

Kid friendly

Moishe's Pippic is a Jewish deli whose décor and menu largely pay tribute to the Windy City. However, mindful of the Big Apple, the "Wrigley Field" (a hot dog with mustard, onions, relish, peppers, tomatoes and pickles) shares menu space with offerings like "The West 57th" (chopped liver and hot pastrami on rye). Midwestern and East Coast transplants will know this isn't quite the real thing, but they'll find spicy dogs and sausages, comforting matzo ball soup and chopped liver that just might make them feel the breeze rising off Lake Michigan.

Breakfast/lunch/dinner Monday-Saturday;
outdoor seating; cash only.

★★★★
$$$$$

Molinari's Deli

North Beach: 373 Columbus Ave. (at Vallejo St.); 415-421-2337

Deli

Good deal

Molinari's, the ultimate San Francisco deli and a city landmark, has been around for more than a century. Crammed into every inch of space are hundreds of imported meats, cheeses, wines and canned goods, including fresh Fior di Latte mozzarella di bufala and some of the highest-rated salami in the nation. A popular lunchtime practice is to order a sandwich— among the city's best—then walk down the street to Vesuvio, North Beach's legendary bar, and wash it down with a cold beer. Don't let the long line at Molinari's fool you: The guys behind the counter are quick.

Breakfast/lunch/dinner daily; no seating; loud;
reservations not accepted; MC, V, checks.

★★★★
$$$$$

Mom Is Cooking

Mission: 1166 Geneva Ave. (between Edinburgh and Naples); 415-586-7000

Mexican

At her hole-in-the-wall Mexican restaurant, "Mom" (chef/owner Abigail Murillo) clearly focuses on the food, not on the decor: faux-wood paneling, red Naugahyde seats patched with green Astroturf, and orange paper placemats on Formica tables. But loyal locals keep coming back for the authentic fare sold at low prices: *boquitas*, cheesy enchiladas, chicken mole, light, airy tomales and a wide range of burritos. The Potpourri Mexicano is great for tasting everything from tamales to cactus on the diverse menu. A cramped but colorful bar offers margaritas, 36 tequilas and Mexican beers on tap.

Lunch/dinner daily; loud; full bar; reservations required for large parties; cash only.

★★★★
$$$$$

Moose's

North Beach: 1652 Stockton St. (between Union and Filbert); 415-989-7800

California

The latest venture of popular restaurateur Ed Moose is hard to miss, facing Washington Square and marked by a big, blue neon moose head hanging over the entrance. Inside, the city's prime movers and shakers gather at the long bar or in the bright, spacious dining room, which serves pricey pasta, chicken, veal, beef and pork dishes, upscale comfort food that neither offends nor excites. A fist-size cut of beef tenderloin is overpriced at $24, but the big $9 Mooseburger is luscious. It's the power and prestige, not the food, that keeps regulars coming back.

Lunch/dinner daily; weekend brunch; late-night dining; live entertainment; full bar; AE, DC, MC, V.

★★★★
$$$$$

Morton's of Chicago

**Downtown: 400 Post St. (at Powell);
415-986-5830**

American/
Steak

**Good
for groups**

With its brass-plated wine lockers, white linens and prominent bar, this branch of the Chicago-based chain has the feel of a men's club. And if you're in the market for a superb 24-ounce porterhouse steak, a 1-pound baked potato and steamed asparagus with hollandaise sauce, you've come to the right place. Morton's buys its prime beef from the most prestigious suppliers (you even get to inspect your meat before it's cooked), and waiters waving around raw broccoli and a live lobster while reciting the menu are part of the Morton's experience. Be prepared to pay a high price for your meal.

Dinner nightly; full bar; jacket and tie required; AE, MC, V.

★★★★
$$$$$

Mo's

**North Beach: 1322 Grant Ave. (between
Vallejo and Green); 415-788-3779**

American

Carnivores from all around come to this burger bastion, where they use only the best-quality, center-cut chuck, grilled to perfection and served between a pair of soft-yet-crusty buns. Burger variations include barbecue, bacon, mushroom, Tex-Mex, California (with avocado), western (with applewood smoked bacon) and alpine (with Swiss and Gruyère cheeses)—each accompanied by a side of French fries, black beans, Spanish rice or cabbage. Steaks, pork chops, chicken and a few vegetarian dishes are also on the menu, as is a dynamite mocha shake, served thick and tall in a shimmering steel container.

Lunch/dinner daily; weekend brunch; late-night dining; reservations not accepted; MC, V.

Moxie Bar & Restaurant

Mission: 2742 17th St. (at Florida);
415-863-4177

Eastern
European

Good
for groups

Romantic

It's difficult to order wrong at Moxie, an eastern European bistro that has developed an adoring clientele since opening in August 1996. Specialties of the chef's fresh, cross-cultural menu include matzo ball soup and roast chicken breast in champagne-vinegar sauce with herb farfel, fava beans and spring garlic shoots. Then there are monthly features such as beef brisket with Sephardic leek fritters, braised greens and beet horseradish sauce or pan-seared lamb loin with whole-wheat couscous, asparagus and baby artichokes. Service can be slow, but the staff seems to try hard.

Lunch weekdays, dinner Tuesday-Saturday; full bar; MC, V.

★★★★
$$$$$

Murasaki Sushi

Richmond: 211 Clement St. (between 3rd
and 4th Aves.); 415-668-7317

Japanese

Along with the homey, happy atmosphere, what's putting everyone in such a jovial mood at this hole-in-the-wall gem is the superb seafood that emerges from behind a glass display case: incredibly fresh sushi, sashimi, the house-specialty soft-shell crab and deep-fried oysters, all washed down with sake and Sapporo beer. If you're adventurous, ask chef Toshihiro Sasaki to choose your sushi—you'll be amazed at the variety on your tray. Prices are a bit steep, particularly for the appetizers, but it's worth the splurge.

Dinner nightly; late-night dining; AE, MC, V.

★★★★
$$$$$

Nanbantei of Tokyo

Downtown: 115 Cyril Magnin St. (between Ellis and O'Farrell); 415-421-2101

Japanese

A rare Japanese restaurant that serves only *yakitori* (skewered and grilled meats and vegetables), Nanbantei, a branch of the Tokyo original, is a home away from home for Japanese tourists. The best seats are at the long yakitori bar, where chefs deftly spear together nearly 30 versions of the meal-on-a-stick. Choices range from grilled octopus dumplings and marinated beef tongue to Japanese eggplant, prawns and duck breast with onions. Top picks are the asparagus spears wrapped in pork and the grilled shiitake mushrooms. Order one pair at a time for maximum savoring, or a half-dozen all at once for a feast.

Lunch/dinner daily; loud; all major credit cards.

★★★★
$$$$$

Narai

Richmond: 2229 Clement St. (between 23rd and 24th Aves.); 415-751-6363

Thai

 Kid friendly

 Good for groups

A reliable charmer, Narai serves cuisine that is simultaneously refined, homey and explosively flavorful, reflecting owner Josephy Komindr's Thai and Chinese background. Start with tofu skins stuffed with crab sausage, the finely balanced sweet-sour-spicy salad of puffed-rice noodles, warm silver-noodle salad with shrimp and pork, or any of the intensely flavorful soups. Excellent entrees include Swatow-style duck simmered in a richly seasoned sauce, stir-fried spicy lamb and seafood hot pots. Taro-root sticky pudding is one of the unusual desserts. The dining room is pleasant enough, though not exceptional.

Lunch/dinner Tuesday-Sunday; validated parking; MC, V.

★★★★
$$$$$

New Eritrea

Sunset: 907 Irving St. (at 10th Ave.);
415-681-1288

African

In a small dining room decorated with East African art and nary a fork or spoon in sight, enormous plates are lined with *injera* (spongy flatbread used instead of utensils), and covered with your choice of toppings such as marinated chicken cooked with onions, tomatoes and spicy red peppers. The braised meat dishes, cooked until tender, are excellent. Several vegetarian dishes appear on the menu, including an Eritrean specialty made from ground fava beans, onions and tomatoes. The dining experience here can be fun, but be sure to keep water or beer handy as it's spicy stuff.

Lunch Tuesday-Sunday, dinner nightly; full bar;
AE, MC, V, checks.

★★★★
$$$$$

Nippon Sushi

Castro: 314 Church St. (at 15th St.);
no phone

Sushi

 Good
deal

Known to all as No-Name Sushi, this signless restaurant attracts an almost cult-like following of folks who patiently wait in the nightly queue for their fix. A wide range of fresh sushi and sashimi priced far below the standard rate is prepared with lightning speed in the tiny, open kitchen by traditionally garbed Japanese chefs; it's served without fanfare in a rather shabby, if funky, room. If you want to drink, you'll need to BYOS (bring your own Sapporo), sold at the market across the street. For the price, you can't go wrong here.

Lunch/dinner Monday-Saturday; no liquor
license; reservations not accepted; cash only.

★★★★
$$$$$

Nob Hill Cafe

Nob Hill: 1152 Taylor St. (between Clay and Sacramento); 415-776-6500

Italian

Good deal

This quaint storefront Italian cafe teems with neighborhood regulars, who come for the heaping portions of robust, casual Italian food and extremely fair prices. Quarters are a bit cramped—try for the larger dining room with terra-cotta floors and dark green walls. The menu emphasizes pastas, but pizza, roasted chicken, calamari steak and other seafood dishes round out the selection. Although the food is usually quite good and the service pleasant and reasonably efficient, all hell can break loose when a big event is happening at nearby Masonic Hall. Come early or be prepared to wait.

Lunch/dinner daily; outdoor seating; reservations not accepted; valet parking; MC, V.

★★★★
$$$$$

North Beach Pizza

Haight: 800 Stanyan St. (between Beulah and Frederick); 415-751-2300
Mission: 4787 Mission St. (between Russia and Persia); 415-586-1400
North Beach: 1310 Grant Ave. (at Vallejo); 415-433-2444
North Beach: 1499 Grant Ave. (at Union): 415-433-2444
Sunset: 3054 Taraval St. (between 40th and 41st Aves.); 415-242-9100

Italian

Kid friendly

People can't seem to agree on which pizzeria makes the best pie in the city, but North Beach Pizza is certainly a contender. Toppings are sparse, but that heavenly layer of whole-milk mozzarella and the hand-spun dough with thick, chewy edges win people over. Either create your own from a list of 20 fresh ingredients (the sausage with black olives is killer), or choose from 10 house specialties, such as the San Francisco Special—clams, garlic and cheese. There's also a huge assortment of pastas, poultry, sandwiches and salads. All North Beach Pizza places deliver; the Haight and Sunset branches are strictly for delivery or takeout.

Lunch/dinner daily; Mission branch is loud; late-night dining (open 24 hours in the Haight); reservations not accepted; all major credit cards.

★★★★
$$$$$

North Beach Restaurant

North Beach: 1512 Stockton St. (between Green and Union); 415-392-1700

Italian

 Good for groups

❤ Romantic

Lorenzo Petroni has added modern styling and a trendy cigar room to his 25-year-old establishment, but the menu, happily, remains traditional. Chef Bruno Orsi's veal scalloppine with pine nuts and mushrooms is his finest dish, a close second to his Chicken-Under-a-Brick. The huge menu includes 22 house-made pastas and an array of fresh fish, among them a particularly good petrale sole. Though perhaps not the best Italian place in the neighborhood, North Beach Restaurant is steeped in the Old San Francisco tradition of charming waiters, heavy-handed cocktails and an ebullient owner.

Lunch/dinner daily; loud; late-night dining; full bar; all major credit cards.

★★★★
$$$$$

Now and Zen Bistro

Japan Center/Fillmore: 1826 Buchanan St. (between Sutter and Bush); 415-922-9696

California/
Vegetarian

😊 Kid friendly

This wonderful, hidden little vegetarian restaurant run by Miyoko Schinner offers gourmet dishes and desserts without dairy, eggs, refined sugar or honey. The stuffed shiitake mushrooms are plump and delicious, filled with tofu, walnuts, rosemary and tomatoes. Other popular appetizers are the seaweed salad and Schinner's "filet of soul," served with a tangy lemon-caper sauce. Entrees range from the best-selling Zen kabobs (grilled seasonal vegetables served over rice) to a hearty portobello and polenta lasagna. The dining room is tastefully decorated, with fresh flowers, modern artwork and a bakery case loaded with Schinner's superb sugar-free cakes and desserts.

Lunch/brunch weekends, dinner Tuesday-Sunday; AE, MC, V.

Ocean Restaurant

Richmond: 726 Clement St. (between 8th and 9th Aves.); 415-668-8896

Chinese

Strictly a purveyor of dim sum, popular Ocean Restaurant is too small to allow the passage of dim sum carts—so check off what you want on the list of dishes and the waiter will take care of the rest. Prices range from $1.10 to $3 a plate, choices from standard to outrageous: deep-fried pork intestines, jellyfish, duck feet with oyster sauce, beef belly, turtle, chicken feet, pork blood. Those who hesitate can order sweet rice with chicken wrapped in a lotus leaf, spareribs with steamed rice in a bowl, or any of the steamed dumplings—all good and amazingly inexpensive.

Breakfast/lunch/dinner daily; MC, V.

Okina Sushi

Richmond: 776 Arguello Blvd. (at Cabrillo); 415-387-8882

Japanese

Inconspicuously tucked into a residential intersection, tiny, tasteful Okina Sushi is well worth seeking out. And once you thread your way through the curtain, friendly greetings instantly fly your way. The chef, clad in a white rolled headband and white jacket, calls hello from inside his kitchen, then proceeds to skillfully turn out artful edible flowers of wasabi, pickled ginger, cucumber and pickled daikon as prelude to the sushi. Try the eel, served warm, and fresh crab, generously wrapped in crisp seaweed. It's all delicious. Okina Sushi has a limited menu, reasonable prices and a local following of regulars.

Dinner Wednesday-Saturday; quiet; cash only.

Old Krakow
Sunset: 385 W. Portal Ave. (between 15th and 16th Aves.); 415-564-4848

Eastern
European

The city's only full-fledged Polish restaurant is a handsome place, with posters of the old country, a collection of antique oak tables and chairs, and recessed lighting, offering hearty dishes to warm chilled bones. For a traditional Krakow *obiad* (main meal), start with a bowl of dumpling-filled borscht, followed by stew thick with mushrooms, sausage, pork, beef and shredded cabbage, accompanied by a mound of mashed potatoes. Spicy beef stew with potato dumplings and caraway seasoning is popular, as are cabbage rolls and kielbasa. *Sernik*, a Polish version of cheesecake, is lemony and studded with raisins.

Lunch/brunch weekends; dinner nightly; MC, V.

Olive's Gourmet Pizza
Marina: 3249 Scott St. (between Lombard and Chestnut); 415-567-4488

Italian

Kid friendly

Good for groups

The secret to Olive's enduring success is its flavorful light and flaky cornmeal crust. Several inventive daily specials are posted, but most customers go for tried-and-true combos such as house-made fennel sausage with roasted green peppers, caramelized onions and a light dose of mozzarella, or the roasted-eggplant and mushroom pie. Assorted pastas, salads, focaccia sandwiches and roasted chicken are offered, too. You can also order your pizza half-baked and have it delivered ready for the oven. Olive's provides crayons for kids to use on the butcher-paper tablecloths.

Lunch/dinner daily; reservations required for large parties; MC, V.

★★★★
$$$$$

One Market

Downtown: 1 Market St. (at Steuart);

415-777-5577

American

 Good
for groups

 Kid
friendly

Dozens of waitstaff clad in matching togs and bow ties dart around a massive, rather chilly dining room trying to keep a couple of hundred customers satisfied. And the food, which continues to reflect celebrity chef/owner Bradley Ogden's Midwestern roots, generally hits the mark. Though chef George Morrone is now in charge, Ogden's hand is still evident in the menu, particularly with his signature Yankee pot roast. The made-from-scratch desserts get mixed reviews. There is something for everyone on the lengthy, consummately Californian wine list. A pianist plays most nights.

Lunch weekdays, dinner Monday-Saturday; view; happy hour; full bar; live entertainment; valet parking; AE, DC, MC, V.

★★★★
$$$$$

O'Reilly's Irish Bar

North Beach: 622 Green St. (between Columbus and Powell); 415-989-6222

Irish

 Good
for groups

A friendly, homey pub that dishes out good, hearty Irish food, O'Reilly's is the dream-come-true of Mike O'Reilly and Larry Doyle (former chef at Stars Cafe). Check out the smoked salmon on boxty, smoked cod in creamy onion sauce, steak and kidney pie and killer Irish stew with rosemary-scented lamb. Vegetarian selections are also served. The food goes down well with a pint of Guinness, though you'll find 19 other beers on draft and many single-malt scotches, as well as a few decent, inexpensive wines by the glass or bottle. Irish coffee is definitely a specialty.

Lunch/dinner daily; weekend brunch; weekday happy hour; live entertainment; full bar; MC, V.

★★★★
$$$$$

Oriental Pearl

Chinese

Good
for groups

Chinatown: 760 Clay St. (between Grant and Kearny); 415-433-1817

One of the finest restaurants in Chinatown serves food from the Chiu Chow region of southern China. Waiters at the spotless and sedately decorated Oriental Pearl deftly deliver steaming baskets of shrimp and scallop dumplings to eager patrons. Dishes are ordered by menu rather than off a cart, guaranteeing their freshness. For dinner, start with the house special—a delicate mix of shrimp, chicken, water chestnuts and ham wrapped in a coating of egg whites. Other smart choices are spicy braised prawns and seafood chow mein, but just about everything on the menu is delicious and definitely worth the slightly higher-than-average prices.

Lunch/dinner daily; full bar; AE, D, MC, V.

★★★★
$$$$$

Osome

Japanese

Good
deal

Good
for groups

Pacific Heights: 3145 Fillmore St. (between Greenwich and Filbert); 415-346-2311

Touted as one of the best Japanese restaurants in town, Osome's light-filled modern dining room and long bar create a cheery environment for friends who want to share some sumptuous sushi and a carafe of warm sake. Several dozen varieties of very fresh sushi and sashimi are available, with grilled and fried items also popular. Particularly good are the deep-fried soft-shell crab roll, kamikaze green-onion roll with tuna and avocado, pork cutlet fried in a crunchy batter, and oysters marinated in teriyaki sauce.

Dinner nightly; AE, MC, V.

★★★★
$$$$$

P J's Oyster Bed

Sunset: 737 Irving St. (between 8th and 9th Aves.); 415-566-7775

Cajun

 Kid friendly

A longtime favorite, P J's Oyster Bed hasn't stopped celebrating Mardi Gras since it opened in 1979. Upon entry, you'll be hit by a blast of spicy Southern smells, thumping zydeco music and a lively party atmosphere. Try chef Pachi Calvo y Perez's all-you-can-eat crawfish, blackened whole Mississippi catfish, a heaping platter of spicy jambalaya (arguably the best in the city) or the house favorite: paella. Appetizers range from Double Trouble Alligator Nuggets to crawfish pie to Papa John's Blue Crab Cakes. Not everything is fiery-hot here or strictly Cajun-style. Cool down with oysters on the half shell.

Lunch/dinner daily; weekend brunch; full bar; all major credit cards.

★★★★
$$$$$

Pacific

Downtown: Pan Pacific Hotel, 500 Post St. (at Mason); 415-929-2087

Pacific

 Good deal

 Romantic

 Good for groups

Hidden in the Pan Pacific Hotel, with an elegant but oddly soulless ambience, this top-notch restaurant is often overlooked by food lovers. Valiantly trying to fill the shoes of former chef Takayoshi Kawai, Yoshi Kojima specializes in intricate, luxurious creations—foie gras with caramelized apples and Calvados, lobster with braised leeks and truffle vinaigrette, duck breast with chutney and wild mushrooms. Desserts are just as refined: pear galette with lemon sorbet, mousse mandarine with kiwi coulis and a magnificent chocolate symphony. A three-course prix fixe menu is offered nightly for $29—a true bargain.

Breakfast/lunch/dinner daily; weekend brunch; quiet; live entertainment; pre-theater menu; prix fixe menu; full bar; valet/validated parking; all major credit cards.

★★★☆
$$$$$

Pacific Cafe

Richmond: 7000 Geary Blvd. (at 34th Ave.); 415-387-7091

Seafood

Good for groups

Open since 1974, this venerable seafood spot, decorated with seafaring photos and mounted game fish, has droves of fans waiting outside (while sipping complimentary house wine) to dine on straight-from-the-docks fish, nicely priced and simply prepared *sans* pomp and circumstance. The chalkboard shows a variety of daily catches, which include such low-priced rarities as sautéed abalone and fresh oyster bisque. Menu items include very good grilled ahi, poached salmon, baked lobster and fried sand dabs (a perpetual favorite). Dinners include sides and salad, and there are wines by the bottle and glass—if you didn't have enough while in line.

Dinner nightly; reservations not accepted; AE, MC, V.

★★★☆
$$$$$

Pad Thai Restaurant

Mission: 3259 Mission St. (between Valencia and 29th St.); 415-285-4210

Thai

Don't be deterred by the dreary location and nondescript interior, this modest establishment offers all the well-prepared, authentic Thai standards you'd expect, plus 15 different seafood dishes and some creative inventions, including three pad thai variations. Service is quietly attentive, and the kitchen prepares each dish to order, paying special attention to artful presentation. Winning choices include tender eggplant slices under sautéed shrimp in a spectacular red-curry coconut sauce, topped with basil and finely julienned kaffir lime leaves, and the chicken *gaeng daeng*, with bamboo shoots and red pepper in that same curry sauce.

Lunch/dinner daily; quiet; AE, MC, V.

★★★☆
$$$$$

Palio d'Asti

Downtown: 640 Sacramento St. (between Kearny and Montgomery); 415-395-9800

Italian

Good for groups

This industrial-chic restaurant, with brilliantly colored banners fluttering from the ceiling, is presided over by the genial Gianni Fassio, who previously ran the late, great, Blue Fox. Almost any dish on the menu is a good bet; the antipasti include grappa-cured salmon and fresh mozzarella with vine-ripened tomatoes and basil oil. Most of the pasta—ranging from half-moon ravioli filled with almonds and fontina cheese to tagliarini with prawns and watercress—is homemade. Other good choices include excellent pizzas, roast chicken salad with Gorgonzola cheese and pancetta and breaded veal cutlet with fontina and prosciutto.

Lunch weekdays; full bar; AE, MC, V.

★★★☆
$$$$$

Palomino Euro-Bistro

South of Market: 345 Spear St. (between Folsom and Harrison); 415-512-7400

California

Good for groups

Part of an upscale Seattle-based chain, this vibrant restaurant has a grand bay view, generally very good food, and one of the loveliest dining rooms in the city—with huge oil paintings, expanses of Italian marble and polished rare woods. Not everything on the menu lives up to the smashing decor, but particularly good are the Gorgonzola potatoes, spit-roasted chicken, applewood-grilled salmon or any of the thin-crust pizzas. Palomino has a comprehensive wine list, and the service is competent and amiable. The bar is crammed most nights with a young, upscale crowd that likes to drink.

Lunch weekdays, dinner nightly; loud; outdoor seating; view; full bar; free parking lot; all major credit cards.

Pancho Villa Taqueria

Mission: 3071 16th St. (between Valencia and Mission); 415-864-3484.

Mexican

Good deal

Good for groups

Kid friendly

If people-per-square-foot is the measure of San Francisco's best Mexican food, Pancho Villa wins hands-down. An array of south-of-the-border standard and specialty dishes are posted on a huge menu above the assembly-line kitchen, where a team of fast-moving cooks and cashiers have trouble keeping up with the demand. Once you get a good whiff of the Super Combo Dinner Platter piled high with grilled garlic prawns, steak tacos and *cebollitas asadas*, you'll know why Mission residents pick Pancho Villa above the rest, despite a very loud, crowded and quite ugly dining room.

Lunch/dinner daily; loud; late-night dining; AE, D, MC, V.

Pane e Vino

Pacific Heights: 3011 Steiner St. (between Union and Filbert); 415-346-2111

Italian

This rustic, bustling trattoria in a charming former carriage house is a neighborhood favorite, with a noisy dining room, spirited service, and Italian-speaking waiters dashing to and fro. For starters, indulge in the chilled artichoke stuffed with bread and tomatoes, followed by one of the perfectly prepared pastas, grilled rack of lamb in red wine sauce or whole-roasted fresh fish. Desserts are traditional, including assorted gelati, luscious crème caramel and a terrific tiramisu. You may need to wait to be seated, even with reservations, but regulars insist the food is worth the patience.

Lunch Monday-Saturday, dinner nightly; loud; AE, MC, V.

★★★☆
$$$$$

Park Grill

**Downtown: 333 Battery St. (at Clay);
415-296-2933**

California

Good
for groups

Kid
friendly

Dramatic woodwork, noise-muffling acoustics and
elegant decor, not to mention memo pads placed at
each table setting, make the Park Grill a favorite with
the power lunch crowd; if only they noticed the
food—an adventuresome take on California cuisine—which happens to be excellent. Artfully
arranged and served with just the right amount of
flourish by a well-trained staff, dishes on the seasonal menu might include an ahi napoleon drizzled
with avocado-mango vinaigrette, butternut squash
soup with banana-bread croutons, basil and sausage
risotto with roasted lobster or sage-rubbed pork tenderloin with sweet potatoes.

*Breakfast/lunch/dinner daily; afternoon tea; late-
night dining; live entertainment; full bar; valet
parking; AE, DC, D, MC, V.*

★★★☆
$$$$$

Parma Ristorante

**Marina: 3314 Steiner St. (between
Lombard and Chestnut); 415-567-0500**

Italian

Good
deal

Romantic

Molded cornices, sculpted friezes and a fine fresco
in a pretty dining room, plus very good classic
Northern Italian cuisine and an animated waitstaff,
have made this small neighborhood trattoria a longtime favorite among locals. Perfectly prepared pastas
are the most popular, but other successes include
paper-thin-sliced carpaccio served with arugula and
Parmesan cheese, garlicky Caesar salad, tender veal
piccata and fine seafood preparations using top-
quality fish. Seating is a bit cramped but that doesn't
seem to deter the loyal customers.

*Dinner nightly; reservations not accepted; AE,
MC, V.*

★★★☆
$$$$$

Pastis

Downtown: 1015 Battery St. (between
Union and Green); 415-391-2555

French

Good
deal

Romantic

Gerald Hirigoyen (also responsible for Fringale) continues his tradition of serving robust, deftly prepared,
moderately priced food at this classy little bistro.
Though it gets less press attention, Pastis has a casually sophisticated European atmosphere, and a warmer,
more exuberant space than Fringale. Hirigoyen and
chef de cuisine Isabelle Alexandre turn out French-
American fusion fare, including an already-legendary
oxtail rouille appetizer, and other tempting starters
such as leeks with sautéed scallops and foie gras
with grapes and verjus. Main courses include baked
halibut with quince risotto and marinated rack of
lamb with squash, peppers and garlic sauce.

*Lunch weekdays, dinner Monday-Saturday; loud;
full bar; AE, MC, V.*

★★★☆
$$$$$

Pat O'Shea's Mad Hatter

Richmond: 3848 Geary Blvd. (between 2nd
and 3rd Aves.); 415-752-3148

American

Sidewalk's
choice

Though Pat O'Shea's looks like just another Irish pub-
cum-sports bar—with 13 TVs, dart boards and pool
tables—Nancy Oakes, now head chef at Boulevard,
got her start here, serving champagne cuisine at Bud-
weiser prices. Oakes' legacy lives on in the oven-
roasted leg of lamb stuffed with fresh herbs and
garlic, served with scalloped potatoes and braised
mushrooms, and pan-roasted salmon on a bed of
garlic mashed potatoes with sautéed spinach. End
your meal with a real vanilla bean crème brûlée. Of
course, you can also get deep-fried zucchini,
nachos, fish and chips or burgers—but with food this
good, why bother?

*Lunch/dinner daily; weekend brunch; loud; full
bar; D, MC, V.*

Pauline's Pizza Pie

Mission: 260 Valencia St. (between Duboce and 14th St.); 415-552-2050

Pizza

Set in a cheery yellow two-level building across from the historic Levi's building on this otherwise drab and somewhat sketchy block, Pauline's does only two things—thin-crusted pizzas and salads—but does them fabulously well. The imaginative menu features eclectic organic toppings, ranging from house-made chicken and Italian sausages to Danish fontina cheese and roasted eggplant, combined with an addictive handmade crust. Salads are just as creative, made with handpicked California produce topped with fresh and dried herbs from Pauline's own gardens. The wine list is notable for its reasonably priced reds and whites, which go well with the simple, spicy food.

Dinner Tuesday-Sunday; reservations required for large parties; MC, V.

Pazzia Ristorante e Pizzeria

South of Market: 337 3rd St. (between Folsom and Harrison); 415-512-1693

Italian

 Romantic

This small, casual, homey trattoria, a Multimedia Gulch landmark, was one of the first local restaurants to provide authentic Italian food, and though ownership has changed hands, chef/owner Marco Sassone has made sure the kitchen remains traditional and inspired, with classic pastas, well-focused salads, fresh focaccia sandwiches, thin-crusted pizzas and a few nightly fish and meat dishes, such as the daring roasted rabbit in rosemary, black olive and red wine sauce. The small wine list features a number of standard Italian varieties, and service is outstandingly friendly.

Lunch weekdays, dinner Monday-Saturday; loud; outdoor seating; full bar; AE, MC, V, checks.

★★★★
$$$$$

Perry's Downtown

Downtown: 185 Sutter St. (between Montgomery and Kearny); 415-989-6895

California

Perry Butler has expanded his original namesake Union Street singles hangout by opening this larger, slightly more upscale clone. Perry's Downtown features friendly barkeeps, a comfortable, pubby decor and typical bar fare—hamburgers, Reubens, potato skins, etc.—but some attempt has been made to bring the menu into the '90s. You'll find such items as vine-ripened tomatoes with fresh mozzarella and basil, Chinese chicken salad, pasta Provençal with shrimp, and chicken and crab pot pie. On Wednesday and Saturday, Perry's Downtown hosts "lobster madness" feasts, with one-and-a-quarter pound Maine lobsters for $12.95.

Lunch/dinner Monday-Saturday; full bar; valet parking; AE, DC, D, MC, V.

★★★★
$$$$$

Pho Tu Do

Richmond: 1000 Clement St. (at 11th Ave.); 415-221-7111

Vietnamese

Most people come to this restaurant strictly for *pho* (the beef noodle soup that's a staple of Vietnamese cuisine), but if soup's not your thing, try the tasty clay-pot catfish or five-spice barbecued chicken over rice. Perk up with a cool, sweet glass of *cafe sua da*, a super-condensed mix of milk and coffee over ice. Don't be afraid to ask the friendly, gracious staff about the proper way to eat pho.

Breakfast/lunch/dinner daily; MC, V.

★★☆☆
$$$$$

Picaro

Mission: 3120 16th St. (between Valencia and Guerrero); 415-431-4089

Spanish

Looking for more room, the owners of the nearby Esperpento revamped this once haggard coffee shop into a tribute to Spain's famed surrealists, complete with melting clocks and Miro-inspired murals. Slow service at least allows time to peruse the enormous menu. Authentic hot and cold Spanish tapas (including grilled mussels, scallop brochette, spicy potatoes and grilled quail) are the main focus, but don't neglect the rabbit stew, fresh snapper or Picaro's specialty, Spanish red peppers stuffed with shrimp and mushrooms and served with spinach béchamel. Sangria is available by the glass or pitcher, and there's a variety of inexpensive Spanish wines.

Lunch Friday-Sunday, dinner nightly; reservations not accepted; cash only.

★★☆☆
$$$$$

Pier 40 Roastery & Cafe
South of Market: Pier 40 (at Townsend); 415-495-3815

American

 Good for groups

 Kid friendly

This attractive cafe takes the quality of its coffee (beans are roasted on-site) and food seriously. And the modern, streamlined dining area, with bold colors and tall windows, is pleasant for lingering. Breakfast offerings include a galaxy of pastries, French toast dipped in homemade hazelnut batter, corned beef hash and a selection of egg dishes (try the gallo pinto, with black beans, rice and tortillas or the Drake's Bay, with chicken apple sausage, mushrooms, red onions and cheddar cheese). Lunch and dinner offerings are beyond typical, with chicken Waldorf salad sandwiches, Chilean sea bass cakes and grilled chiles stuffed with cheese and chorizo.

Breakfast/lunch/dinner daily; outdoor seating; view; live entertainment; free parking lot; AE, D, MC, V, checks.

★★★ ☆
$$ $$

Plouf

Downtown: 40 Belden St. (between Bush and Pine, Kearny and Montgomery); 415-986-6491

French

Good deal

Located on an alley within the Financial District, this curbside bistro is recognizable by the bevy of umbrellas and tables filled with dining elite, who come as much for the cosmopolitan ambience as the cuisine. The hybrid French and California menu is mostly successful, such as sautéed medallions of monkfish in a ragout of savoy cabbage, pearl onions and bacon. Or, for $10, try a bounteous bowl of the house specialty: mussels slathered in a choice of seven sauces, such as apple cider, sweet and hot pepper, escargot butter or their show-stopping crayfish and tomato.

Lunch/dinner daily; loud; outdoor seating; full bar; AE, DC, MC, V.

★★★ ☆
$$ $$

PlumpJack Cafe

Marina: 3127 Fillmore St. (between Filbert and Greenwich); 415-563-4755

California

Good deal

Romantic

Co-owned and run by Billy Getty and new San Francisco supervisor Gavin Newsom, this exotic California-Mediterranean bistro is one of San Francisco's leading restaurants. The consistently excellent food is overseen by chef Maria Helm (former chef of The Sherman House and a top culinary talent) whose seasonal menu is primarily French-inspired, with Asian and Italian influences. Highlights are the appetizers, including bruschetta topped with roasted beets, goat cheese and garlic or eggplant, sweet peppers and chèvre. Don't miss the remarkable risottos, flavored with artichokes, applewood-smoked bacon and goat cheese, or smoked salmon and shiitake mushrooms. The extensive wine list is studded with fine bottles at

near-retail prices. The well-trained staff provides
excellent service.

*Lunch weekdays, dinner Monday-Saturday; loud;
full bar; valet parking; AE, DC, MC, V.*

★★★★
$$$$$

Polker's Gourmet Burgers
**Russian Hill: 2226 Polk St. (at Vallejo);
415-885-1000**

American

**Labeling itself a gourmet hamburger place, this
snazzy bistro features menus in the shape of artist's
palettes, jazz playing on the sound system, and
burgers that come recommended with merlot,
cabernet, or chardonnay (particularly tasty with the
chicken, turkey and tofu burgers). Fifteen varieties of
burgers are available, including the North Beach,
with garlic pesto and melted Jack, and the Haight-
Ashbury, topped with sautéed eggplant, garlic and
tomato. Other offerings include sandwiches wrapped
in lavash, Marina Green salads, shakes, floats and
for breakfast, big platefuls of pancakes, French toast
and potato scrambles.**

*Breakfast/lunch/dinner daily; late-night dining;
cash only.*

★★★★
$$$$$

Port Cafe
**Castro: 3499 16th St. (at Sanchez);
415-552-7645**

Cuban

 Good
deal

**This Cuban-American restaurant is alive with color,
from the red, copper, and tangerine paint job to the
brunch hostess, Birdie, a congenial and wildly
dressed drag queen who entertains folks waiting for a
table. Dinner is also a lively affair—especially on
weekends when a crowd of folks savor sangria and
an array of Cuban dishes such as roasted leg of pork
with garlic, fried chicken pieces and seasoned
ground beef hash. All come with soup or salad, rice
and black beans. To satisfy American palates, the**

cafe also offers more than two dozen hot or cold sandwiches and burgers.

Breakfast/lunch/dinner daily; weekend brunch; loud; AE, MC, V.

★★★★
$$$$$

Postrio

Downtown: 545 Post St. (between Mason and Taylor); 415-776-7825

California

Romantic

Good for groups

An immediate sensation when it opened in 1989, Wolfgang Puck's Postrio crackles with energy the moment you set foot in this elegant, modern space designed by Pat Kuleto. The spacious dining room provides a lovely setting for the terrific food, an exciting hybrid of California/Asian/Mediterranean cuisine crafted by brothers Mitchell and Steven Rosenthal: grilled quail accompanied by spinach and a soft egg ravioli with port wine glaze; sautéed salmon with plum glaze, wasabi mashed potatoes and miso vinaigrette; or roasted leg of lamb with garlic potato puree and niçoise olives. Be sure to save room for the sensational desserts. Service can be frosty for nonregulars, fawning for socialites and visiting celebs.

Breakfast/lunch/dinner daily; weekend brunch; pre-theater menu; full bar; live entertainment; valet parking; all major credit cards.

★★★★
$$$$$

Powell's Place

Hayes Valley: 511 Hayes (between Gough and and Octavia); 415-863-1404

Southern

Powell's, owned by local gospel singer Emmit Powell, has been serving authentic soul food to a mostly African-American clientele for the past 20 years (and in recent years to Hayes Valley hipsters.) The well-worn, window-fronted space is nothing fancy, but the staff is friendly, there's plenty of seating and the food is authentic and quite good. The house specialty is crispy, juicy Southern-fried chicken, served with a corn muffin and sides. Other choices include oxtails, ribs and smothered pork chops and chitterlings. Avoid the canned-tasting veggies, but try the savory greens. Finish with some house-made sweet potato pie.

Breakfast/lunch/dinner daily; AE, MC, V.

★★★★
$$$$$

Pozole Restaurant

Castro: 2337 Market St. (between Castro and 16th St.); 415-626-2666

Latin American

Decked out with Day of the Dead decor, this exuberant little Mexican restaurant is the brainchild of talented chef and owner Jesse Acevedo, who prepares fresher, lighter and less spicy fare than that typically found in local Mexican restaurants. Try the quesadilla with smoked chicken, mild chorizo sausage and diced potatoes; the California burrito with cactus, baby corn, lime juice, tomatoes and roasted garlic; or the sublime pink bean puree with smoked tomatoes, mild chiles and strips of homemade tortilla. The lime- and cilantro-marinated fish tacos and the chicken tamale made with the airiest of masa are equally delicious.

Dinner nightly; late-night dining; reservations not accepted; cash only.

★★★★
$$$$$

Prego Ristorante

Pacific Heights: 2000 Union St. (at Buchanan); 415-563-3305

Italian

Once the exclusive bastion of singles, Prego has opened the door to families, too, slightly altering the menu and the attitude. Though no longer a culinary trendsetter (it was heralded for introducing authentic trattoria fare to the city), it's still reliable and offers a variety of fresh pastas, juicy rotisserie meats and good brick-oven-baked pizzas with thin crusts and unique toppings (the lobster sausage, mozzarella, tomato and frisée combo is probably the most unusual). A well-edited wine list includes some reasonably priced bottles. The young, talented owners

have also launched the successful Il Fornaio, Pane e Vino and Bix.

Lunch/dinner daily; weekend brunch; loud; outdoor seating; late-night dining; full bar; AE, DC, MC, V.

$$ SSS

R & G Lounge
Chinatown: 631 Kearny St. (between Clay and Sacramento); 415-982-7877

Chinese

Good for groups

This mecca for connoisseurs of authentic Cantonese cuisine is one of San Francisco's top regional Chinese restaurants. The utilitarian downstairs dining room is fine for lunch, while the more formal shoji-screened dining room upstairs is pleasant for a leisurely dinner. Many of the best dishes aren't on the English menu, so check out what others are eating or interrogate your waiter about what's fresh. The salt-and-pepper prawns or fresh oysters in a clay pot are bona fide winners; other excellent dishes include mustard greens in garlic, mushrooms with tender greens, roasted Dungeness crab and soy sauce chicken.

Lunch/dinner daily; validated parking; AE, MC, V.

★★☆☆
$$ SSS

Radicchio Trattoria
Marina: 1809 Union St. (at Octavia); 415-346-7373

Italian

Good deal

Romantic

As you might expect, radicchio rules the kitchen at this simply designed, refreshing Northern Italian restaurant and it's creatively incorporated into many dishes. Favored entrees include the grilled scallop kebabs wrapped in radicchio and Italian speck, simple but juicy rib-eye steak, Italian sausage paired with grilled polenta and a roasted bell-pepper stew or rock shrimp and tagliolini noodles bathed in a saffron-infused squid-ink sauce. The reasonably priced wine list is heavily Italian, with a few well-chosen California varietals. Top off your meal with an eye-opening dessert: hazelnut gelato sunk in a cup of espresso.

Dinner Tuesday-Sunday; AE, MC, V.

The Ramp
China Basin: 855 China Basin St. (at Pier 64); 415-621-2378

American

 Sidewalk's choice

 Good for groups

 Kid friendly

A favorite bayside retreat, the Ramp is best enjoyed on a sunny afternoon, when you can hang out on the large deck and gaze at the rusting ships. Hugely popular is the weekend brunch, where Bloody Marys flow like water and enormous omelets are consumed with gusto. At lunch you'll find standard sandwiches, salads and burgers. The food's not great, but that's not the point—people trek out here for the salty wharf-side atmosphere and the live music on the weekends. The Ramp's a bit hard to find (giving it more cachet), and is only open until about 8 p.m.

Breakfast/lunch daily, weekend brunch; full bar; view; outdoor seating; live music; reservations not accepted; AE, MC, V.

Rasoi
Mission: 1037 Valencia St. (between 21st and 22nd Sts.); 415-695-0599

Indian

Though relatively new, a loyal following swears this attractive restaurant serves the freshest, healthiest Indian food in town. The gourmet Indian pizza is a treat, topped with tandoori chicken, mushrooms, green peppers and cilantro, as are chicken kabobs roasted with cashew paste and skewered prawns coated with sesame seeds. Savory vegetarian entrees include chile peppers stuffed with cottage cheese and scallions in anise and cumin sauce, and a zesty medley of sautéed cauliflower, potatoes, tomatoes and green peas seasoned with cumin and coriander. Meat-eaters should sample the lamb in a spicy onion-

curry sauce or tandoori chicken simmered in creamy tomato sauce.

Dinner nightly; AE, MC, V.

Rassellas
Pacific Heights: 2801 California St. (at Divisadero); 415-567-5010

Ethiopian

 Romantic

Good for groups

This Ethiopian restaurant and club is best known for its nightly live jazz and blues but the food, often overlooked, is authentic and has a loyal following. Though not always distinctive, Rassella's serves ample portions of several delicious, spicy vegetarian stews, made with varying combinations of lentils, okra, zucchini and potatoes. There's also a juicy lamb stew seasoned with *berbere* sauce and beef cubes sautéed in butter with peppers, onions and zesty spices—all mopped up with traditional spongy *injera* bread. The charms of the beautiful, turn-of-the-century room (a former saloon) are somewhat lost amid the crowds and overly dim lighting.

Dinner nightly; full bar; live entertainment; reservations required; AE, CB, DC, MC, V.

Red Balloon
Mission: 2763 Mission St. (between 23rd and 24th Sts.); 415-285-1749

Nicaraguan

 Good deal

 Good for groups

Despite its name, this appealing Nicaraguan restaurant's interior is entirely done up in blue, from the carpets to the walls. Start with a savory combination plate of fried cheese, fried banana and pork wrapped in steaming banana leaves for less than $10. Move on to one of the traditionally prepared soups, light and flaky whole fried snapper or grilled pork. Tamales, fried plantains and yucca dishes round out the menu. Wash it all down with one of the exotic, non-alcoholic Nicaraguan drinks.

Breakfast/lunch/dinner daily; no liquor license; checks.

★★★★
$$$$$

Rendezvous du Monde

Downtown: 431 Bush St. (between Grant and Kearny); 415-392-3332

Mediterranean **Homey and humble, this small, family-run restaurant is prized for its tasty California-Mediterranean fare offered at reasonable prices, and chef/owner Sam Mogannam makes sure his robust food is enjoyed by his faithful patrons. The wild mushroom and mascarpone ravioli is lovely, as are the warm goat cheese salad, yellow Finn potatoes with herb aïoli and roasted Moroccan chicken breast. Even the cheeseburger reaches gourmet heights, topped as it is by Gruyère and a house-made focaccia bun. Desserts include espresso pots de crème and pear skillet cake with vanilla gelato. The small, quality wine list has some good values.**

Breakfast/lunch weekdays, dinner Tuesday-Saturday; Saturday brunch; loud; outdoor seating; prix fixe menu; AE, DC, MC, V.

★★★★
$$$$$

Restaurant Aya

Marina: 2084 Chestnut St. (at Steiner); 415-929-1670

Japanese **The dining room here, with its small, glimmering sushi**

Good deal

Romantic

Good for groups

bar, is as tranquil as the lush garden glimpsed through the back windows, making it a great resting spot for weary Chestnut Street shoppers. Take a seat at the bar and watch the sushi chef, who wins praise for his creations using fantastic flying fish and salmon roe, as well as some fresh-from-the-sea octopus. Other than sushi, Aya offers a nice selection of cooked Japanese fish. Winners are the miso-marinated eggplant *shigeyaki* **appetizer and the chicken** *amiyaki* **entree, broiled and brushed with a zesty teriyaki sauce.**

Dinner nightly; quiet; AE, DC, MC, V.

Restaurant LuLu

South of Market: 816 Folsom St. (between 4th and 5th Sts.); 415-495-5775

Mediterranean

Sidewalk's choice

Good for groups

San Franciscans are in love with LuLu, and despite occasional past lapses, co-chefs Jody Denton and Mark Valiani have helped put this bustling restaurant serving robust Mediterranean family-style fare back in favor. Swoon over starters like the hearty helping of roasted mussels served in a cast-iron skillet, or grilled chèvre wrapped in grape leaves. Popular follow-ups are the wood-fired rotisserie chicken, juicy pork loin, or any of the roasted, superbly seasoned fish or shellfish dishes. Pizzas are wonderful, topped with ingredients like prosciutto and fontina, and oyster lovers rejoice at the staggering variety available from the raw bar. The well-organized wine list is an eclectic mix of international standards and boutique wines.

Lunch/dinner daily; loud; late-night dining; full bar; AE, DC, MC, V.

★★★☆
$$$$$

Ristorante Bonta

Pacific Heights/Marina: 2223 Union St. (between Fillmore and Steiner); 415-929-0407

Italian

A popular Italian restaurant on bustling Union Street, Bonta serves very good food in an intimate dining room. Pass through the front door and you'll feel as though you've walked into a friend's home for a specially prepared pasta dinner. Especially good is the smoked mozzarella and mushroom appetizer and the savory ravioli stuffed with sea bass. For dessert, don't miss the traditional tiramisu or the warm pear crisp with hazelnut gelato. The room holds only about a dozen small tables, so you'll want to make reservations.

Dinner Tuesday-Sunday; MC, V.

★★★★
$$$$$

Ristorante Ecco

Italian

South of Market: 101 South Park (between Brannan and Bryant, 2nd and 3rd Sts.); 415-495-3291

Owned by the South Park Cafe team, Ecco has earned a reputation for its professional service and masterful execution of rustic Italian fare with an urbane twist. Its stylish dining room sports soaring windows, crisp table linens and a sleek palette of grays and neutrals. Lunchtime brings sparkling salads, such as ahi tuna, green beans, arugula, fennel, potatoes, beets and olives, thin-crusted pizzas and tasty panini. Dinner offers more venturesome options, such as deep-fried squid with fennel and red onion, Tuscan boar stew with wild mushrooms and white beans, and the namesake linguine, with pears, pecans, Gorgonzola and Parmesan.

Lunch weekdays, dinner Monday-Saturday; loud; view; full bar; AE, MC, V.

★★★★
$$$$$

Ristorante Ideale

Italian

Romantic

Good for groups

North Beach: 1309 Grant Ave. (at Vallejo); 415-391-4129

This little oasis of a restaurant with red-tile floors, soothing yellow walls and a Mediterranean-villa atmosphere, offers some of the best northern Italian cooking in the city. Start with the superb antipasto of marinated vegetables followed by pappardelle with wild boar-tomato sauce. The equally enticing *secondi piatti* include such delights as leg of lamb baked with artichokes and white wine. If you're unsure about which wine to order, Ideale's ebullient owner, Maurizio Bruschi, will happily help you out. From its attentive and exceedingly charming staff to very satisfying rustic fare, this modest spot delivers with seemingly effortless grace.

Dinner Tuesday-Sunday; full bar; AE, D, MC, V.

Ristorante Milano

Nob Hill: 1448 Pacific Ave. (between Hyde and Larkin); 415-673-2961

Italian

For more than a dozen years, Ristorante Milano has attracted a steadfast clientele, partly due to the two owners from Rome, who are sticklers about serving only authentic northern Italian dishes. In addition to dishes like superb mushroom risotto, house-made gnocchi and penne puttanesca, there are meat dishes such as a grilled combo of sausage, chicken breast and lamb, and grilled white veal chop infused with rosemary and sage. The intimate dining room is draped in shades of gray and black with black-and-white photos of Italian landmarks adorning the walls. The staff is Italian-accented and perpetually accommodating.

Dinner Tuesday-Sunday; AE, MC, V.

Ristorante Umbria

South of Market: 198 2nd St. (at Howard); 415-546-6985

Italian

A small menu, carefully conceived and executed, is the hallmark of this Italian eatery owned by Giulio Tempesta, formerly of Pazzia. An array of delicious sandwiches is offered at lunch (try the vinaigrette-drizzled pork or chicken focaccia). Grilled and roasted meats and fish, pizzas and superb roasted potatoes are some of the menu mainstays, bolstered by a roster of daily specials. Tempesta has an especially pleasing way with rabbit, chicken and lamb and the prices are extremely reasonable. The restaurant is simply furnished, with white-linen-topped tables, fresh flowers, terra-cotta tile floors and large windows.

Lunch weekdays, dinner Monday-Saturday; AE, DC, MC, V.

Riverside Seafood Restaurant

Sunset: 1201 Vicente St. (at 23rd Ave.);
415-759-8828

Chinese

Good
deal

Good
for groups

Kid
friendly

What river this friendly, placid and pleasingly decorated Chinese restaurant is next to is unclear, but a steady stream of Chinese patrons, who know what a good deal they're getting for such high-quality Mandarin Cantonese cooking, flows through here. Be sure to start with the fried sesame prawn appetizer and the Hong Kong-style pan-fried noodles. Look to the specials board on the back wall—that's where you'll find the best entrees, such as fresh rock cod in black bean sauce or deep-fried halibut and excellent crab preparations.

Lunch/dinner daily; MC, V.

Rocco's Seafood Grill

Nob Hill: 2080 Van Ness Ave. (at Pacific);
415-567-7600

Seafood

Kid
friendly

Though the name (formerly Kiki's) and menu have changed at this classic Parisian-style brasserie, the ambience largely remains the same. The reasonably priced, straightforward menu appeals to an older audience, who like their steaks rare and their fish plain and simple: prime rib and potatoes, sautéed sand dabs flavored with a bit of fresh lemon, seared halibut topped with herb butter. The simple yet sublime shrimp-in-the-shell appetizer is worth the work. Though its claim to having San Francisco's largest seafood bar probably wouldn't hold up, you can get seafood fresh and by the platter.

Dinner nightly; full bar; valet parking; all major credit cards.

★★★★
$$$$$

Roosevelt Tamale Parlor

Mission: 2817 24th St. (between Bryant and York); 415-550-9213

Mexican

Good deal

Since 1922, this cramped restaurant, festooned with black-and-white photos of its mascot, Teddy, has been the *sine qua non* of home-style Mexican cooking. Tamales, slow-cooked pork or chicken slathered with a zesty chili sauce, are the specialty. Tacos, enchiladas and an outstanding chile verde (pork in a tomatillo sauce spiced with green chiles) are accompanied by a side of beans and rice. The guacamole is some of the best in town. Enormous portions and a relaxed and friendly atmosphere make this an inviting place to hang out and fill up.

Lunch/dinner Tuesday-Sunday; cash only.

★★★
$$$$$

Rose Pistola

North Beach: 532 Columbus Ave. (between Union and Green); 415-399-0499

Italian

This boisterous, perpetually packed, sleek restaurant ranks among the hottest spots in the city, possessed of the same Midas touch that chef/restaurateur Reed Hearon has had with Restaurant Lulu and Cafe Marimba. The rustic food, served family-style, is southern Italian with a California flair. Exceptional wood-fire oven entrees include roast rabbit with fresh shell-bean ragout and polenta, roast pork chop with panzanella, and roasted whole fish in tomato broth. Practically all the pastas, seafood, pizzas and antipasti are expertly prepared. The only flaw at this otherwise outstanding restaurant is the service, which has ranged from poor to outright rude.

Lunch/dinner daily; ear-shattering; outdoor seating; late-night dining; full bar; live entertainment; valet parking; AE, MC, V.

★★★☆
$$$$$

Rosmarino

Richmond: 3665 Sacramento St. (between Locust and Spruce); 415-931-7710

 Mediterranean

Romantic

Though the cuisine at this small, serene, sequestered restaurant is labeled "rustic Mediterranean," the kitchen creates mostly Italian selections, ranging from house-made ricotta gnocchi topped with Parmesan and wild mushrooms to Moroccan braised chicken with pomegranates, spinach and quince or roast rack of lamb, stuffed with fig olivada. For dessert, order the fresh fruit crumble. They have a lovely lunch menu and an extensive Sunday brunch, including baked eggs with red peppers, tomatoes, onions and parmesan and amaretto French toast with almond-ricotta filling. For a romantic splurge or a beautiful alfresco linger, Rosmarino is highly recommended.

Lunch/dinner Tuesday-Sunday; Sunday brunch; outdoor seating; AE, DC, MC, V.

 ★★★★
$$$$$

Rosti

Marina: 2060 Chestnut St. (between Steiner and Fillmore); 415-929-9300

Italian

 Good deal

 Kid friendly

This L.A.-based Italian chain, specializing in rustic Italian dishes served fast and priced to move, has been an instant success (call it a Boston Market with class). The house special, an herbed roast chicken cooked under a brick and served with rosemary potatoes, is deliciously authentic. Other standouts are superb seafood risotto and pasta puttanesca. The menu also features white bean soup, grilled baby salmon, a dozen types of pasta, thin-crust wood-oven pizza and focaccia sandwiches. Sit-down service is available, and the dining room is pleasant, with high ceilings, arched windows and an open grill.

Lunch/dinner daily; loud; reservations not accepted; AE, DC, MC, V.

★★★★
$$$$$

Rubicon

Downtown: 558 Sacramento St. (between Sansome and Montgomery); 415-434-4100

French/
California

Sidewalk's
choice

Good
for groups

Though executive chef Scott Newman recently took over for star chef Traci des Jardins, his stint as her sous chef convinced him to preserve key elements of her menu. A mix of California and French influences, the menu features dishes like duck with dried figs and port, salmon carpaccio with cucumber-mint vinaigrette and crème brûlée. Tasting menus pair carefully chosen wines with each course. Rubicon's beamed ceilings, dark wood and large windows give it a roomy, almost loft-like feel, and celebrity watchers can only hope investors Robert De Niro, Francis Ford Coppola or Robin Williams might drop by.

Lunch Monday-Friday, dinner Monday-Saturday; full bar; reservations required; valet parking; AE, DC, MC, V.

★★★★
$$$$$

Rumpus

Downtown: 1 Tillman Place (off Grant between Post and Sutter); 415-421-2300

California

Good
for groups

Kid
friendly

Tucked away on a small, dead-end alley, this popular, casually sophisticated bistro pulls in crowds with its attractive, colorful decor and wonderful cooking. The kitchen's California cuisine, with French and Italian influences, serves great renditions of risotto, Caesar salad and roasted chicken. The smoked chicken ravioli, tamales with rock shrimp and arugula salads make delicious starters; pork chops fragrant with honey and rosemary and seasonal fish dishes are successful entrees. Standout desserts range from chocolate brioche cake to pineapple-rhubarb chutney ice cream. The small, playful, thoughtful wine list features unique varietals at great value.

Lunch Monday-Saturday, dinner nightly; loud; full bar; AE, DC, MC, V.

Saigon Saigon

Mission: 1132 Valencia St. (between 22nd and 23rd Sts.); 415-206-9635

Vietnamese

Good deal

Flavorful, inexpensive Vietnamese fare is offered within this simply furnished, high-ceilinged one-room restaurant. Lunch specials are a particularly good deal, and prices are only slightly higher at dinnertime. Good appetizers include lightly battered, deep-fried soft-shell crabs seasoned with garlic and white pepper, golden pan-fried quail and the aromatic tofu and vegetable soup flavored with lemongrass. Standout entrees are papaya-beef salad, tender lemongrass chicken or lamb and black-pepper catfish fillet with fresh mango tempura; nice desserts include dark- and white-chocolate mousse or fried banana topped with coconut ice cream.

Lunch/dinner daily; reservations required for large parties; AE, MC, V.

Sam's Grill

Downtown: 374 Bush St. (between Kearny and Montgomery); 415-421-0594

American

Good for groups

Step through the velvet-draped doorway of Sam's Grill and enter another era. The dark-wood wainscoting and brass fixtures are a perfect setting for longtime regulars, who order chops, traditional seafood dishes and creamed spinach from veteran waiters. Unless you like your food heavy and overly sauced, you'd do best to stick to simply prepared fish or grilled meats. For a real blast to the past, request one of the private curtained booths, complete with buzzers for summoning the waiters.

Lunch/dinner weekdays; loud; full bar; AE, DC, MC, V.

★★★★
$$$$$

Samui Thai Cuisine

Marina: 2414 Lombard St. (between Scott and Divisadero); 415-563-4405

Thai

 Good deal

 Romantic

Good for groups

The tropics are definitely the theme here, with fake palm trees, an attractive aquarium and bamboo decor dominating the somewhat kitschy dining room, which specializes in southern Thai cuisine. Reflecting island flavors, the extensive menu features many interesting and well-prepared seafood entrees and starters, including an excellent hot-and-sour *tom yam goon* soup, rich with shrimp and seasoned with lemongrass. The curry dishes are also good, and the crunchy green-papaya salad is refreshing. Be sure to try the savory beef seasoned with chile, garlic and mint leaves, or the daily specials.

Lunch Monday-Saturday, dinner nightly; reservations not accepted; AE, MC, V.

★★★★
$$$$$

San Tung

Sunset: 1031 Irving St. (between 11th and 12th Aves.); 415-242-0828

Chinese

San Tung's dumplings have become almost legendary as the most delicious in the city. Wrapped in a thick, smooth semi-translucent blanket of dough and exploding with flavor, the bestsellers are the shrimp and keek with minced shrimp and Chinese garlic chives, followed by the pork. Also a big hit are the long-noodle dishes, such as Three Deluxe Spicy Sauce Noodles, teeming with squid, onion, zucchini and shrimp. The spotless interior is built for speed, not comfort; if you get the feeling you're being rushed, you are.

Lunch/dinner daily except Wednesday; MC, V.

★★★★
$$$$$

Sanppo

Fillmore: 1702 Post St. (at Buchanan);
415-346-3486

Japanese

This small country-style restaurant has been cramming in locals for decades with its reliable, fresh, perfectly prepared food, cheerful staff and very reasonable prices. Along with the fine tofu and *tonkatsu* standbys, there's a range of adventurous specials. Tried-and-true favorites include tempura dishes, barbecued eel plate and a cast-iron pot filled with Japanese pot stickers floating in broth, teeming with noodles, tofu and vegetables. How the small, partially open kitchen cranks out such a variety of dishes is a mystery, but if you want sushi, sashimi, donburi, ramen or a side of cod roe, they've got it.

Lunch/dinner daily; reservations not accepted;
validated parking; MC, V.

★★★★
$$$$$

Sanraku Four Seasons Japanese Restaurant

Downtown: 704 Sutter St. (at Taylor);
415-771-0803

Japanese

Good
deal

This small Japanese restaurant serving high-quality food at reasonable prices may be sterile, but the chefs behind the sushi bar are lively and talented, conversing easily with patrons and occasionally even wrapping up a rose from a vase at hand for tourists to take with them. Sushi offerings include house specials like eel and avocado or the hand-rolled, deep-fried soft-shell crab. The fish is noticeably fresh and well prepared. A full dinner menu includes noodles, tempura, teriyaki, sukiyaki and donburi—well-executed, in generous portions. A dozen different sakes are also available.

Lunch weekdays; dinner nightly; AE, MC, V.

★★★★
$$$$$

Savor

Noe Valley: 3913 24th St. (between Noe and Sanchez); 415-282-0344

Mediterranean

Kid friendly

The three brothers who opened this popular neighborhood restaurant with an airy, high-ceilinged interior work hard to provide savory flavors on their mixed menu of Mediterranean, Southwest and French cuisine; and what it boils down to is hearty sandwiches, crisp salads and very good crepes. For a breakfast twist, try crab cakes and poached eggs served on homemade biscuits covered with Cajun hollandaise sauce. Later, try the Milano crepe filled with grilled eggplant, roasted garlic, artichoke hearts, roasted peppers and provolone cheese, or a mushroom-cheddar burger. The dessert crepes are worth the calorie splurge.

Breakfast/lunch/dinner daily; outdoor seating; late-night dining; fireplace; MC, V.

★★★★
$$$$$

Scala's Bistro

Downtown: 432 Powell St. (between Post and Sutter); 415-395-8555

French

Good for groups

In 1995, new owners Donna and Giovanni Scala, who operate Napa's Bistro Don Giovanni, transformed this glamorous spot into a stylish, welcoming setting that buzzes with energy on busy evenings, serving exceptional Italian and French regional cooking to an enthusiastic following. Standout appetizers include grilled portobello mushrooms and crispy calamari. Dynamite pastas range from porcini tagliatelle to rigatoni with Conchetta's veal meatballs. The seared salmon fillet and pork tenderloin are two excellent entrees, and a selection of risottos, salads and pizzas rounds out the menu. Portions are generous, but try to save room for the Chocolate I.V. and Bostini cream pie.

Breakfast/lunch/dinner daily; loud; full bar; valet parking; AE, DC, D, MC, V.

Scoma's at Fisherman's Wharf

★★★☆
$$$$$

Fisherman's Wharf: Pier 47 (between Jefferson and Jones); 415-771-4383

Seafood

 Good for groups

 Kid friendly

In its three decades of existence, this weather-beaten, rambling institution has achieved a national reputation for excellence, which seems deserved to some and mystifying to others. Scoma's perch on the pier endows it with wonderful views of the bay and a certain irresistible waterfront character, and the place is always packed. Offering a lineup of seafood dishes, as well as pasta and steak, the most popular dish is the shellfish sauté, but baby lobster tail, cioppino and grilled fresh fish are also favorites. The service is usually efficient, though not particularly charming.

Lunch/dinner daily; view; full bar; reservations not accepted; valet parking; all major credit cards.

Sears Fine Food

★★★☆
$$$$$

Downtown: 439 Powell St. (between Post and Sutter); 415-986-1160

American

 Good deal

 Good for groups

 Kid friendly

Fans of this San Francisco institution, known for its breakfasts, swear by the Swedish pancakes (fluffy dollar-sized morsels, 18 to a portion), baked Rome apples, strawberry waffles and corned beef hash. Lunch-goers chow down on braised lamb shanks, grilled salmon steaks and such diner classics as BLTs, egg-salad sandwiches, slabs of delicious strawberry shortcake and homemade fruit pies. Critics complain about the circus atmosphere, with pushy crowds and staff of pink-uniformed waitresses who are a little overeager to collect the check, but those naysayers are outnumbered by longtime loyalists who give both food and service thumbs-up.

Breakfast/lunch daily; loud; cash only.

Seoul Garden

★★★☆
$$$$$

Fillmore: 22 Peace Plaza (between Post and Geary); 415-563-7664

Korean

Good for groups

Kid friendly

This Korean country inn-style restaurant manages to be romantic and fun at the same time, with waitresses dressed in traditional Korean garb escorting you to one of the two dining rooms, each covered with fine woodwork and Korean art. When you place your order, the food comes raw and sliced into manageable pieces, then tossed onto the grill at your table and barbecued to exact specification. Standard dishes include varieties of marinated chicken, pork and beef, as well as seafood and fresh vegetables. Prices are a bit steep, but portions are huge.

Lunch/dinner daily; full bar; validated parking; AE, D, MC, V.

Silks

★★★★
$$$$$

Downtown: Mandarin Oriental Hotel, 222 Sansome St. (between Pine and California); 415-986-2020

Asian

Popular with downtown lunching businessman, the Mandarin Oriental Hotel's flagship restaurant hasn't caught on as an evening destination, despite a decade of critical acclaim for its exceptional California-Pacific Rim cuisine. The latest chefs continue the tradition of flavorful, beautifully presented dishes, such as the elegant Dungeness crab and smoked salmon parfait or crisp chicken, pork and shiitake spring rolls for starters, with roast Sonoma lamb loin with portobello mushrooms or roasted artichoke and portobello strudel among the entrees. For dessert, try the exotic chilled mint, mango and lime soup with vanilla ice cream. The latest remodel makes the dining room slightly more amiable, with dramatic modern art, wood-latticed windows and soaring floral arrangements.

Breakfast/dinner daily, lunch weekdays; prix fixe menu; full bar; jacket and tie required; reservations required; valet parking; all major credit cards.

★★★☆
$$$$$

Slow Club

Mission: 2501 Mariposa St. (at Hampshire); 415-241-9390

American

Although its postindustrial-chic decor can be forbidding—cement floors, metal railings, low lighting, exposed pipes and ducts—this small, hard-to-find bistro amid warehouses and garages is worth tracking down for its terrific California cuisine. The tiny menu changes nightly, featuring such robust fare as oven-roasted marinated chicken with grilled polenta and Belgian endive; potato gnocchi with black chanterelles, spinach and cream; and a Niman Schell hamburger with fries. Tuesday is tapas night: try small plates of polenta with Parmesan cheese, poblano chiles stuffed with goat cheese, and other exotic specialties. Service—perhaps fittingly, given the establishment's name—can be rather slow.

Lunch weekdays, dinner Tuesday-Saturday; outdoor seating; full bar; reservations not accepted; MC, V.

★★★☆
$$$$$

Socca

Richmond: 5800 Geary Blvd. (at 22nd Ave.); 415-379-6720

French

 Romantic

 Good for groups

The food at this romantic spot, decorated in warm shades of yellow and blue, stays close to the hearty cuisine of Provence, but is given a twist by Italian chef John Caputo. Highlights on the seasonally changing menu include the incredible wild mushroom risotto, succulent New Zealand grouper on a bed of cauliflower encircled by red and black caviar and topped with potato crust (the best fish you'll ever

taste), cassoulet and braised lamb shank. The menu's Mediterranean flair is reflected in the small, though reasonably priced, wine list. Socca's signature warm chocolate cake with chantilly cream offers a perfect ending.

Dinner Tuesday-Sunday; loud; prix fixe menu; full bar; valet parking; all major credit cards.

★★★★
$$$$$

South Park Cafe

South of Market: 108 South Park (between Brannan and Bryant, 2nd and 3rd Sts.); 415-495-7275

French

 Romantic

Everything from the zinc bar and pale yellow walls to the selection of French newspapers hanging on wooden rods evokes the Parisian bistro experience, and the food at this popular neighborhood cafe is as authentic as you'll find this side of the Left Bank. The lunch and dinner specials are always good, as are staples such as mussels, rabbit and duck. At lunchtime, the place is packed with artsy types from Multimedia Gulch. Things are more civilized at dinner or during the cocktail hour, when a small array of tapas complements a selection from the comprehensive, well-priced wine list.

Lunch weekdays, dinner Monday-Saturday; loud; full bar; AE, MC, V, checks.

★★★★
$$$$$

Spaghetti Western

Fillmore: 576 Haight St. (between Steiner and Fillmore); 415-864-8461

Southwestern

 Good deal

Check out the funky Spaghetti Western at breakfast for food that's good in a hearty, hangover-cure way. The Pesto Scram with home fries and a homemade biscuit is tasty, as is the Homeboy, with two eggs, home fries and biscuits smothered in country gravy. Lunch offers everything from salads to tuna melts to tofu burgers. The decor is Vegas Western: Cattle skulls, old guns and pictures of Elvis from his B-movie days adorn the walls, cacti lurk in the corner

and waitstaff dress in jeans and T-shirts. Tunes range
from acid-punk to Tom Jones.

*Breakfast/lunch daily; loud; reservations not
accepted; cash only.*

★★★★
$$$$$

Speckmann's
Noe Valley: 1550 Church St. (at Duncan);
415-282-6850

German

 Good
for groups

At this quaint, dimly lit restaurant, with red-and-
white-checked tablecloths, dark-wood chairs and
Bavarian music, waitresses dressed in dirndls spout
German while serving bowls of goulash and platters
of bratwurst. After a few swigs of one of the 25 beers
available, you might believe you're in Munich.
Speckmann's offers about two dozen traditional
German favorites, most served with lentils, goulash,
thick potato leek soup or salad, and vegetables or
potatoes. If you're a hearty soul, indulge in the
Bavarian Peasant Platter, a feast for two that
includes ham hock, blood and polish sausage,
smoked pork loins, red cabbage, sauerkraut, potatoes and vegetables.

Lunch/dinner daily; AE, MC, V.

★★★★
$$$$$

Spiazzo
Sunset: 33 West Portal Ave. (between
Vicente and Ulloa); 415-664-9511

Italian

This popular neighborhood eatery with an odd but
pleasing purple, peach and gray color scheme does a
brisk business, serving modern Italian-American
dishes at reasonable prices. In addition to pastry-thin
pizzas from the wood-burning oven, the menu
includes a small selection of predictably pleasing
dishes such as spinach tortellini with sun-dried
tomatoes in roasted garlic cream sauce and grilled
pork loin with rosemary. Daily specials are the best
bet, such as grilled rainbow trout or wild mushroom

risotto. A modest wine list offers California and Italian wines. The service is friendly and helpful.

Lunch/dinner daily; free parking lot; all major credit cards.

★★★★
$$$$$

Splendido

Downtown: 4 Embarcadero Center (between Clay and Sacramento at Drumm); 415-986-3222

California/
Mediterranean

 Good
for groups

Kid
friendly

Pat Kuleto's playful Mediterranean village design, with its profusion of stone, brick and tile, suggests a medieval fantasy land, and the restaurant's California-Mediterranean menu is equally exuberant. For example, there's seafood soup with toasted country bread, excellent pizzas from the wood-burning oven, imaginative pasta dishes such as linguine with tender Manila clams, roasted vegetables with toasted parsley orzo or grilled lamb loin with wilted spinach and toasted couscous. Desserts include warm apricot brioche and a twice-baked bittersweet chocolate cake.

Lunch weekdays, dinner nightly; loud; outdoor seating; full bar; validated parking; AE, DC, D, MC, V.

★★★★
$$$$$

Stars

Civic Center: 555 Golden Gate Ave. (between Van Ness and Polk); 415-861-7827

American

A San Francisco landmark, Jeremiah Tower's Stars is vast and noisy, with the longest bar in the city and acres of gleaming wood, brass and mirrors, attracting luminaries from all spheres. Stars' legendary status has superseded its food, and even devoted fans grumble that the uberchef sometimes seems more interested in expanding his culinary empire than in maintaining standards here. But when his inspired culinary creations are carried out, the results can be truly wonderful. Exhibit A: dishes such as grilled salmon with celery root puree and roasted lamb with

mint pesto. The wine list is large and carefully compiled. Desserts are usually top-notch. And the service is friendly and adept, even if you're not a star.

Lunch weekdays, dinner nightly; loud; full bar; AE, DC, MC, V.

★★★★
$$$$$

Stoyanof's

Sunset: 1240 9th Ave. (between Irving and Lincoln); 415-664-3664

Greek

An old standby amid all the chic new eateries, this quiet, relaxing place, modestly decorated with hanging rugs, ceiling fans and exposed wood beams, is one of San Francisco's top Greek restaurants. The menu is unfalteringly Greek—*dolmades*, *tzatziki*, Greek salad, *moussaka*, *spanakopita*—and it's all fresh, wholesome and surprisingly inexpensive. Start with zesty soup, made with chicken, egg yolk, rice and lemons; follow that with the excellent leg of lamb, roasted with an herb marinade and served au jus, or the popular grilled swordfish kabob.

Lunch/dinner Tuesday-Sunday; reservations required for large parties; AE, MC, V.

★★★★
$$$$$

Straits Cafe

Richmond: 3300 Geary Blvd. (at Parker); 415-668-1783

Singaporean

Owner/chef Chris Yeo offers superb authentic Singaporean dishes in a unique, picturesque setting resembling a Southeast Asian village. Dine family-style to get the full effect of Yeo's mastery of spices and herbs in a wide array of unusual chicken, beef, lamb, seafood and vegetable dishes. Preparations range from delicate salmon fillet seasoned with fresh chile and lemongrass and grilled in a banana leaf to the fiery marinated beef simmered in kaffir lime leaves. Be sure to order a side of fried coconut rice with prawns and vegetables. In addition to a solid wine list, the bar offers pungent tropical cocktails.

Lunch/dinner daily; full bar; AE, DC, MC, V.

★★★★
$$$$$

Suppenküche

**Fillmore: 601 Hayes St. (at Laguna);
415-252-9289**

German

 Good
deal

Good
for groups

Suppenküche's got delicious updated German fare, a
young, hip crowd clad in black and a dining room
straight out of some remote European monastery.
Here, classics like *sauerbraten*, Wienerschnitzel and
bratwurst are executed delicately, with less cream,
butter and fat than usual German cooking. Sauteed
venison in red wine sauce is tender and flavorful,
potato pancakes are crisp and light, and at least
three fabulous vegetable soups are on the menu.
Diners sit family-style on the long benches. There are
20 beers on tap, 18 of them German.

*Dinner nightly; weekend brunch; reservations
required for large parties; AE, MC, V.*

★★★★
$$$$$

Sushi Groove

**Russian Hill: 1916 Hyde St. (between Union
and Green); 415-440-1905**

Japanese

The food at this hip new sushi bar lives up to its
motto—"raw talent on Russian Hill"—and a talented
hand was evidently behind the restaurant's design,
which features halogen lamps resembling inverted
martini glasses, highly lacquered wood tables and
purple velvet curtains that contrast with the mustard-
colored walls. There's the standard array of nigiri and
maki rolls, as well as unique twists: jungle rolls (yellowtail tuna with papaya) and monkey rolls (sea
urchin, eel and avocado). High-grade seafood, crafty
presentation, friendly service and suave surroundings will undoubtedly attract a steady stream of customers.

*Dinner nightly; reservations required for large
parties; valet parking; AE, DC, D, MC, V.*

Sushi-A

★★☆☆
$$$$$

Fillmore: 1737 Buchanan St. (between Sutter and Post); 415-931-4685

Japanese

 Romantic

For a more subdued, intimate environment, try this little restaurant, serving exceptional Japanese cuisine and sushi expertly prepared by the legendary owner Yoshi Motoda, who has perfected his craft over the past decade. Eschewing the flashy presentation and boisterous atmosphere of some competitors, Sushi-A focuses its energy on producing top-quality food. Start with miso soup and a simple unagi appetizer, followed by a sampler of meat, seafood and vegetable appetizers. The standard teriyaki, sukiyaki and tempura dinners are available and the clay-pot seafood dishes, brimming with noodles, fresh vegetables and tofu in a flavorful broth, are particularly good.

Lunch/dinner Thursday-Monday; AE, MC, V.

Swan Oyster Depot

★★☆☆
$$$$$

Nob Hill: 1517 Polk St. (between California and Sacramento); 415-673-1101

Seafood

This is a one-of-a-kind San Francisco experience for die-hard shellfish fans, and fortunately it's the type of place tourists walk right past. You won't find white linen tablecloths, or even tables, at this oyster bar— since 1912, patrons have balanced themselves on the 19 hard, rickety stools lining the long, narrow marble counter cluttered with bowls of oyster crackers, fresh-cut lemons, and Tabasco sauce. A congenial, quick-shucking team is always eager to serve. Along with bivalves, lunch specialties include sizable salads (crab, shrimp, prawn or a combo), seafood cocktails, lobster and cracked Dungeness crabs.

Lunch Monday-Saturday; loud; checks.

★★★★ $$$$$

Sweet Heat

Marina: 3324 Steiner St. (between Chestnut and Lombard); 415-474-9191
Haight: 1725 Haight St. (between Cole and Shrader); 415-387-8845

Mexican

Good deal

Kid friendly

The friendly young owners of this casual but spirited pair of restaurants offer what they've dubbed "healthy Mexican food to die for" at unbeatable prices. Reggae fills the air, palm fans swing in unison and a faux toucan perches over the minibar, creating a beach-like ambience. Try the red snapper or crispy calamari tacos filled with cabbage, fresh tomato salsa and *cotija* cheese. Other good choices are the spicy Mexican Caesar salad, zesty chicken wings served with nonfat cilantro-yogurt dipping sauce or the very popular calamari or grilled salmon burritos.

Lunch/dinner daily; full bar; reservations not accepted; MC, V.

★★★★★ $$$$$

Sweet Max's

Downtown: 1 California St. (between Market and Drumm); 415-781-6297
235 Montgomery St. (between Bush and Pine Sts.); 415-398-6297

Deli

Sweet Max's (part of the chain that includes Max's Opera Cafe, Max's Eatz and Max's Market) is everything you'd expect from a New York-inspired deli. This branch is the original, and the owners roast their own meats, bake their own breads and pastries, serving it to the business-lunch crowd, who come for their trademark sandwiches—no one makes them taller, thicker, drippier or more delicious. In addition to the standards, Max's provides vegetarian and low-fat dining options, offering salads and daily specials, such as tandoori chicken or blackened snapper with tomato relish. Sinful desserts include strawberry

shortcake, chocolate mousse, cheesecake and brownies. Go early and expect a line.

Breakfast/lunch weekdays; loud; no liquor license; reservations not accepted; AE, DC, MC, V.

★★★★
$$$$$

Tadich Grill

Downtown: 240 California St. (between Battery and Front); 415-391-1849

Seafood

Good for groups

This Financial District establishment, with cable cars clattering out front, boasts a crew of starchy old-time waiters, a roster of competently prepared seafood dishes, and a convoluted pedigree that somehow stretches back to an 1849 tented, waterfront coffee stand. Although you'll find such rich retro fare as lobster Thermidor and turbot à la Newburg on the menu, it's probably best to stick to fresh fish simply prepared; other good bets include clam chowder, seafood cioppino, and shrimp or crab Louis salad. The dark-paneled walls, private booths, ornate ceiling and dim lighting lend a wonderful, old San Francisco feel.

Lunch/dinner Monday-Saturday; loud; historic interest; full bar; reservations not accepted; MC, V.

★★★★
$$$$$

Tanuki

Richmond: 4419 California St. (between 6th and 7th Aves.); 415-752-5740

Japanese

Little-known and well-hidden behind a tree in a parking lot off California Street, homey little Tanuki with its dark wood trim and rice paper walls is adored by locals. They pile in for wonderfully fresh sushi, sashimi and sukiyaki, as well as traditional noodle bowls, soups and combination plates. You'll be hard pressed to find such great service and acceptable prices at any other Japanese restaurant in the city. The most popular sushi choice is a soft-shell crab roll. For lunch, order the box lunches—different

combinations of sashimi, tempura, tonkatsu, beef, chicken or fish, served with soup and rice.

Lunch weekdays, dinner nightly; reservations not accepted; free parking lot; MC, V.

★★☆☆
$$$$

Taqueria Cancun

Downtown: 1003 Market St. (at 6th St.);
415-864-6773
Mission: 2288 Mission St. (at 19th St.);
415-252-9560
Mission: 3211 Mission St. (at Valencia);
415-550-1414

Mexican

 Sidewalk's choice

 Good deal

This little slice of paradise serves what many say are the best burritos in the city. The Market Street branch is the seediest of the bunch, drawing a roughneck crowd from nearby transient hotels. If you brave the Mission-and-19th locale, be prepared to push through crowds of homeboys hanging around outside (this is gang territory) and then head to the back of the smoky, cramped space to listen to the jukebox while you wait. If that's too rough for you, head further down to the Mission-at-Valencia location: Its small, spare room with yellow Formica tables and paintings of voluptuous Aztec warrior princesses and princes is less crowded and less smoky than the one up the street. The burritos are heads above others, featuring lightly grilled, parchment-like shells, moist, well-seasoned rice and big chunks of fresh avocado. The veggie burrito is the most lauded; other fillings include greasy-good marinated pork, average *carne asada*, beef head-meat and tongue and nicely grilled chicken. Don't miss the refreshing house-made fruit drinks, especially the peach and cantaloupe, or the cinnamony *horchata*.

Breakfast/lunch/dinner daily; loud; late-night dining; reservations not accepted; cash only.

Taqueria El Balazo

★★☆☆
$$$$$

Haight: 1654 Haight St. (between Clayton and Cole); 415-864-8608

Mexican

Kid friendly

Perpetually in a state of near-chaos, this popular corner taqueria is a riot of red and yellow paint, pressed copper, Mexican folk art and pumping music. Patrons line up for the fat burritos and corn-tortilla tacos piled high with meat. Enchiladas, tamales, quesadillas, *carne asada* plates, fish tacos, nachos—they're all on the menu, all wonderful and priced to move. Sample from two vegetarian burritos dedicated to Jerry Garcia and Grateful Dead band mate Bob Weir, or try the Burrito Vallarta, filled with sautéed rock shrimp, fresh nopales (cactus leaves), sweet red peppers, saffron rice, black beans and salsa.

Lunch/dinner daily; loud; late-night dining; cash only.

Taqueria San José 1/2/3

★★☆☆
$$$$$

Mission: 2830 Mission St. (between 24th and 25th Sts.); 415-282-0203
Mission: 2839 Mission St. (between 24th and 25th Sts.); 415-282-0283
North Beach: 2257 Mason St. (between Chestnut and Francisco); 415-749-0826

Mexican

Sidewalk's choice

Good for groups

With three locations, Taqueria San Jose is consistently voted as one of the best, if not the preeminent, burrito and taco joint in the city. Best known for its huge portions and wide variety of fillings, such as nopal cactus leaves, boiled beef head or grilled calf brains, the chain also serves up a specialty double-layered taco filled with spicy spit-roasted pork and topped with salsa and cilantro. You can also get a dynamite version of the standard charcoal-grilled steak, spicy pork or chicken burrito, as well as chiles rellenos, enchiladas, tostadas, and other authentic specialties. Prices are cheap, and high turnover insures freshness.

Lunch/dinner daily; loud; late-night dining (at 1 and 2 only); reservations not accepted; cash only.

Tay Viet

Marina: 2034 Chestnut St. (between Fillmore and Steiner); 415-567-8124

Vietnamese

At this tiny, unprepossessing Vietnamese restaurant, tantalizing, spicy aromas engulf you the moment you walk in the door. Chef/owner Thuy Diep ran restaurants in Saigon and Paris, and it's clear that her time served her well. Start with her delicate, fragrant imperial rolls, and for a truly scintillating experience, sample the marinated lemongrass beef, seasoned with mint, cilantro, chopped peanuts and a savory fish-based sauce. The nightly special might feature a whole Dungeness crab or charbroiled jumbo prawns, with garlic noodles and wine, for $17.95. The minimalist, ultramodern decor of the dining room reflects Diep's passion for art.

Lunch/dinner daily; AE, D, MC, V.

Ten-Ichi

Pacific Heights: 2235 Fillmore St. (between Clay and Sacramento); 415-346-3477

Japanese

This festive Japanese restaurant is serious about serving excellent sushi (both the standard and the unorthodox), udon, tempura and teriyaki in a simple but elegant environment. The popular Indian Summer marries green-bean tempura and avocado with layers of grilled eel, while the Fat Tuesday roll is a decadent mix of smoked salmon and cream cheese rolled in seaweed, and the Popeye combines steamed spinach and shiitake mushrooms. The tempura is crisp but never greasy, and the teriyaki wins kudos for its delicate spicy-sweet coating. Particularly good is the seafood udon, heavy with shrimp, scallops, calamari and halibut.

Lunch/dinner daily; MC, V.

The Terrace

Nob Hill: Ritz Carlton Hotel, 600 Stockton St. (at California); 415-296-7465

California

With a brick courtyard, elegant fountain and profusion of flowers, this is the loveliest, most civilized venue for alfresco dining in the city; and the interior with delicate French decor is just as charming for enjoying terrific California-Mediterranean food. Complex signature dishes include mussels sautéed with shallots and white wine; salad of baby beets, goat cheese, arugula and curried croutons; superb monkfish; and rack of lamb with sweet-potato gnocchi. The small wine list is traditional in both selection and price. Desserts are sensational, and the lavish afternoon teas and Sunday jazz brunches have their fans.

Breakfast/lunch/dinner daily; weekend brunch; afternoon tea; outdoor seating; full bar; live entertainment; valet parking; all major credit cards.

Thai Bar-B-Q

Civic Center: 730 Van Ness Ave. (between Turk and Eddy); 415-441-1640

Thai

Skip the fast-food burger and taco joints in the area and go straight to Thai Bar-B-Q for a cheap fix of tasty grilled meats and noodle combinations in a pleasant, chic setting near Opera Plaza. Barbecued squid, chicken, meatballs, lamb, oysters, trout and salmon are only a few of the choices on the extensive menu. Try the addictive barbecued duck on noodles or mildly spicy sautéed eggplant with black bean sauce. Entrees arrive with shredded carrot salad, sweet, sticky rice and warm bread.

Lunch Monday-Friday, dinner Monday-Saturday; cash only

★★★☆
$$$$$

Thai

Thai House

**Castro: 151 Noe St. (at Henry);
415-863-0374**

A cozy neighborhood joint serving the best Thai food in a neighborhood rife with Thai restaurants, this convivial, crowded spot is known for its pad thai and roast duck renditions such as in spicy red-curry with pineapple and basil. The tom kha gai (hot and sour chicken soup) is also very good, and Thai beer is available in bottles. Flowers grace every table, the waitstaff wears traditional clothing and miniature Thai paintings hang on the walls. If it's too crowded when you go, try its larger, less cozy sister restaurant around the corner on Market.

Dinner daily; MC, V.

★★★☆
$$$$$

Thai

 Good for groups

Thanya & Salee

**Potrero Hill: 1469 18th St. (at Connecticut);
415-647-6469**

This exuberant Thai restaurant serves good, traditional fare in a room busy with tropical decor: bamboo wainscoting, orchids and potted palm trees, and a huge saltwater fish tank below an old fishing net. Fortunately, the chefs take their jobs more seriously than the decorators did. Try any of the Thai classics—coconut soup flavored with chicken and lemongrass, chicken satay with peanut sauce—or sample the thick red curry sauce with prawns, deep-fried catfish filets, or barbecued salmon. For dessert, go with coconut or Thai tea ice cream served with a honey-laced fried banana.

Lunch weekdays, dinner nightly; full bar; AE, MC, V, checks.

Thep Phanom

Haight: 400 Waller St. (at Fillmore);
415-431-2526

Thai

Sidewalk's
choice

With a permanent line out its door, no Thai restaurant is more highly lauded than Thep Phanom is. Using garden-fresh ingredients in its creative and colorful renditions of Thai specialties, Thep Phanom seamlessly blends complex flavors into dishes such as boneless duck in a light honey sauce served on a bed of spinach (one of the city's great entrees); superb minty, spicy calamari salad; warm duck salad with mint, chiles, lemon and onion; and velvety, basil-spiked seafood curry served on banana leaves. The service is charming and efficient, and the decor is upscale for the grungy neighborhood.

Dinner nightly; AE, MC, V.

Thirsty Bear Brewing Company

South of Market: 661 Howard St.
(between 2nd and 3rd Sts.); 415-974-0905

Spanish

Good
for groups

Everything about this hot new brew pub draws kudos. A hip crowd comes to the industrial-chic bi-level space as much for the food as for the superb well-crafted microbrews. Chef Daniel Olivella, a Catalonia native, prepares what is arguably the best, most authentic Spanish cuisine in San Francisco. All three versions of paella are outstanding, as are the majority of hot and cold tapas—particularly the spinach sautéed with garlic, pine nuts and raisins, and the roasted vegetables. Finish with the signature twin chocolate mousse-filled sugar cones on a bed of Chantilly cream and fresh berries.

Lunch Monday-Saturday, dinner nightly; full bar; AE, DC, MC, V.

Ti Couz

Mission: 3108 16th St. (at Valencia);
415-252-7373

French

Sidewalk's choice

Good deal

This incredibly popular crepe joint serves delectable, paper-thin crepes in a stucco-and-wood dining room reminiscent of an old Breton inn, with a menu based on classic recipes from that region. French chef/owner Sylvie LeMer creates numerous fillings to choose from: crepes stuffed with ham and Gruyère to a shrimp and scallop combo. For dessert, how about a crepe full of coffee ice cream and warm chocolate, or with fresh berries and ice cream drizzled with a sweet berry sauce? There are several beers on tap, but most choose hard cider. The crowd is mixed.

Lunch/dinner daily; loud; reservations not accepted; MC, V.

Timo's

Mission: 842 Valencia St. (between 19th and 20th Sts.); 415-647-0558
Russian Hill: Ghirardelli Square, 900 North Point St. (between Polk and Larkin); 415-440-1200

Spanish

These lively restaurants serve some of San Francisco's best tapas in colorful settings. The original branch in the Mission has bright yellow Formica tables, pumpkin-and-purple walls, and a full-size classic bar that has its own history. The Ghiradelli location is also colorful and boasts a pleasant enclosed patio sports bar with sweeping bay views. Start with the terrific sangria, and follow it with the well-known *tortilla Espanola*, made with layers of lightly browned, thinly sliced potatoes and onions. Other great bets are sautéed prawns, ahi tuna *ceviche* with avocado, and Catalan-style spinach sweetened with raisins, apricots and pine nuts. Service in both locations is relaxed, if

not downright slow. A flamenco guitarist plays every
Thursday at the Valencia Street branch.

*Dinner nightly in the Mission; lunch/dinner daily;
view and validated parking at Ghiradelli Square;
loud; full bar; live entertainment; AE, MC, V.*

★★★★
$$$$$

Tokyo Sukiyaki Restaurant and Sushi Bar

**Fisherman's Wharf: 225 Jefferson St.
(at Taylor); 415-775-9030**

Japanese

Kid
friendly

This oasis of calm civility amidst the touristy bustle
has tables and chairs with windows overlooking the
wharf, or classic tatami rooms with low wooden
tables and mats for more private dining. Tasteful artwork and a collection of lovely ceramics add to the
charm, and kimono-clad waitresses prepare many of
the dishes tableside. Beef sukiyaki, consisting of
thinly sliced beef, bamboo shoots, fresh mushrooms,
tofu cubes, noodles and assorted vegetables, is the
restaurant's most popular dish, but the *shabu-shabu*
and teriyaki specials attract their own fans. However,
it all comes with a rather high price tag.

*Lunch weekends, dinner nightly; view; full bar;
validated parking; AE, DC, MC, V.*

★★★★
$$$$$

Tommaso's

**North Beach: 1042 Kearny St. (between
Broadway and Pacific); 415-398-9696**

Italian

Good
for groups

Kid
friendly

From the outside, Tommaso's looks particularly unap-
pealing—a dark, windowless facade surrounded by
porn shops. Step through the heavy wooden door,
however, and you'll find a clean, cheery Italian
restaurant bustling with local families and well-
informed tourists, who know that Tommaso's serves
what many consider San Francisco's best thin-crust
pizza. (Even Francis Ford Coppola is a regular.) For a
winning dinner combo, start with fresh vegetables
antipasto, followed by the Pizza Super Deluxe,

loaded with mushrooms, anchovies, peppers, ham and house-made sausage and fired in Tommaso's ancient brick oven. The lasagna and the enormous calzone are also popular.

Dinner Tuesday-Sunday; reservations not accepted; AE, DC, MC, V.

★★★★
$$$$$

Tommy Toy's Haute Cuisine Chinoise

Downtown: 655 Montgomery St. (between Washington and Clay); 415-397-4888

Chinese

♥ Romantic

Good for groups

Tommy Toy's inspires feelings of either loyalty or loathing for its haute Chinese-French cuisine and luxurious, 19th-century empress-dowager (some say Disney) style of the dining room. It's popular with expense-accounters, who enjoy being treated as visiting dignitaries. The six-course "signature dinner" provides an excellent introduction to the kitchen's fusion fare, including seafood bisque in a coconut shell crowned with puff pastry; Maine lobster sautéed with pine nuts and mushrooms with peppercorn sauce and crystal noodles; Peking duck with lotus buns; charred medallions of beef with garlic, wine and rosemary; and peach mousse in a strawberry compote.

Lunch weekdays, dinner nightly; quiet; menu; full bar; valet parking; all major credit cards.

★★★★
$$$$$

Ton Kiang

**Richmond: 5821 Geary Blvd. (between 22nd and 23rd Aves.); 415-387-8273
Richmond: 3148 Geary Blvd. (at Spruce); 415-752-4440**

Chinese

Sidewalk's choice

Good for groups

Ton Kiang has a reputation as one of the best Chinese restaurants in San Francisco when it comes to dim sum (served only at the far prettier 5821 Geary location) and Hakka cuisine, no easy feat considering the competition. In addition to the celebrated clay-pot casseroles, proven dishes include chicken wonton soup, steamed salt-baked chicken and any of the stuffed tofu dishes. The dim sum at 5821 Geary is phenomenal—fresh, flavorful, not the least bit greasy—particularly the crispy taro root or wonderful steamed meat dumpling.

Lunch/dinner daily; AE, MC, V.

★★★★
$$$$$

Town's End Restaurant & Bakery

South of Market: 2 Townsend St. (at Embarcadero); 415-512-0749

American

 Sidewalk's choice

 Good deal

 Kid friendly

This affable, casual restaurant and bakery offers one of the best brunch menus in the city. The renowned house-baked bread and pastry selection that arrives right away is so fresh and delicious you might want to make a meal of it—but don't. With such choices as excellent crab cakes, eggs Benedict, smoked chicken hash and Swedish oatmeal pancakes, you'll want to save some room. It's particularly pleasant when the sun shines through the large windows overlooking the bay or on the coveted patio tables. Dinner is less celebrated, offering delicately prepared pastas, seafood, chicken and meat dishes.

Breakfast/lunch/dinner Tuesday-Sunday; weekend brunch; view; outdoor seating; AE, MC, V.

★★★★
$$$$$

Truly Mediterranean

Mission: 3109 16th St. (at Valencia); 415-252-7482
Haight: 1724 Haight St. (at Cole); 415-751-7482

Middle Eastern

Very fresh, spicy and delicious Middle Eastern fast food is served in a tiny storefront by a friendly and expert staff who work at breakneck speed assembling meals. The substantial falafels, rolled in lavash and served with tahini sauce, cucumber salad, onions and extras such as feta, potatoes or tabbouleh, are always excellent. Also popular is the *shwarma* and a variety of pita sandwiches filled with feta, hummus, and baba ghanouj. Though it's often very busy, even the longest lines dissipate quickly. There are only five counter stools and a couple of outdoor tables.

Lunch/dinner daily; outdoor seating; late-night dining; no liquor license; reservations not accepted; cash only.

Tu Lan

South of Market: 8 6th St. (between Market and Mission); 415-626-0927

Vietnamese

 Sidewalk's choice

 Good deal

 Kid friendly

In one of the worst sections of San Francisco resides one of the city's best Vietnamese restaurants; even Julia Child is a fan. Don't expect much in the way of service: There's only one waiter, and the eight rickety tables are always filled. The food is prepared behind a greasy-looking Formica counter, but what emerges is fresh and delicious. Try the imperial rolls on a bed of rice noodles, lettuce, peanuts and mint, the lemon beef or chicken salad and the pork kebabs. Other favorites are fried fish in ginger sauce and ginger duck, along with the noodle soups.

Lunch/dinner Monday-Saturday; reservations not accepted; cash only.

Universal Cafe

Mission: 2814 19th St. (between Bryant and Harrison); 415-821-4608

California

 Sidewalk's choice

 Good deal

Hidden in an industrial/residential neighborhood, this chic little cafe has been the big meeting-and-munching spot for those in the know for several years. And now that chef Julia McClaskey (formerly of Palo Alto's L'Amie Donia) is at the helm, watch out. The salads are stellar, and grilled flat breads with assorted toppings are some of the city's best. McClaskey prepares a mouth-watering pan-seared filet mignon, and the grilled pepper ahi is practically perfect; don't miss the mashed potatoes. Service can be inconsistent, but the food makes up for the inconvenience.

Lunch Tuesday-Saturday, dinner Tuesday-Sunday; AE, DC, MC, V.

★★★★
$$$$$

Val 21

Mission: 995 Valencia St. (at 21st St.);
415-821-6622

California

Over the years this stylish, upscale restaurant has become a neighborhood favorite, thanks in part to the top-notch ingredients from owner Nidal Nazzal's Valencia Whole Foods store next door. A friendly staff serves eclectic dishes that are a blend of international cuisines, such as fresh mussels steamed in a spicy curry sauce, pinenut- and pepper-crusted ahi tuna or triple polenta torte with sun-dried tomato pesto served on a wild-mushroom ragout. Some work surprisingly well; others suffer from a flawed medley of exotic ingredients. Green tables paired with red-cushioned chairs and cobalt-blue vases filled with flowers soften the effect.

Lunch weekends, dinner nightly; weekend brunch; validated parking; AE, DC, MC, V.

★★★★
$$$$$

Valentine's Cafe

Noe Valley: 1793 Church St. (at 30th St.);
415-285-2257

Vegetarian

This cozy, casual cafe has captured the hearts of vegetarians and meat-eaters alike with its international organic vegetarian fare served in an airy dining room with pleasant bistro seating. While some entrees are inconsistent, most are a hit: samosas filled with Indian-spiced potatoes and cool mint chutney; spicy jambalaya featuring house-made seitan "sausage" in a tomato-based broth over red rice; and citrus-tea-smoked tofu on basmati rice with eggplant and a Thai coconut curry sauce. Weekend breakfast is equally inventive, from butternut-squash pancakes topped with sweet onion sauce to the tofu Benedict with walnut-pesto cream.

Dinner nightly; weekend brunch; MC, V.

★★★★
$$$$$

Venticello Ristorante

Nob Hill: 1257 Taylor St. (at Washington); 415-922-2545

Italian

This lively neighborhood restaurant is known for its house-made pasta and inventive sauces, grilled meats and other fine trattoria fare. Its sponge-painted ochre walls, splashes of cobalt blue tiles, rustic furniture and airy feel create a warm Tuscan air. The only flaw is the service, which can be anything but inviting; still regulars are willing to tolerate the occasional lapses in exchange for such dishes as ravioli filled with spinach and ricotta with lemon-grappa sauce and fire-grilled prawns wrapped in pancetta with spicy red-chili sauce.

Dinner nightly; valet parking; AE, MC, V.

★★★★
$$$$$

Vertigo

Downtown: Transamerica Pyramid, 600 Montgomery St., (between Montgomery and Sansome); 415-433-7250

California

Good
for groups

Named after the Hitchcock classic, this splashy restaurant lives up to its moniker with a dizzying jumble of playful design elements tamed by soothing blond woods and large windows overlooking redwoods. The fusion of French, Italian and Asian cuisines can be as interesting as the décor, with combinations such as foie gras with peach and raspberry strudel, scallops with lime risotto, and venison with mashed sweet potatoes and huckleberry demiglace. A voluminous (and expensive) wine list complements the food. Service is cordial and efficient.

Lunch weekdays, dinner Monday-Saturday; loud; outdoor seating; full bar; live entertainment; valet parking; AE, DC, MC, V.

★★☆☆
$$$$$

Vicolo Pizzeria

Civic Center: 201 Ivy St. (at Franklin);
415-863-2382

Pizza

Hayes Valley regulars and concert patrons on their way to Symphony Hall order at the counter of this alley gourmet pizza joint, which is tops in San Francisco. In an industrial-chic shack with cathedral ceilings and steel-framed windows, Vicolo specializes in crisp, cornmeal-crust pizzas topped with an eclectic array of fresh ingredients, including sweet corn, baked eggplant, asparagus and roasted potatoes. A favorite item is the Andouille, with smoked mozzarella, spicy sausage and fresh Parmesan. A half dozen versions are offered daily, whole or by the slice—but, alas, they don't come cheap.

Lunch/dinner daily; reservations not accepted; MC, V.

★★☆☆
$$$$$

Vino e Cucina

South of Market: 489 3rd St. (between
Bryant and Harrison); 415-543-6962

Italian

Look for a huge red tomato, and you'll easily find this trattoria, which serves large portions of well-prepared, though traditional, Italian fare. Some of the appetizers and especially the soups—a hearty minestrone and a tangy tomato soup thickened with chunks of bread—are quite filling. The savory pasta puttanesca has a pungent sauce with olives and anchovies. For lighter fair, try the chicken salad served on a paper-thin flat bread. Service can be slow.

Lunch weekdays, dinner Monday-Saturday; D, MC, V.

Vivande Porta Via

★★★☆
$$$$$

Pacific Heights: 2125 Fillmore St. (between
California and Sacramento); 415-346-4430

Italian

The atmosphere at this deli/cafe/bookstore is refined
but casual: white linen tablecloths on small tables, a
prominent deli counter and an assortment of colorful
tiles lining the brick wall. Prices are steep, but the
helpful staff and cheerful sounds from the open
kitchen make for a pleasant meal. Chef/owner Carlo
Middione's menu changes daily, but might include
blanched asparagus spears wrapped in prosciutto
with Parmesan cheese for lunch, and savory pan-
broiled fillet of beef with a dry Marsala and veal
demi-glace or excellent risotto cooked in chicken
stock and studded with fresh portobello mushrooms
for dinner.

*Lunch/dinner daily; reservations not accepted;
all major credit cards, checks.*

Vivande Ristorante

★★★☆
$$$$$

Civic Center: 670 Golden Gate Ave.
(between Van Ness and Franklin);
415-673-9245

Italian

Romantic

Good
for groups

Chef/owner Carlo Middione's large restaurant is
delightfully broken up into cozy nooks, with slate and
marble floors and antique Italian light fixtures. Even
the bathrooms reflect Middione's sense of whimsy,
with erotic murals copied from Pompeiian ruins.
Vivande's seasonal menu reflects the diversity of
Italian regional cooking: prosciutto di Parma with
Marsala-soaked figs and grilled polenta triangles
with roasted portobellos are two spectacular
antipasti offerings, and the risotto is among the best
around. Osso buco and chicken splashed with balsamic vinaigrette rank high among the second
courses; and the "earthquake cake" for dessert will
shake any chocolate lover's world.

*Lunch/dinner daily; loud; full bar; live entertain-
ment; all major credit cards, checks.*

★★★★
$$$$$

Washington Square Bar & Grill

North Beach: 1707 Powell St. (at Union); 415-982-8123

American

When it comes to hearty American food, dry martinis and even drier bar jokes, Washington Square Bar & Grill (dubbed the Washbag by Herb Caen) is the perennial old-time favorite. Humphrey Bogart and Ernest Hemingway would have loved this place for its clatter of dice at the bar, smoke-permeated front dining area and great view of the park through the large, open windows. The menu isn't the main draw here. Stick with solid classics like a burger with mushrooms and onions or grilled New York steak sandwich rather than the more updated experiments. A surprising number of offbeat producers appear on the small wine list.

Lunch/dinner daily; weekend brunch; full bar; live entertainment; valet parking; AE, MC, V.

NR
$$$$$

The Waterfront Restaurant

Downtown: Pier 7 (Embarcadero at Broadway); 415-391-2696

East-West

A success for more than 20 years, the Waterfront is especially popular for sipping a glass of wine and gazing out at the fading light on the bay. A million-dollar renovation was completed in 1997 and the brilliant chef Bruce Hill (formerly of Oritalia) was brought in to revamp the menu. Look for East-West combinations. *Note: The restaurant opened too close to press time to review.*

Lunch/dinner daily; weekend brunch; view; outdoor seating; full bar; valet parking; AE, DC, MC, V, checks.

★★★★
$$$$$

We Be Sushi

Richmond: 3226 Geary Blvd. (between Spruce and Parker); 415-221-9960
Sunset: 94 Judah St. (at 6th St.); 415-681-4010
Mission: 538 Valencia St. (between 16th and 17th Sts.); 415-565-0749
Mission: 1071 Valencia St. (between 21st and 22nd Sts.); 415-826-0607

Sushi

Good deal

"Sushi Like Mom Used to Make," is the motto of this simple chain (four San Francisco locations) serving fresh sushi at very good prices. Expect the full range of sushi—nigiri-, maki-, or sashimi-style—and a selection of vegetable rolls. The usual miso soup and side dishes of rice are also served. It all goes nicely with sake or Japanese beer. The Geary branch also serves delicious, if sometimes bony, grilled fish at dinnertime; choose from salmon, pike (including the head and teeth), cod and mackerel. The Valencia branches cater to a young, bohemian crowd. Near the UCSF medical center, the Judah branch is filled with students and other locals.

Lunch weekdays (and on weekends, 538 Valencia location only), dinner nightly; reservations not accepted; cash only.

★★★★
$$$$$

Woodward's Garden

Mission: 1700 Mission St. (at Duboce); 415-621-7122

Mediterranean

Sidewalk's choice

Tucked under a busy highway overpass on a gritty, windy, noisy corner stands one of the Bay Area's best restaurants. The kitchen takes up at least half the room in this diminutive restaurant: You not only see and smell your food being prepared by chef/owners Margie Conard and Dana Tommasino, you even feel the heat of the stove. Blending American and Mediterranean influences, the constantly changing menu features five appetizers and five entrees each night, such as divine sweet potato-ginger soup, sautéed scallops with endive, Meyer lemon beurre blanc and caviar, and perfectly roasted duck breast paired with grilled polenta, a cherry-onion marmalade and braised chard.

Dinner nightly (reserved seating); reservations required; MC, V.

★★★★
$$$$$

Wu Kong Restaurant

South of Market: 101 Spear St. (at Mission); 415-957-9300

Chinese

Good for groups

Chandeliers, stylish modern furniture and fine art characterize this spacious Chinese restaurant, which specializes in Shanghai-style cuisine. Exotic offerings include drunken squab (marinated in rice wine and served chilled), jellyfish salad with sesame dressing and the celebrated vegetarian goose (fried bean curd with mushroom stuffing); other favorites are the Shanghai-style onion cakes and steamed flounder in a light gingery broth. When the kitchen gets busy, the quality sometimes suffers, but the attractive setting, efficient service and unusual, often wonderful food secure Wu Kong's place among the city's finest Chinese restaurants.

Lunch/dinner daily; loud; outdoor seating; full bar; validated parking; AE, DC, MC, V.

★★★★
$$$$$

Ya Halla From Nadia

Lower Haight: 494 Haight St. (between Webster and Fillmore); 415-522-1509

Middle Eastern

Good deal

Capitalizing on the city's romance with ethnic food, healthy vegetarian options, ambience and value, Ya Halla covers its bases with a winning combination: inexpensive, fresh Middle Eastern fare served in an exotic environment—ochre walls accented with red and decorated with Christmas lights and kilim-style cushions. The tiny kitchen, which takes up half of the room, manages to produce satisfying falafels, garlicky hummus, a smooth baba ghanouj and luscious lamb kebabs, which come with olives, pickles, feta cheese and pita bread.

Lunch/dinner daily; loud; late-night dining; live entertainment; MC, V, checks.

★★★★
$$$$$

Yabbies Coastal Kitchen

Russian Hill: 2237 Polk St. (between Green and Vallejo); 415-474-4088

Seafood

Sidewalk's choice

This new, high-style, glass-tiled seafood restaurant is packed most nights, featuring a wildly popular oyster bar that also offers scallops, crayfish, mussels, sashimi and six kinds of clams. Chef Mark Lusardi (formerly at Vertigo) has put together a sophisticated, international menu: pepper-seared ahi with Japanese eggplant and soy-citrus juices, grilled swordfish flavored with Sicilian capers and green olives, king salmon with Vietnamese rice-noodle salad, chile lime juice and mango, as well as pasta, beef fillet and grilled chicken. The wine list offers a wide range of reasonably priced California, French and Italian wines.

Dinner nightly; validated parking; MC, V.

★★★★
$$$$$

Yank Sing

South of Market: 49 Stevenson St. (between 1st and 2nd Sts.); 415-541-4949
Downtown: 427 Battery St. (between Sacramento and Clay); 415-781-1111

Chinese

Yank Sing's two locations are some of the best places to get dim sum in the city. Fans come in droves for the vast number of items, rolled around on carts by numerous servers. Don't miss the cart of Peking duck with scallions and plum sauce on semisweet buns. Other favorites are pot stickers, plump shrimp dumplings, fried taro, spicy sautéed snap peas in chili oil and sesame balls stuffed with sweetened red-bean paste, rice water and baked custard. The Stevenson Street dining room is less appealing and is closed on Saturdays. Service is helpful at both branches; if you don't see what you're looking for, just ask.

Lunch Sunday-Friday on Stevenson, daily on Battery; Battery location is loud; outdoor seating on Stevenson; MC, V.

YaYa Cuisine

Sunset: 1220 9th Ave. (between Lincoln and Irving); 415-566-6966

Middle Eastern

 Sidewalk's choice

Chef/owner Yahya Salih, hailing from northern Iraq, prepares his mother's recipes (with some California twists) in this handsome restaurant of blue-tiled archways and elaborate murals of ancient Babylon. The menu is filled with unfamiliar dishes, but the affable servers provide guidance. Popular dishes are ravioli stuffed with dates and cinnamon, eggplant in pomegranate sauce, and baby chicken stuffed with rice, raisins and cashew nuts. Some of the hybrid dishes are the most interesting: salmon with a tamarind aïoli, steamed oysters topped with a cooling yogurt-mint sauce. The exuberant, Salih often appears to greet customers and explain exactly what they're eating.

Lunch Tuesday-Friday, dinner Tuesday-Sunday; AE, MC, V, checks.

Yo Yo's

Downtown: 318 Pacific Ave. (between Sansome and Battery); 415-296-8273

Japanese

 Good deal

There's nearly always a line stretching out the door of this tiny, pristine takeout sushi shop at lunchtime. No wonder: The fresh, bargain-priced sushi, udon and soba have made this spot a neighborhood favorite. Among the offerings: tempura, bean curd or seaweed soup; neatly packaged sushi rolls of crab, eel and vegetables; and chicken teriyaki served with rice and a small lettuce salad. Drinks, fortune cookies and Japanese rice crackers complete the menu.

Lunch weekdays; quiet; no liquor license; reservations not accepted; cash only.

★★★★
$$$$$

Yoshida-Ya

Pacific Heights: 2909 Webster (at Union); 415-346-3431

Japanese

Good for groups

The stylish, bold interior of Yoshida-Ya—lacquered tables and stark black, Kyoto-red and apricot color scheme—might not be to everyone's liking, but the food usually is; it's very popular, despite slightly elevated prices (and many Japanese eat here, which is a good sign). *Yakitori* (skewered meat and vegetables, barbecued to your liking) is the specialty, and the yakitori bar is one of the few in the city. The vast menu offers an array of other dishes, including very good teriyaki and tempura, a full lineup of sushi rolls and 60 kinds of appetizers.

Lunch weekdays, dinner nightly; full bar; validated parking; AE, DC, D, MC, V.

NR
$$$$$

Yoyo Bistro

Japan Center/ Fillmore: 1611 Post St. (at Laguna); 415-922-7788

California

Sidewalk's choice

Kid friendly

Romantic

Good for groups

Formerly Elka's, Yoyo Bistro underwent multiple chef changes in the last few years and emerged in the fall of 1997 with a modified décor and a new menu that is includes French as well as Pacific Rim flavors. The appetizer menu features a wide range of tsunamis, the Japanese version of tapas, served in a wooden bento box such as ginger-pickled salmon with wasabi crème fraîche and ahi tartare with pickled plum vinaigrette. Traditional bistro dishes such as pan-roasted chicken and grilled filet mignon dominate the entrees. *Note: The renovated restaurant was too new to review at press time.*

Breakfast/lunch/dinner daily; full bar; valet and validated parking; AE, DC, MC, V.

★★★★ $$$$$

Yuet Lee

Chinatown: 1300 Stockton St. (at Broadway); 415-982-6020
Mission: 3601 26th St. (between Valencia and Guerrero); 415-550-8998

Chinese

Good for groups

Kid friendly

An impossible-to-miss, lime-green fixture in Chinatown (and now the Mission), this bright utilitarian restaurant serves some of the freshest seafood in town. A perennial favorite is the salt-and-pepper squid, lightly pan-fried with a hint of Chinese spices and yanked from the pan before it loses its soft texture. The fresh steamed oysters in black bean sauce are delightful, and fans of fresh crab can enjoy a number of preparations: with silver noodles and satay sauce in a clay pot, sautéed with pepper and black-bean sauce or simply steamed. The Chinatown branch is open until 3 a.m.

Lunch Monday-Saturday, dinner nightly; closed Tuesday; late night; MC, V.

★★★★ $$$$$

Yukol Place Thai Cuisine
Marina: 2380 Lombard St. (between Scott and Pierce); 415-922-1599

Thai

Good deal

Good for groups

Locals continue to pack this homey, 55-seat restaurant despite a relocation, and while the decor is not particularly elaborate or colorful, Yukol Place's lovingly prepared food and eager-to-please service are truly some of the best. Chef/owner Yukol Nieltaweephong turns out fabulous fare, including a spicy duck salad seasoned with lemon and mint; sliced sirloin in a hot-pepper sauce; and red-curry chicken with bamboo shoots. Other popular dishes are pad thai, chicken satay and lemon-chicken soup with coconut milk. For dessert, try the homemade ice cream with lychee or a fried banana dish.

Dinner nightly; MC, V.

Zarzuela

★★★★
$$$$$

**Russian Hill: 2000 Hyde St. (at Union);
415-346-0800**

Spanish

Sidewalk's choice

A hit since it opened, this Spanish restaurant specializing in tapas and paella has expanded to accommodate the hordes of diners. Inside, Spanish music bounces off tiled floors and walls adorned with hand-painted plates, and good bread and a dish of olives arrive at the table immediately. While there've been some recent complaints about inconsistent tapas, they're generally excellent, particularly the spicy shrimp with aïoli, sautéed mushrooms and fresh squid. Foremost among the entrees is the paella Valenciana, which ranks among the best around. Other classics include a rich seafood stew, oxtail casserole and grilled lamb. Prices are very reasonable, but service is slow.

Lunch/dinner Monday-Saturday; reservations not accepted; MC, V.

Zax

★★★★
$$$$$

**North Beach: 2330 Taylor St. (between
Chestnut and Francisco); 415-563-6266**

California

Sidewalk's choice

Romantic

Hailed as one of San Francisco's better restaurants—a perfect blend of informality, excellent cuisine, artistic decor and reasonable prices—Zax is not known to many because of its hidden location. But a buzz has started about the California-Mediterranean cuisine of husband-and-wife team Mark Drazek and Barbara Mulas. Their small, seasonal menu changes frequently, but the food is consistently healthy, well balanced and flavorful, without heavy sauces. Recent hits were pan-fried sand dabs with roasted new potatoes and artichokes, roasted Sonoma duck breast with grilled fig vinaigrette and spicy braised short ribs with excellent horseradish mashed potatoes. Don't miss the house specialty, the light and savory goat-cheese soufflé.

Dinner Tuesday-Saturday; MC, V.

Zazie

★★☆☆
$$$$$

Haight: 941 Cole St. (between Carl and Parnassus); 415-564-5332

French

The secret's out about this cheerful little French bistro with colorful checkered flooring, an antique hutch, and stylish French posters adorning brick and pale-yellow walls. Though the food's had mixed reviews, the majority of dishes are pretty good to excellent, and the roast chicken with vegetables and Provençal fish soup are solid standbys. Specials might include artichoke and crab ravioli, roasted trout with goat cheese and fresh thyme or spinach and zucchini risotto. For breakfast, the Miracle Pancakes are always a hit. Owner Catherine Opoix keeps lunch simple—soups, salads, French sandwiches, and a few plats du jour. Live musicians perform Sunday nights.

Breakfast/lunch Monday-Saturday, dinner nightly; weekend brunch; outdoor seating; live entertainment; MC, V.

Zingari

★★★☆
$$$$$

Downtown: Donatello Hotel, 501 Post St. (at Mason); 415-885-8850

Italian

Airy and bright, Zingari has an authentic, carefree atmosphere, where chef/owner Giovanni Scorzo takes pride in creating traditional, regional Italian dishes. Aside from the authenticity of the cooking, part of Zingari's allure is its interesting menu: You'll find old favorites like linguine and clams and pasta e fagioli along with more daring fare, such as wild boarstudded pappardelle and veal loin stuffed with fontina and truffles. The deeply seasoned homemade sausage, featured in various pasta preparations, is prepared by Scorzo by hand, as are all the breads. Select California bottles dot the overwhelmingly Italian wine list.

Dinner nightly; full bar; live entertainment; valet/validated parking; AE, MC, V.

★★★★
$$$$$

Zinzino

Marina: 2355 Chestnut St. (between Scott and Divisadero); 415-346-6623

Italian

Sidewalk's choice

Good deal

In this restaurant-saturated neighborhood, Spago-sired Andrea Rappaport, one of the latest hot new chefs, helps distinguish this trattoria. A wizard with the wood-fired oven, Rappaport makes outstanding thin-crust pizzas, oozing with feta and mozzarella (try the heavenly eggplant or Italian sausage). Other smash hits are the roasted half-chicken served with superb goat cheese salad, enormous focaccia sand-wiches and one of the best calamari appetizers in the city. Formerly a laundromat, Zinzino's interior has all the elbow room of a submarine, but it's adorned with chic furnishings and old Italian movie posters.

Dinner nightly; loud; outdoor seating; MC, V.

★★★★
$$$$$

Zuni Cafe

Civic Center: 1658 Market St. (at Gough); 415-552-2522

Mediterranean

Sidewalk's choice

Romantic

This trendy restaurant has become a popular San Francisco institution, as the line out the door every night attests. Twenty-year-old Zuni still possesses a timely chic, with its long, copper bar, exposed-brick walls, roaring brick oven and trays of glistening oys-ters that rush by. Chef Judy Rodgers's sophisticated, Mediterranean-influenced food is divinely simple: a plate of mild, house-cured anchovies sprinkled with olives, celery, and Parmesan cheese; heavenly polenta with delicate mascarpone; perfectly roasted chicken over Tuscan bread salad; grilled rib-eye steak accompanied by sweet white corn piqued with fresh basil. Service is wildly uneven: first-rate for regulars and the appropriately hip, indifferent to the rest.

Breakfast/lunch Tuesday-Saturday, dinner Tuesday-Sunday; weekend brunch; outdoor seating; late-night dining; full bar; live entertain-ment; AE, MC, V.

East Bay

Reviews and neighborhood maps

Berkeley/ Albany/ Emeryville

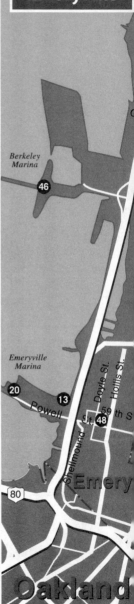

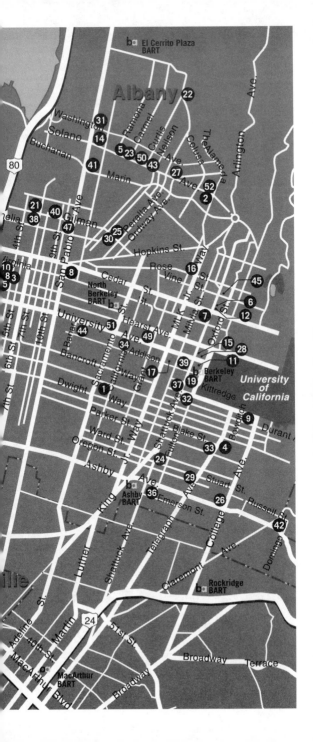

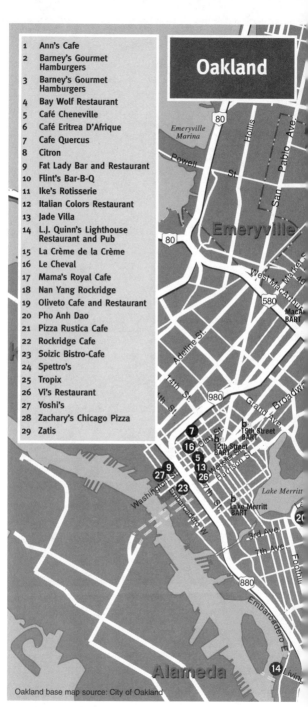

1	Ann's Cafe
2	Barney's Gourmet Hamburgers
3	Barney's Gourmet Hamburgers
4	Bay Wolf Restaurant
5	Café Cheneville
6	Café Eritrea D'Afrique
7	Cafe Quercus
8	Citron
9	Fat Lady Bar and Restaurant
10	Flint's Bar-B-Q
11	Ike's Rotisserie
12	Italian Colors Restaurant
13	Jade Villa
14	L.J. Quinn's Lighthouse Restaurant and Pub
15	La Crème de la Crème
16	Le Cheval
17	Mama's Royal Cafe
18	Nan Yang Rockridge
19	Oliveto Cafe and Restaurant
20	Pho Anh Dao
21	Pizza Rustica Cafe
22	Rockridge Cafe
23	Soizic Bistro-Cafe
24	Spettro's
25	Tropix
26	Vi's Restaurant
27	Yoshi's
28	Zachary's Chicago Pizza
29	Zatis

Oakland

Oakland base map source: City of Oakland

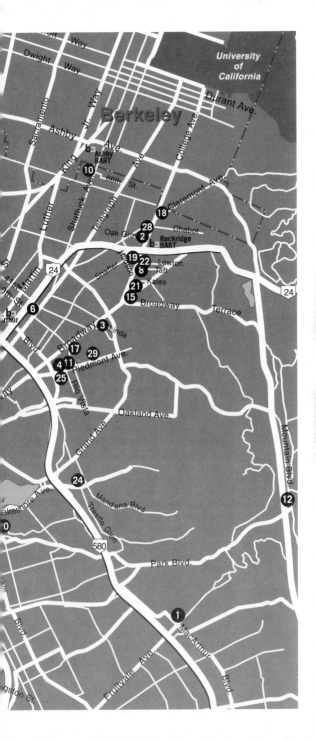

★★★★
$$$$$

A la Carte

Berkeley: 1453 Dwight Way
(at Sacramento); 510-548-2322

Mediterranean

 Romantic

 Kid friendly

This longtime neighborhood favorite changed hands in 1996, but the romantic Provençal atmosphere, reasonable prices, good service and appealing bistro food remain intact. The menu changes seasonally, offering a California twist on traditional Mediterranean recipes: ricotta gnocchi with roasted red pepper sauce, wild mushroom ragout, Yucatan-spiced cod, pumpkin bread pudding. The younger set is welcome here, but don't expect the usual children's menu; mini-gourmets recently feasted on duck breast with yam puree and tangerine sorbet for $3.95. A three-course prix fixe menu is served on Sunday.

Dinner Wednesday-Sunday, afternoon tea by appointment; quiet; MC, V, checks.

★★★☆
$$$$$

Ajanta

Berkeley: 1888 Solano Ave.
(at The Alameda); 510-526-4373

Indian

 Sidewalk's choice

Intrepid diners forge beyond the usual tandoori dishes and curries at this Berkeley favorite, which presents specialties from different regions of India each month. The elegant, serene dining room sets the stage for a culinary adventure with intricate woodwork, golden fabrics and graceful reproductions of the murals found in the Ajanta cave temples of India. Among the standout dishes are lamb rib chops, *murg ularthu* (boneless chicken simmered in a sauce made with onions, mustard seeds, fennel, garlic and ginger) and prawn curry, as well as vegetarian dishes, including the wonderful *baigan ki boorani* (pan-fried eggplant slices topped with a garlic-lemon-yogurt sauce).

Lunch/dinner daily; major credit cards.

Ann's Cafe

Oakland: 3401 Fruitvale Ave.
(at MacArthur Blvd.); 510-531-9861

American

Fran (daughter of Ann), the fireball proprietor of this tiny, single-counter establishment, embraces newcomers and regulars alike with old-fashioned hospitality and teasing banter while single-handedly preparing massive servings of Italian-American diner food. An antiquated menu board lists items such as eggs, hot cakes, sandwiches, and the renowned oversized omelets. Rotating daily lunch specials listed simply as meatloaf and chicken arrive with a mountain of mashed potatoes smothered in thick gravy, garlic cheese toast, and a slice of chocolate cake, all for $5.50. Plan to spend a few hours at Ann's; you'll want to put off going back to the outside world.

Breakfast/lunch Tuesday-Friday; free parking lot; cash only.

Barney's Gourmet Hamburgers

Oakland: 4162 Piedmont Ave. (between
Linda and 41st St.); 510-655-7180
Oakland: 5819 College Ave. (between
Chabot and Oak Grove); 510-601-0444

American

The best thing about Barney's is its wide selection: You can get any of its 21 burgers with chicken breast or ground-turkey patty, and some even with tofu. Try the Popeye chicken burger with sauteed spinach and feta cheese or the California burger with Jack cheese, bacon, green chiles and sour cream. The menu is not for the heart-smart; the spinach salad comes with oily vinaigrette, feta cheese, and thick strips of fatty bacon. If you're not pondering the replica of the Sistine Chapel ceiling on the wall at the Piedmont Avenue eatery, outdoor seating in the Roman-style courtyard is a big attraction.

Lunch/dinner daily; loud; outdoor seating; reservations not accepted; cash only.

Bay Wolf Restaurant
Oakland: 3853 Piedmont Ave. (at Rio Vista); 510-655-6004

California

 Romantic

Housed in an attractive Victorian, Bay Wolf continues its tradition of serving subdued yet flavorful California-Mediterranean food, now under chef Lauren Lyle. Fresh ingredients and careful preparation are the focus, with the menu changing frequently. Typical first courses include spiced scallop and endive salad or rich, smoky asparagus and hazelnut soup. Main courses vary from tender braised lamb shanks with white beans, artichokes and rosemary to flavorful seafood stew. For dessert, there might be a sweetly spiced peach pie with a scoop of cinnamon ice cream. Enophiles will enjoy Bay Wolf's unique and well-priced wine list.

Lunch weekdays, dinner nightly; quiet; outdoor seating; MC, V, checks.

Bette's Oceanview Diner
Berkeley: 1807-A 4th St. (between Hearst and Virginia); 510-644-3230

American

 Sidewalk's choice

 Good for groups

 Kid friendly

The charm of this small updated diner is in its red vinyl booths, chrome stools, checkerboard tile floor, hip waitstaff, the best jukebox around, and damn fine breakfasts and desserts. On weekends, expect a 45-minute wait, but consider the payoff: enormous souffle-style pancakes stuffed with pecans and ripe berries, farm-fresh eggs scrambled with prosciutto and Parmesan, corned beef hash and quintessential huevos rancheros with black beans. If you can't bear the long wait, pop into Bette's-to-Go next door. In the afternoon, the diner offers superlative focaccia, pizzas, kosher hot dogs, fruit pies and sundaes.

Breakfast/lunch daily; loud; reservations not accepted; MC, V, checks.

★★★☆
$$$$$

The Blue Nile

Berkeley: 2525 Telegraph Ave. (between Parker and Dwight); 510-540-6777

Ethiopian

Sidewalk's choice

Good for groups

The Blue Nile's bamboo-shrouded walls, marimba music and posters of Africa set the stage for some of the best Ethiopian food in the Bay Area. The chicken dishes (such as pan-fried chicken simmered in an aromatic sauce) and plentiful vegetarian entrees (try the veggie platter, which includes lentil *wat*, split pea *wat*, *kiche*, *gomen* and rice) are especially recommended, and you might want to order a cold Nogoma beer to wash down the sometimes spicy fare. Although the setting is modest, the prices are right, and the servings are generous.

Lunch Tuesday-Saturday, dinner Tuesday-Sunday; MC, V.

★★★☆
$$$$$

Britt-Marie's

Albany (see Berkeley map): 1369 Solano Ave. (at Ramona); 510-527-1314

Mediterranean

As inviting as a pair of favorite slippers, Britt-Marie's offers comfort food from many corners of the globe in a European wine-bar atmosphere. Dishes include the Portuguese sandwich (garlic-rubbed toast topped with salt cod and potatoes), cucumbers in garlic sour cream, roast chicken with herbs, and pork schnitzel with buttered noodles. A new California-style menu supplements the roster of continental classics (the fresh fish and risotto items are especially delightful additions). A well-priced, well-chosen wine list promotes the European notion of wine's place at the dinner table.

Lunch Tuesday-Saturday, dinner Tuesday-Sunday; reservations not accepted; checks.

★★★☆
$$$$$

Cafe at Chez Panisse

Berkeley: 1517 Shattuck Ave. (between Cedar and Vine); 510-548-5049

California

 Sidewalk's choice

Romantic

A less expensive alternative to Alice Waters' four-star eatery Chez Panisse, this lively upstairs cafe with redwood, copper light fixtures and French bistro-style posters, serves an excellent California-Mediterranean menu to upscale, food-savvy diners. The daily menu exhibits the same eye to freshness and quality as its formal sibling. For example: Sonoma goat cheese baked on a fig leaf with toasted almonds and olives; crispy-crusted pizza with escarole, olives and fontina and spicy pan-fried rock cod. Whimsical desserts might include strawberry-orange sherbet or passion fruit ice cream with gingersnaps. Though the wine list is the same as the one downstairs, the bistro fare dictates more playful choices.

Lunch/dinner Monday-Saturday; prix fixe menu;
AE, MC, V, checks.

★★★☆
$$$$$

Café Cheneville

Oakland: 499 9th St. (at Washington); 510-893-5439

Mediterranean

 Sidewalk's choice

 Good deal

 Romantic

 Kid friendly

Café Cheneville is a graciously restored restaurant—featuring a beautiful mosaic entryway, original mahogany, and William Morris-type fabrics—that serves splendid Mediterranean-inspired dishes. The weekend morning menu offers savory, gutsy dishes such as omelets with smoked trout and chives or baked eggs with roasted peppers and Parmesan; the wood-burning oven produces terrific pizzas and focaccia. Dinners are an ambitious mix of the same high flavors and seasonal produce: Greek lamb stew with baby artichokes, fennel and tomato, or specially featured oysters and clams. The wine list is exclusively European and carefully chosen. Service is slow, but the waitstaff is knowledgeable and enthusiastic.

Lunch/dinner Tuesday-Sunday, weekend brunch;
loud; DC, MC, V.

Cafe de la Paz

★★★★
$$$$$

**Berkeley: 1600 Shattuck Ave. (at Cedar);
510-843-0662**

Latin American

Good
for groups

This small restaurant offers plates of lively, well-prepared dishes in a genial, vibrant, gently political environment. The Latin American tapas (Venezuelan corn pancakes, sweet potato and chile sauté, Ecuadoran potato cakes) are sweet, spicy and freshly made. The Venezuelan tapas (masa-based cakes with fresh corn and sage) come with sauces that don't quite offset the sweetness. African-Brazilian stews and expertly grilled meats round out this ambitious menu; there are also lots of vegetarian dishes. Service is earnest but not overly polished. You'll be off to a good start with the sangria garnished with hibiscus blossoms or Brazilian black beer.

Lunch weekdays, dinner nightly; AE, MC, V.

Café Eritrea D'Afrique

★★★★
$$$$$

**Oakland: 4069 Telegraph Ave. (at 41st St.);
510-547-4520**

African

Good
deal

Good
for groups

Kid
friendly

"A Cozy Place to Be" reads the sign outside this warm little cafe offering an eclectic, multiethnic menu, including hummus, tabbouleh and spaghetti. But the real reason to come is the fine Ethiopian cuisine, which is served family-style on one large platter. Try the fava beans with tomatoes, bell pepper, onion and yogurt; beef cubes in butter, garlic, onion and pepper; or the chicken stew. *Injera*, a spongy bread, functions as your utensil. To accompany your meal, try an African beer or some *mes* (honey wine). The cafe also serves as a meeting place for local Ethiopians.

*Breakfast/lunch/dinner daily; outdoor seating;
MC, V.*

Cafe Fanny

Berkeley: 1603 San Pablo Ave. (at Cedar);
510-524-5447

California

Alice Waters' diminutive corner cafe can handle
fewer than a dozen stand-up customers at once, but
that doesn't deter anyone from coming here for the
simple, inexpensive breakfasts or lunches. Named
after Waters' daughter, this spot recalls a French
neighborhood cafe, right down to the zinc countertop.
Breakfast on crunchy Cafe Fanny granola, jam-filled
buckwheat crepes or perfect soft-boiled eggs served
on sourdough toast with house-made jam, and sip
cafe au lait from a bowl. For lunch, order a small
pizza or one of the seductive sandwiches, such as
grilled mozzarella with olive paste.

Breakfast/lunch weekdays; outdoor seating; free
parking lot; MC, V, checks.

Cafe Grace

Berkeley: 2625 Durant Ave. (between
Bowditch and College); 510-548-4366

California

 Romantic

 Good for groups

 Kid friendly

In the sculpture garden of the UC Berkeley Art
Museum and Pacific Film Archive, surrounded by tall
poplars, cypress and olive trees, Cafe Grace is a
favorite spot for UC faculty, staff and students, as
well as notable visitors. You could judge this restaurant simply by its Caesar salad—garlicky with the
distinct-but-not-overpowering hint of anchovy, sprinkled with crunchy house-made croutons. The kitchen
also serves up a seasonally changing menu of
salads, soups, sandwiches, pizzas and main courses.

Lunch daily; outdoor seating; checks.

Cafe Quercus

Oakland: 1233 Preservation Park Way (between 12th and 13th Sts.); 510-832-2500

American

In a restored Victorian in Preservation Park, Cafe Quercus serves extraordinarily good comfort food at astonishingly reasonable prices in a bucolic setting. Owner Susan Nelson (original owner of the Fourth Street Grill) shows dedication to wholesome ingredients from small local farms through the food that she and chef Murray Gorson offer, and her association with food luminaries is reflected in menu items such as Alice Waters' Egg Salad Sandwich (served openface with sundried tomatoes and anchovies) and Mark Miller's Caesar Salad. This is a stellar addition to the Bay Area restaurant scene.

Breakfast/lunch weekdays; quiet; outdoor seating; reservations required for large parties; MC, V.

Cafe Rouge

Berkeley: 1782 4th St. (between Hearst and Virginia Sts.); 510-525-1440

California

Chef/owner Marsha McBride (formerly of Zuni Cafe) insists on high quality ingredients, so it's hard to go wrong on this bistro's small-but-beguiling menu. Her passions are oysters and charcuterie, but there are creative salads and pastas, great grilled steaks and juicy spit-roasted chicken. Desserts are absolute knockouts. Though small, the wine list offers clever choices. Many of the house-smoked charcuterie items are available in the market in back of the airy twolevel restaurant, which boasts a long zinc counter, modern wall sconces, and skylights. Service is inconsistent, but most customers seem to be forgiving.

Lunch weekdays, dinner Tuesday-Sunday; full bar; free parking lot; MC, V.

Cambodiana's

Berkeley: 2156 University Ave. (between Shattuck and Oxford); 510-843-4630

Cambodian

Good for groups

This tiny, colorful, popular Cambodian restaurant has a surreal interior and equally exotic fare. The menu is organized around six regional Cambodian sauces, each designed to complement delectable renditions of meat, poultry, and seafood. To start, try the shrimp and coconut milk soup or wonderful stuffed chicken wings. Both the specialty of the house—buttery grilled pork chops marinated in a mixture of garlic, lemongrass, galanga, paprika and soy sauce—and the country-style smoky eggplant—roasted and tossed with pork, shrimp, green onions and garlic—win raves. The atmosphere is quiet, the food reasonably priced and the service gracious.

Lunch weekdays, dinner nightly; quiet; AE, CB, DC, MC, V, checks.

Cha-Am

Berkeley: 1543 Shattuck Ave. (at Cedar); 510-848-9664

Thai

Sidewalk's choice

One of the best Thai restaurants in the Bay Area, Cha-Am offers innovative, aromatic Asian cooking, with an emphasis on fresh ingredients, in a cheery, comfortable setting graced by a glass-enclosed porch. Start with one of the superb soups (such as *tom ka gai*, chicken simmered in coconut milk, and *tom ka talay*, the seafood equivalent), the beef satay or the deep-fried Golden Triangles. Good choices off the main menu include the salmon curry, tamarind duck or sautéed gluten with chili and garlic sauce. A sleek and modern second branch is located in San Francisco.

Lunch/dinner Monday-Saturday; AE, DC, MC, V.

★★★★
$$$$$

Charley Brown's Steakhouse

Emeryville: 1890 Powell St. (at Frontage Road); 510-658-6580

Steak

Good for groups

Kid friendly

On the bay in Emeryville, this traditional, family-style steakhouse serves standard, predictably satisfying food. The Baseball, a thick cut of sirloin with mushrooms, is a top choice, as is the classic steak, marinated in bourbon, wine and garlic, then flame-broiled. Another good bet is the balsamic grilled chicken, served with sautéed spinach. You get plenty to eat, and prices are comparable to those at other steakhouses. Come here when you want to eat a substantial meal in peace and quiet, or just to contemplate the panoramic bay view while sipping a drink at the bar.

Lunch/dinner daily, weekend brunch; view; senior discount; full bar; free parking lot; AE, D, MC, V.

★★★★
$$$$$

Chez Panisse

Berkeley: 1517 Shattuck Ave. (between Cedar and Vine); 510-548-5525

California

Sidewalk's choice

Romantic

Kid friendly

Chez Panisse, the world-renowned birthplace of California cuisine started by Alice Waters in 1971, is a required destination for any serious gastronome. Her exquisitely orchestrated meals are as sublimely understated and satisfying as the dining room's spare yet elegant redwood decor. A different prix fixe dinner is offered each night: An autumnal feast might include grilled scallop salad, buttery gnocchi rich with mushrooms and spinach, perfectly roasted goose accompanied by Savoy cabbage tossed with fall nuts and root vegetables. Approachable and interesting wines define the eclectic wine list. Despite its daunting credentials, Chez Panisse is not just for the elite but for anyone who appreciates nature's bounty.

Dinner Monday-Saturday; prix fixe menu; reservations required; AE, MC, V, checks.

★★★☆
$$$$$

Citron
Oakland: 5484 College Ave. (at Tell); 510-653-5484

French

Sidewalk's choice

Romantic

Smart, stylish, and unpretentious, Citron was an immediate hit when Craig Thomas opened it in 1992, and appears to be settled in for the long run under the recent owner/chef Chris Rossi. Appetizer options on this contemporary French-Mediterranean menu might include a grilled quail salad or a corn soup topped with roasted garlic-sage butter and fried sage leaves. Italian features include wild mushroom cannelloni with chanterelles, ricotta and Swiss chard, and lamb osso buco. Or taste the chicken with 40 garlic cloves, and you'll think you've been transported to Provence. The wine list is significant, and the sommelier has taken care to include a balanced selection of less expensive wines.

Dinner nightly; outdoor seating; AE, D, MC, V.

★★★☆
$$$$$

Daniel's Fine Food and All That Jazz
Albany: 827 San Pablo Ave. (at Solano); 510-524-0157

Italian

Kid friendly

Daniel's, a cozy art deco-style supper club, is known as much for its quality jazz as it is for its upscale food. Chef Diane Posner, of the legendary Enoteca trattoria, has created a menu that's distinctly Italian, including fettuccine carbonara, fresh pasta infused with nutmeg, then tossed with crisply sautéed pancetta, garden-sweet English peas and parmesan and excellent meat dishes. During the day, the restaurant is definitely a diner, where standard breakfast and lunch fare is served. Whether you come for the camaraderie of the lunch counter or the jazzy ambience at dinnertime, you're sure to get an excellent meal for a pittance.

Breakfast/lunch daily, dinner Friday-Saturday; smoke-free; prix fixe menu; live entertainment; free parking lot; AE, D, MC, V, checks.

★★☆☆
$$$$$

Europa

Berkeley: 1981 Shattuck Ave. (at University); 510-841-1981

Mediterranean

Kid friendly

Its quaint interior featuring murals of a coastal village on one wall and the Acropolis on another, with a bubbling fountain in the back, Europa serves Mediterranean-Arabic fare with a California twist: standards like spanakopita, Greek salad and an assortment of kabobs, in addition to pomegranate chicken with apricots, skewered swordfish and grilled lamb with figs. Nice touches stand out: The pita bread is served warm; the vegetarian combo plate includes grilled eggplant; and an ordinary spinach salad is spruced up with medjool dates, toasted almonds and oranges. Quench your thirst with *jalab* (rose water and dates), freshly made lemonade or Arabic tea.

Lunch weekdays, dinner nightly; MC, V.

★★☆☆
$$$$$

Fat Lady Bar and Restaurant

Oakland: 201 Washington St. (at 2nd St.); 510-465-4996

American

Good for groups

It's said that the namesake of this 25-year-old establishment once ran the most popular brothel on the wharf, counting Jack London among her clientele. Now this second-generation family-run restaurant/bar, which resembles a Hollywood version of a Gold Rush bordello, draws a weekday lunch crowd that doesn't seem to mind paying high prices for the standard continental food; dinner, served only on Friday and Saturday, offers the same. The weekend brunch features (again, pricey) items like eggs Florentine, omelets, or the thick and delicious Grand Marnier French toast. A trio plays jazz and R&B Thursday to Saturday evenings.

Lunch weekdays, dinner Friday and Saturday, weekend brunch; outdoor seating; full bar; live entertainment; AE, MC, V.

★★★★
$$$$$

Fatapple's Restaurant & Bakery
Berkeley: 1346 Martin Luther King Jr. Way (at Rose); 510-526-2260

American

Sidewalk's choice

Kid friendly

When nothing but a burger will do, head for this comfortable, all-American spot packed with wood tables and images of Jack London. Fatapple's makes its patties with lean, high-quality beef, serving them on homemade wheat rolls with a variety of toppings, including five very good cheeses. The soups are good, and the spinach salad is delicious, tossed with feta cheese, walnuts and marinated black beans. Standout desserts include the flaky pecan pie, thick milkshakes, and cheese puffs. With an ever-present smell of fresh baked goods, Fatapple's also serves one of the best brunches around. Expect to wait for a table, but the line moves quickly.

Breakfast/lunch/dinner daily; reservations not accepted; cash only.

★★★★
$$$$$

Flint's Bar-B-Q
**Oakland: 6609 Shattuck Ave. (at 66th St.); 510-653-0593
Oakland: 3114 San Pablo Ave.; 510-658-9912**

Barbecue

Sidewalk's choice

Owned by the Flintroy family for over three decades, this original, strictly takeout rib joint has red-eye hours and the best barbecue in town. The pork ribs and hot links are the thing to order, retaining their succulent juiciness after slow cooking in the massive oven (skip the dried-out chicken). The sweet, thick sauce comes in mild, medium, or sinus-blasting. All barbecue comes with white bread, useful for mopping up the extra sauce. Sides of potatoes and baked beans are nothing special, but do add variety.

Lunch/dinner daily, late-night dining; takeout only; free parking lot; cash only.

Gertie's Chesapeake Bay Cafe

Berkeley: 1919 Addison St. (between Milvia and Martin Luther King Jr. Way); 510-841-2722

Seafood

For more than 15 years, Gertie's has been dishing up hearty and satisfying Chesapeake Bay-style seafood to an appreciative and diverse crowd. The lively, pink-toned eatery is known for its generous portions of Maryland crab cakes and crab soup, but you'll also find gumbo, blackened catfish and shrimp steamed in beer on the menu, which also includes non-seafood selections. The high-spirited and loud atmosphere makes Gertie's a fun place to go with a large group, whether you're celebrating a birthday or attending a nearby Berkeley Rep performance.

Lunch weekdays, dinner nightly; loud; outdoor seating; AE, DC, MC, V.

Ginger Island

Berkeley: 1820 4th St. (between Hearst and Virginia); 510-644-0444

Asian

Though the original chef and owner Bruce Cost has since left this lively restaurant, it serves much of the original pan-Asian menu, but with a lot less panache and consistency. Ginger is the favored ingredient, and a number of menu items are inspired by Asian lands: Indonesian chicken satay, Vietnamese spring rolls and Thai green curry noodles with scallops and chives. The drink of choice is ginger ale, which is mixed from fresh ginger syrup and lime. Service can be spotty, the noise level unbearable and prices increased, but still the noodle dishes win raves.

Lunch/dinner daily; loud; outdoor seating; full bar; free parking lot; AE, DC, MC, V.

★★★☆
$$$$$

Great China Restaurant
Berkeley: 2115 Kittredge Ave. (between Shattuck and Oxford); 510-843-7996

Chinese

 Good deal

Good for groups

Tiny, with too many tables crammed into its two rooms, this is one of the most popular Chinese restaurants among the many that surround the UC Berkeley campus and is distinguished by the fine fresh vegetables that appear in almost every dish. There are 124 menu selections, so the kitchen can offer budget items as well as celebratory dishes such as black bean crab and savory tea duck. With so many items to choose from, it's best to defer to the experts. Just avoid the busy noon hour, when university types line up out the door.

Lunch Monday-Saturday, dinner nightly; loud; MC, V.

★★★☆
$$$$$

Hong Kong East Ocean
Emeryville: 3199 Powell St. (at Emeryville Marina); 510-655-3388

Chinese

 Good deal

 Good for groups

 Kid friendly

In Hong Kong East Ocean's vast, sleek dining room, where every table has a magnificent three-bridge bay view, you'll find superlative seafood and dynamite dim sum. Weekend dim sum is a great treat: Try the sweet, crunchy, deep-fried meat, Shanghai dumplings, or tender steamed shrimp dumplings swirled in rice noodles. Be sure to flag down the roving waiters with trays of specials—perhaps soft, sticky barbecued pork buns or flaky daikon-mushroom pastries. For lunch or dinner, try any seafood (particularly the whole black cod in a velvety soy, ginger-garlic sauce) or anything with gossamer egg noodles.

Lunch/dinner daily; view; full bar; free parking lot; AE, MC, V.

Ike's Rotisserie

Oakland: 3859 Piedmont Ave. (between 38th and 39th Sts.); 510-450-0453

Middle Eastern

 Good deal

 Good for groups

 Kid friendly

Don't let the name fool you—Ike's is a Middle Eastern cafe serving some of the best tahini around, drizzled over crisp and grease-free falafel and other regional specialties. The courteous staff delivers your order quickly, but you may be tempted to linger, watching the cook slice thin layers off the *shawarma*—compacted, marinated chicken and beef roasted on a vertical spit and served with tomatoes and seasoned onions. The ambience isn't much; decor in the dining area, which offers 20 or so tables, consists mostly of posters from the Jordanian Tourism Authority.

Lunch/dinner Monday-Saturday; outdoor seating; no liquor license; checks.

Italian Colors Restaurant

Oakland: 2220 Mountain Blvd. (between Snake and Park); 510-482-8094

Italian

 Kid friendly

Neighborhood locals have embraced this spot, filling it each evening for dinner. Some of the pizzas and pastas on the menu are reminiscent of another local Oakland favorite, Zza's; in fact, Italian Colors was started by one of its co-founders. Moving beyond Italian standards, some entrees are more upscale but tend to be too contrived; stick to the more straightforward dishes. Portions are large, and service is attentive. Desserts are noteworthy—don't miss the ultra-lemony Mom's lemon cake with strawberries and whipped cream or the white chocolate banana tart.

Lunch weekdays, dinner nightly; outdoor seating; live entertainment; full bar; free parking lot; AE, MC, V.

Jade Villa

**Oakland: 800 Broadway (at 9th St.);
510-839-1688**

Chinese

The top dim sum house in Oakland, this restaurant takes up nearly a quarter of a block in Chinatown, and its ornate dining room is packed with Chinese families at lunch time. The kitchen offers a tempting array of entrees, but the real reason to come is the dim sum. Servers circulating through the room pushing carts laden with delicacies will pause to let you inspect barbecued pork buns, stuffed dumplings, wedges of green pepper filled with shrimp and lots of other tasty treats. Hold out for at least one order of steamed prawns in the shell, Jade Villa's best dish.

Breakfast/lunch/dinner daily; loud; MC, V.

★★★★
$$$$$

Jimmy Bean's

**Berkeley: 1290 6th St. (at Gilman);
510-528-3435**

California/
Mediterranean

Offering dynamite food at affordable prices in a converted warehouse, this bustling modern semi-self-serve restaurant (self-serve at lunch, table service at dinner) immediately attracted a following when launched in 1995 by the same folks responsible for the special-occasion Lalime's. The menu concentrates on California grill fare, with a half-dozen types of quesadillas (including duck, shiitake, fennel and eggplant), burgers, salads and assorted sandwiches (such as Mediterranean chicken with eggplant, tomato, feta, spinach and pesto). At night, the food is more Italian, with offerings like risotto alla Milanese, tagliatelle with assorted seafood, and various pizzas.

Lunch/dinner daily; loud; AE, MC, V.

★★★☆
$$$$$

Kensington Circus

Kensington (see Berkeley map): 389 Colusa Ave. (at Berkeley Park and Curtis); 510-524-8814

English

Sidewalk's choice

Good for groups

Kid friendly

This up-market East Bay enclave with an unassuming, low-key, neighborhood style attracts locals who come for a solid selection of English and Irish beers and ciders on tap. Although the food leans toward traditional English fare (fish and chips or shepherd's pie), items such as low-fat lemon chicken sausage served with black beans and grilled chicken breast topped with sautéed mushrooms and roasted red pepper sauce go beyond simple pub grub. Larger-than-traditional portions compensate for what may seem like slightly higher prices. There's live acoustic music most Wednesdays and Fridays.

Dinner nightly; loud; live entertainment; fireplace; MC, V, checks.

★★★☆
$$$$$

Khayyam's

Albany (see Berkeley map): 1373 Solano Ave. (between Ramona and Carmel); 510-526-7200

Middle Eastern

Good for groups

Named after the renowned 11th-century Persian poet, this oasis, with sunlight streaming onto the front courtyard and a large fountain gurgling in the dining room, provides artful, complex Middle Eastern food. Delicious, warm flat bread is the perfect accompaniment to wonderful appetizers, including the Mediterranean platter (hummus, garden-fresh tabbouleh and chunky baba ghanouj) or the roasted eggplant with a tangy side of yogurt. For your main dish, try the *kabob barreh*—marinated lamb, tomato, bell pepper and onion on a perfectly cooked mound of rice. Also satisfying is the sautéed spinach, tofu chunks, fava bean, lemon and saffron served with rice and salad.

Lunch/dinner daily; full bar; reservations required for large parties; free parking lot; all major credit cards.

★★★★ ☆
$$$$$

Kirala

**Berkeley: 2100 Ward St. (at Shattuck);
510-549-3486**

Japanese

Good deal

Kid friendly

As you enter this mecca for sushi lovers, be prepared to wait. This corner restaurant fills up with regulars who come for the best, freshest sushi in town. Try tuna so rich it could be a dessert, or prawns that are always plump and fresh. Make sure you order one of the stellar grill items: The lobster tail and corn win raves, and grilled skewers of seafood, vegetables and meats are done to perfection. Even the old standards—tempura, teriyaki and delicate Japanese pot stickers—are light, flavorful and taken to new heights.

*Lunch weekdays; dinner nightly; reservations
not accepted; free parking lot; AE, MC, V.*

★★★★ ☆
$$$$$

L.J. Quinn's Lighthouse Restaurant and Pub

**Oakland: 51 Embarcadero Cove
(at Livingston); 510-536-2050**

American

Kid friendly

Once a working lighthouse, this rustic, seafaring-atmosphere tavern with its view of the Oakland estuary is a local institution, serving seafood, burgers and other pub-type food. Choose from among 60 beers, well drinks and several types of wine. On Thursdays, the old lighthouse sways with the sounds of the Sons of the Buccaneers, a group that sings "salty sea chanteys" and the like, accompanied by dulcimers, bells and harmonicas.

*Lunch/dinner daily; outdoor seating; view; live
entertainment; full bar; MC, V.*

La Crème de la Crème

**Oakland: 5362 College Ave. (at Hudson);
510-420-8822**

California

Romantic

Located in what once was a private home, this beautiful little restaurant turns out light California-French fare, such as delicate individual pizzas, fresh pastas and heartwarming French comfort food. Even heartier dishes such as lamb brochettes with polenta and cassoulet are prepared with a light touch. For dessert, the warm pear brioche pastry with vanilla bean crème pâtissière and orange crème anglaise are spectacular. The interior is airy and pretty, with fresh flowers everywhere. Or, if the weather's right, sit outside on the lush, trumpet vine-draped patio.

Lunch Monday-Thursday, dinner nightly; Sunday brunch; outdoor seating; AE, DC, MC, V, checks.

La Méditerranée

**Berkeley: 2936 College Ave. (at Ashby);
510-540-7773**

Mediterranean

Good deal

Kid friendly

A popular local chain, La Méditerranée skillfully blends the sun-splashed cuisines of Greece and North Africa. Try the savory sandwiches of lahvosh bread layered with cream cheese, herbs, cucumbers, lettuce, feta cheese and tomato. Traditional Greek phyllo pie gets a twist with chunks of tender chicken, almonds, chickpeas, currants and cinnamon, or with lean ground beef seasoned with pine nuts, onions and spices. Everything is reasonably priced, although one of the best deals is the "Mediterranean meza," an assortment of 10 house specialties for two or more that runs $10.50 per person.

Lunch/dinner Monday-Saturday; outdoor seating; reservations not accepted; AE, MC, V, checks.

★★★☆
$$$$$

Lalime's

Berkeley: 1329 Gilman St. (between Neilson and Peralta); 510-527-9838

Mediterranean

Kid friendly

Located in a white stucco house, this restaurant serves sublime food in a radiant dining room with colorful quilts on the walls and candle-lit tables cloaked in white linens. The menu changes nightly, with features such as soup made with Finn potatoes, golden beets and ginger; roast garlic and shiitake ravioli; juniper berry-cured pork chops; or parchment-wrapped sea bass. Desserts are equally splendid. Zenophiles will adore the small selection of heavy-hitting wines on this well-priced wine list. Not all the complex dishes on the menu are equally well executed, but the knowledgeable staff can direct you to the gems.

Dinner nightly; prix fixe menu; MC, V, checks.

★★★☆
$$$$$

Le Cheval

Oakland: 1007 Clay St. (between 9th and 10th Sts.); 510-763-8495

Vietnamese

Good deal

Romantic

Good for groups

Kid friendly

Forget the borderline neighborhood location of this French/Vietnamese restaurant; unforgettable sauces—served in a spiffy high-ceilinged dining room—bring many people back again and again. The food is delicious, the portions large and the selection enticing. Simple shrimp rolls touched with mint and served with spicy peanut sauce make a favorite starter. Try the bean curd and eggplant simmered in a rich black bean sauce, chicken shish kebab with a sensational fish dipping sauce, or pan-fried beef spiked with lemongrass and hot pepper. About a dozen beers are on tap at the bar, including lots of Asian imports.

Lunch Monday-Saturday; dinner nightly; full bar; AE, D, MC, V.

Liu's Kitchen

Berkeley: 1593 Solano Ave. (at Ordway);
510-525-8766

Chinese

Good deal

Good for groups

Kid friendly

This casual spot with incongruous decor and a loyal following serves lots of flavorful (though decent at best) Chinese food for less than 10 bucks per person. Try the succulent whole fish special, the green-bean beef with garlic and ginger sauce, or the won tons the size of plums. You'll find many families happily chowing down on huge portions; unless you want leftovers, order less than you normally would. And as you eat, sit back and watch the incredible tag-team service that Liu's delivers.

Lunch Monday-Saturday, dinner nightly; loud;
MC, V, checks.

Long Life Vegi House

Berkeley: 2129 University Ave. (between
Walnut and Shattuck); 510-845-6072

Chinese

Good deal

Kid friendly

What this simply decorated, barn-like restaurant lacks in charm, it makes up for in value. The menu features a long roster of Chinese vegetarian and seafood dishes, and while portions are big, prices are small. The mu-shu vegetables, Chinese chive ravioli and tan-tan noodles with peanut sauce are outstanding, as are the faux-meat items, barbecued tofu with onions and straw mushrooms, curried prawns, and the scallops with string beans and black bean sauce. The varied menu eschews MSG. Dim sum is available on weekends.

Lunch/dinner daily; loud; AE, DC, D, MC, V.

Lucio's

Berkeley: 2826 Telegraph Ave. (between Oregon and Stuart); 510-841-4149

Spanish

Sidewalk's choice

Romantic

Good for groups

Paul Carrara's latest venture stands out as the best place to enjoy Spanish food in the Bay Area—and you can't miss this spot with a striking mosaic decorating its facade and an interior lit by bare orange bulbs and votive candles. You could make a meal from the selection of extraordinary flavorful tapas, but then you'd miss the tender, delicately prepared entrees like grilled skate wings with herbs, grilled chicken with saffron and lemon or the excellent paella, made from scratch when you place your order. Desserts range from good to superb.

Lunch/dinner daily; late-night dining; full bar; MC, V, checks.

Mama Lan's Vietnamese

Berkeley: 1316 Gilman St. (at Neilson); 510-528-1790

Vietnamese

Good deal

This tiny, often-crowded North Berkeley cafe turns out very flavorful dishes and is especially well known for its Vietnamese-style seafood preparations. The fresh crab is a standout dish; also try the whole fish that melts in your mouth. This spot is truly one of those places where everything's good, from crispy spring rolls to soothing desserts. Trouble is, if you're there when it's crowded (and it often is), the heady aromas wafting out of the kitchen can be excruciating.

Lunch/dinner Monday-Saturday; free parking lot; MC, V, checks.

Mama's Royal Cafe

Oakland: 4012 Broadway (between 40th and 41st Sts.); 510-547-7600

American

Eclectic decor and good food served in large portions keep the bohemian/boomer crowd coming back for some of the heartiest breakfasts in the East Bay, despite high prices and slow service. Breakfast includes 31 types of omelets and such specials as fresh fruit crepes and a burrito with chipotle tortilla. Lunch features a selection of burgers and sandwiches, including the Dagwood sandwich, a BLT with chicken, avocado, chiles and a fried egg. While you wait, check out the vintage apron and radio collection on the walls, as well as the annual napkin art contest.

Breakfast/lunch daily; weekend brunch; cash only.

$$\$\$\$

Mangia Mangia
Albany (see Berkely map): 755 San Pablo Ave. (at Washington); 510-526-9700

Italian

 Kid friendly

This cozy, likable eatery has a stylized Mediterranean look, with sponge-painted walls and small manzanita trees hung with bright peppers and other vegetables. The creative antipasto plate is one of the best things on the menu, featuring grilled shrimp wrapped in prosciutto, baby greens in vinaigrette and lemony marinated carrots in a red-pepper puree. Standouts among the generous entrees include spaghetti cartoccio pasta with prawns, salmon, shellfish and scallops baked in parchment and topped with spicy tomato sauce and risotto with mushrooms and artichokes. Don't miss the melt-in-your-mouth tiramisu made by Mama every day.

Lunch Wednesday-Friday, dinner Tuesday-Sunday; free parking lot; all major credit cards.

$$\$\$\$

Maxim
Berkeley: 2190 Bancroft Way (at Fulton); 510-843-6989

Mediterranean

 Good for groups

Drawing on California, Mediterranean, Southwestern and Asian cuisines for inspiration, Maxim creates imaginative dishes in an unassuming dining room, with pleasing Mediterranean accents. Prix fixe meals are the best deal: A three-course dinner, ranging in price from $13 to $16, might include gazpacho, excellent Moroccan lamb and chocolate-espresso torte with strawberry sauce. You can also order à la carte; choose from among an assortment of fresh pastas, a seafood clay pot, and house-made sun-dried tomato and chicken sausage. A limited selection of beer and wine is offered.

Lunch weekdays, dinner nightly; fireplace; prix fixe menu; free parking lot; all major credit cards.

★★★★
$$$$$

Nan Yang Rockridge

Oakland: 6048 College Ave. (at Claremont); 510-655-3298

Burmese

Good deal

Long lines of customers clamor for chef/owner Philip Chu's highly spiced, wonderful delights at this Burmese eatery (the first in the Bay Area) which have been conjured out of recipes from monasteries, street vendors, festival food booths and families. Favorites include his five-spice chicken, spicy fried potato pancakes and crunchy, textural ginger salad with 16 ingredients. The generous curry dishes come with giant chunks of lamb, beef, chicken or fish, and there are plenty of seductive vegetarian variations. Although simply decorated and brightly lit, Nan Yang continues to be a neighborhood favorite.

Lunch/dinner Tuesday-Sunday; outdoor seating; MC, V.

★★★★
$$$$$

New Delhi Junction

Berkeley: 2556 Telegraph Ave. (between Blake and Parker); 510-486-0477

Indian

Romantic

Kid friendly

Hidden away on the second floor of a funky mini-mall, this soothing little jewel of a restaurant serves rich, smoky tandoori and fine curries. Its claim to fame is its "Gourmet Tour of India," a monthly menu drawn from different regions and ethnic groups of India. Each month, owner B. Fra pores over his vast collection of cookbooks and chooses three distinctive regional dishes, such as the Uttar Pradesh delicacy kava chicken (boneless chicken and cashew nuts cooked with coconut, ginger, coriander and cinnamon). Other noteworthy items are the flaky vegetarian pakoras, samosas, and garlic- and onion-studded nan.

Lunch/dinner daily; quiet; free parking lot; AE, DC, MC, V.

★★☆☆
$$$$$

North Beach Pizza

Berkeley: 1598 University Ave. (at California); 510-849-9800

Italian

Kid friendly

North Beach Pizza is ranked among the best of the Bay Area's pizzerias, and though this Berkeley location is unusual, the menu is the same as at the others. Toppings are sparse, but that heavenly layer of whole-milk mozzarella and the hand-spun dough with thick, chewy edges wins people over. Either create your own from the list of 20 fresh ingredients (sausage with black olives is killer), or choose from the house's 10 specialties, such as the San Francisco Special—clams, garlic and cheese. Besides pizza, there's a huge assortment of pastas, poultry, sandwiches and salads.

Lunch/dinner daily; late-night dining; no liquor license; reservations not accepted; all major credit cards.

★★★☆
$$$$$

O Chamé

Berkeley: 1830 4th St. (at Hearst); 510-841-8783

Asian

Sidewalk's choice

Good deal

Romantic

Even jaded food fanatics are bewitched by chef David Vardy's elaborate Buddhist-Taoist-inspired culinary fare at this exotic Asian-California restaurant. The menu changes often, but typical dishes include a vinegared wakame seaweed and cucumber salad, tofu dumplings with burdock and carrot, grilled river eel with endive and chayote, and soba noodles with shiitakes and daikon sprouts. The food is pricey and the portions small, but O Chamé's serene interior—crafted in the style of a rustic Japanese wayside inn, with a magnificent Oriental rug and rough-hewn wooden chairs—seems to lull most patrons into a Zen-like calm.

Lunch/dinner; quiet; outdoor seating;
AE, DC, MC, V.

Oliveto Cafe and Restaurant

Oakland: 5655 College Ave. (at Shafter); 510-547-5356

Italian

 Sidewalk's choice

 Romantic

Chef Paul Bertolli's passion for the Italian table and his careful interpretations of rustic Italian cuisine make Oliveto's a top East Bay destination, attracting a cosmopolitan crowd with its Florentine trattoria-style decor. A longtime veteran of Chez Panisse, Bertolli changes the menu to reflect the seasons, featuring strikingly unusual dishes—tripe with English peas, charcoal-grilled pigeon—along with pastas, grilled meats and rustic appetizers. The casual cafe downstairs, serving an identical menu in the evenings and an abbreviated version at lunch, catches the overflow. Espressos, good wines by the glass, exotic beers, expensive Scotch and sidewalk tables add to the European ambience.

Lunch/dinner daily; weekend brunch; outdoor
seating; AE, DC, MC, V, checks.

Omnivore

Berkeley: 3015 Shattuck Ave. (between Ashby and Emerson); 510-848-4346

California

 Good for groups

Chef/owner Andy Lee's cozy restaurant is one of the best bargains around, combining high-quality food made from scratch and a pleasing ambience. The dining room is enhanced by rice-paper screens and antiques, and the food is a delectable fusion of California, Mediterranean and Asian cuisines. Try, for example, the pan-fried breaded sea scallops with a dipping sauce of wasabi, lemon juice, ginger and scallions, the inventive Thai fish soup or the smoked leg of lamb with pistachio demi-glace. There's a good selection of wines on the sensibly priced list. Desserts range from a pistachio-nut ice cream pie to fresh fruit tarts.

Dinner Wednesday-Sunday; AE, MC, V.

★★★★
$$$$$

Pasand

Berkeley: 2286 Shattuck Ave. (between Bancroft and Kittredge); 510-549-2559

Indian

 Good for groups

Opened in 1975, Pasand remains one of the East Bay's top spots for southern Indian food, with its use of fresh ingredients and light preparations. Try a regional specialty such as lentil-flour crepes from Madras stuffed with vegetable curry, or deep-fried pastry from Andhra. Other good choices are ginger masala chicken, lamb biriyani in curry and vegetarian *mutter panir* curry. Pasand's decor is minimal, but the live Indian music performed most nights creates an authentic feel. Club Pasand downstairs has a dance floor and hosts live music—blues, reggae, swing, jazz, hip-hop—five nights a week.

Lunch/dinner daily; weekday happy hour;
full bar; live entertainment; AE, MC, V.

★★★★
$$$$$

Pho Anh Dao

Oakland: 280 E. 18th St. (between Park Boulevard and 3rd Ave.); 510-836-1566

Vietnamese

An essentially one-dish restaurant specializing in *pho*, the anise-scented beef-and-noodle soup that hails from Hanoi. Many Vietnamese eat the soup every day, and after tasting Pho Anh Dao's version, you'll see why—the aromatic meal-in-a-bowl is cheap, delicious, filling and healthful. Asian basil, sliced green chiles, a lime or lemon wedge and bean sprouts arrive on the side. Add as many of the garnishes as you like and then, with chopsticks in one hand and a soup spoon in the other, dive in.

Breakfast/lunch/dinner daily; cash only.

★★★☆
$$$$$

Picante Cocina Mexicana

Berkeley: 1328 6th St. (near Gilman);
510-525-3121

Mexican

 Sidewalk's choice

 Good deal

 Good for groups

 Kid friendly

Jim Maser, owner of Cafe Fanny and brother-in-law of Alice Waters, studied cooking in Mexico before taking over this casual, lively neighborhood spot in 1994, and his extensive research shines in every bite. Just about everything on the menu reveals Maser's passion for fresh ingredients and careful cooking, from the tortillas made by hand throughout the day to the variety of savory sauces. The chiles rellenos and tamales are outstanding, especially a chicken version bathed in tomatillo sauce and a vegetable tamale with butternut squash and roasted poblano chiles. The two dining areas are always bustling, and service is efficient and amiable.

Lunch/dinner daily; weekend brunch; outdoor seating; live entertainment; free parking lot; MC, V, checks.

★★★☆
$$$$$

Pizza Rustica Cafe

Oakland: 5422 College Ave. (at Kales);
510-654-1601

California

 Good deal

 Good for groups

 Kid friendly

Impeccable pizzas and unusual rotisserie chicken dishes are served at tiny tables in Rustica's cramped, noisy dining room. It's a jazzy nouveau pizza joint with pop art on the walls, where you can get the usual margherita, mixed vegetable, pepperoni and mushroom toppings, or go for the exotic, such as Thai pizza topped with roasted chicken in spicy ginger and peanut sauce, mozzarella, carrots, scallions, daikon, peppers and sesame seeds. Another highlight is the rotisserie chicken, done Greek-, Jamaican- and Tuscan-style. Salads and appetizers are available, too.

Lunch/dinner daily; loud; outdoor seating; reservations required for large parties; MC, V.

★★★☆
$$$$$

Plearn Thai Cuisine

Berkeley: 2050 University Ave. (between Milvia and Shattuck); 510-841-2148

Thai

 Good deal

For more than a decade, Plearn has had a reputation for serving some of the best Thai food in the East Bay. Regulars come for wonderful and unusual seafood dishes like green-lipped mussels; prawns sautéed in coconut milk with carrots, sugar peas and a spicy sauce; and salmon with ginger and green onions baked in banana leaves. The fragrant pork, chicken and seafood curries are popular as well. There's often a long wait for a table, even though the restaurant is large, the tables are packed together, and the staff often exhibits a move-'em-in-move-'em-out attitude.

Lunch/dinner daily; reservations not accepted; MC, V.

★★★☆
$$$$$

Pyramid Brewery & Alehouse

Berkeley: 901 Gilman St. (at 7th); 510-528-9880

American

 Good for groups

It may look like an enormous industrial auto plant from the outside, but inside, earthy tones and a funky design warm up the cavernous space of the Seattle-based brew pub and restaurant. Though Pyramid beer can be found in many stores, it's better fresh from the spout (there are 20 to 25 beers on tap). As for food, in addition to standbys like nachos and burgers, there are a number of ambitiously concocted dishes: wood-roasted halibut with roasted garlic, rosemary,

lemon and capers; smoked mahogany half-chicken; tasty barbecue ribs; and the sausage sampler.

Lunch/dinner daily; loud; outdoor seating; reservations not accepted; free parking lot; AE, MC, V.

$$$$

Restoran Rasa Sayang
Albany (see Berkeley map): 977 San Pablo Ave. (at Buchanan); 510-525-7000

Malaysian

Good deal

Good for groups

Kid friendly

If you dream of an exotic paradise, feed your fantasy with Rasa Sayang's reasonably priced, exceptionally flavorful food, which draws on Malaysian, Thai and Indian cuisines. Start your culinary adventure with the Malaysian salad, an interesting and spicy combination of cucumber, red onion, pineapple, chiles and tomatoes tossed with a coconut milk dressing or fried dal, onion and chile fritters. Such items as tandoori chicken, Malaysian bread stuffed with minced lamb, spicy marinated fish simmered in tamarind juice, chicken cooked with lemongrass in coconut gravy and enticing Malaysian noodle dishes are also on the menu. The amiable staff happily offers suggestions.

Lunch/dinner daily; free parking lot; AE, MC, V.

$$$$

Rick & Ann's
Berkeley: 2922 Domingo Ave. (between Ashby and Russell); 510-649-8538

California

Good for groups

Kid friendly

Rick and Ann's mission to combine American comfort food with healthy, inventive California cuisine results in large portions of fresh, satisfying fare. It's served in a homey restaurant with a diner-style counter and sea-blue vinyl booths, in the shadow of the Claremont Hotel. At breakfast, the challah French toast is legendary, as are the red flannel hash, Ann's tofu scramble, terrific omelets, millet muffins and a variety of pancakes. Burgers, sandwiches (from tofu to BLT), soups and salads are on the luncheon menu.

Dinner choices include pork chops with fruit chutney, chicken pot pie, meatloaf and vegetarian moussaka.

Breakfast/lunch/dinner daily; weekend brunch; outdoor seating; reservations required for large parties; validated parking; MC, V.

★★★☆
$$$$$

Rivoli

Berkeley: 1539 Solano Ave. (at Neilson); 510-526-2542

California

Sidewalk's choice

Kid friendly

Modest digs, funky decor and unexceptional service haven't stopped chef Wendy Brucker and Roscoe Skipper from making Rivoli one of Berkeley's dining hot spots, serving casual but refined California-Mediterranean cuisine. The one constant on the menu is Brucker's incredible portobello fritter appetizer, but look for other outstanding starters such as smoked trout with vegetable *anchoiade* or any of the wonderful soups. Stews, fish dishes and roasts are always first-rate, and braised lamb shank with white beans and rosemary aïoli is the essence of good country cooking. Appropriately, the small wine list is an eclectic but interesting jumble with reasonable prices.

Dinner nightly; loud; MC, V.

★★☆☆
$$$$$

Rockridge Cafe

Oakland: 5492 College Ave. (between Taft and Lawton); 510-653-1567

American

Good deal

Kid friendly

A top contender in the ongoing burger wars, this classic American diner offers good food and lots of it. The juicy burgers and succulent, honey-mustard chicken sandwiches are good bets. Add thick-cut homemade fries or onion rings and a Ben and Jerry's shake, and you've hit the basic food groups. For dessert, the chewy fudge pie and tangy olallieberry pie are standouts. Stick to the standards here and eschew more complicated offerings (such as the gruel-like Apache stew). For breakfast, choose delicate ricotta pancakes or one of the hearty egg-and-potato dishes.

Breakfast/lunch/dinner daily; MC, V.

★★★★
$$$$$

Santa Fe Bar & Grill

Berkeley: 1310 University Ave.
(between Acton and Bonar); 510-841-1110

American

❤ Romantic

Though the white stucco facade and vaguely Southwestern interior of this restaurant—a former railroad station—haven't changed over the years (and now look rather dated), the quality of the food has varied dramatically; currently it's just OK. The changing American menu shows touches of Mediterranean influences, with starters such as fried calamari with cilantro-garlic-and-yogurt dipping sauce and entrees featuring fettuccine with scallops, mushrooms and shrimp or smoked Petaluma duck with wild rice and a Cointreau demi-glace. A jazz pianist plays nightly, and there's a lively bar scene.

Lunch weekdays, dinner nightly; loud; outdoor seating; full bar; live entertainment; AE, MC, V.

★★★★
$$$$$

Saul's

Berkeley: 1475 Shattuck Ave. (between
Vine and Rose); 510-848-3354

Jewish

 Good deal

 Kid friendly

At this New York Jewish-style deli, not only is the food authentic, but the service is of the snooze-you-lose variety. Breakfast offerings include challah French toast, Noah's bagels with lox and cream cheese, and Russian yogurt (laced with honey, fruit and toasted nuts). Good bets from the impressive lunch roster are Tel Aviv salad (diced vegetables, lettuce, feta cheese, pita, olives and eggs) or Manhattan Madness sandwich (corned beef, turkey and tongue with Russian dressing). Dinner brings an array of deli platters, including Niman Schell braised brisket of beef and grilled chicken livers and onions.

Breakfast/lunch/dinner daily; live entertainment; reservations not accepted; MC, V, checks.

★★★☆
$$$$$

Skates on the Bay

Berkeley: 100 Seawall Drive (at University); 510-549-1900

American

 Romantic

 Good for groups

Kid friendly

With expansive views of the bay, a stone fireplace and cherry-wood trim, attractive, cozy Skates features a competently prepared American menu and is a popular destination for tourists and locals alike. Starters range from New England clam chowder to crab-artichoke dip, while entrees include prime rib, penne with seafood sausage, blackened salmon Caesar salad and grilled pork chops. A rich chocolate cake topped with Lappert's vanilla ice cream and raspberry coulis towers over the dessert menu. While not exactly gourmet fare, the food is tasty and hearty, and the service good-natured.

Lunch/dinner daily; weekend brunch; fireplace; view; full bar; free parking lot; all major credit cards.

★★★☆
$$$$$

Soizic Bistro-Cafe

Oakland: 300 Broadway (at 3rd St.); 510-251-8100

California

 Good deal

 Romantic

 Good for groups

Two blocks from Jack London Square, this exquisite artsy bistro with warm golden colors occupies a converted warehouse with 18-foot ceilings and a second-floor loft dining room. The owners, a Korean husband-and-wife team, once owned Berkeley's critically acclaimed Cafe Pastoral. He's an architect; she's a painter and head chef. The food is Mediterranean-inspired California cuisine: mouth-watering eggplant with goat cheese and mushrooms served with polenta or savory smoked chicken sandwiches with sun-dried tomatoes, watercress aioli and spinach. For dessert, try their famous ginger-spiked custard. Service is extremely efficient, making Soizic a surprisingly luxurious dining destination.

Lunch Tuesday-Friday, dinner Tuesday-Sunday; quiet; MC, V.

Spettro's

★★★★ ☆
$$ $ $ $

Oakland: 3355 Lakeshore Ave. (between
Trestle Glen and Mandana); 510-465-8320

California

 Good
deal

 Good
for groups

Kid
friendly

Spettro's ("spirit" in Italian) has an other-worldly
theme with a skeleton at the entrance and macabre
gravestone photography. But you'll be brought back
to earth once you get a whiff of these international
dishes, concocted with a twist (including baby greens
tossed in blueberry vinaigrette or bacon, cheese and
peanut butter on pizza). The owners (former owners
of Topless Pizza) give new life here to some of Top-
less' unusual pies; additional creations include
smoked chicken and oyster gumbo and Brazilian *fei-
joada* with black beans and linguica on rice. Many of
the strange combinations were dreamed up by and
named after the waitstaff.

Dinner nightly; all major credit cards.

Sushi Banzai

NR
$$ $ $ $

Berkeley: 1019 Camellia St. (at 10th);
510-524-6625

Japanese

Tucked away in a warehouse in West Berkeley, this
noteworthy little restaurant is a true family operation
run by Hide Nagano and his wife (their son Max is
often found doing his homework at the counter). It's
a favorite of local chefs on their day off, who have
discovered that the fish is unfailingly fresh, the
selection is outstanding, and the show is always
entertaining. In addition to the usual sushi offerings,
Sushi Banzai features the B-29, a thick roll that's
dipped in tempura batter and deep-fried.

*Lunch/dinner Tuesday/Sunday; reservations not
accepted; MC, V.*

Townhouse Bar & Grill

★★★★
$$$$$

Emeryville: 5862 Doyle St. (between
Powell and 59th St.); 510-652-6151

California

 Romantic

 Good for groups

Around long enough to attract a loyal following, this
surprisingly good grill evokes a neighborhood feel in
a busy location. The decor is upscale, reminiscent of
a garden restaurant—light, airy, and refreshing. So is
the food: fish tacos with tomatillo-avocado salsa; an
incredible grilled lamb salad with onions, peppers,
white cheddar and red wine sauce; and an ethereal
butternut squash ravioli touched with tarragon and
walnut cream sauce.

> *Lunch/dinner Monday-Saturday; loud; outdoor
> seating; full bar; live entertainment; fireplace;
> free parking lot; MC, V.*

Tropix

★★★★
$$$$$

Oakland: 3814 Piedmont Ave. (between W.
MacArthur and 40th St.); 510-653-2444

Caribbean

Good for groups

Kid friendly

This Caribbean-style cafe is a fun spot with a zingy
mix of flavors; in fact, it offers some of the most fan-
ciful combinations you'll find this side of the islands.
A sampling of these creations includes fettuccine
and vegetables in roasted squash and coconut sauce,
sprinkled with walnuts and more coconut, and a jerk
chicken salad with mango, red cabbage and carrot.
The decor is snazzy with a black-and-white checkered floor, sherbet-colored walls and a huge, colorful
mural depicting an island beach scene.

> *Breakfast weekends, lunch/dinner daily; outdoor
> seating; AE, MC, V, checks.*

Venezia

Berkeley: 1799 University Ave. (at Grant); 510-849-4681

Italian

Kid friendly

The atmospheric murals, amiable hustle and bustle of the dining room, and free crayons make this a favorite with kids, but even if you don't come with little ones in tow, you'll enjoy the hearty Italian food, festive ambience and abondanza portions. The antipasti include fried calamari with lemon aioli, and a salad of baby spinach with persimmons and pomegranate. The ravioli, risotto, and pasta noodles are all made in-house, and the pasta puttanesca is a tried-and-true favorite. The rotisserie chicken and grilled steak served with spinach and polenta are also recommended.

Lunch weekdays, dinner nightly; AE, MC, V.

★★★★
$$$$$

Vi's Restaurant

Oakland: 724 Webster St. (between 7th and 8th Sts.); 510-835-8375

Vietnamese

Good deal

Good for groups

Look closely at your fellow diners slurping Vi's famous braised-duck noodle soup and you may notice familiar faces from some of the best eateries around. This is where the professionals from places such as Chez Panisse come for their fix of very good Vietnamese food. The fresh, steamed rice-noodle crepes contain dried mushrooms, onions, ground pork and shallots and come with bean sprouts and Vietnamese pork sausage on the side. Prices are cheap; five-spice chicken, for example, is only $4.95. Though the place is usually full, turnover is quick.

Breakfast/lunch/dinner Friday-Wednesday; reservations not accepted; cash only.

Walker's Pie Shop and Restaurant

Albany: 1491 Solano Ave. (at Curtis); 510-525-4647

American

Beloved by families and senior citizens, Walker's Pie Shop is a throwback to days when friendly waitresses called you "honey" and urged, "How about a nice piece of pie?" The pies, made from scratch and bursting with their fillings, come in many flavors—from strawberry rhubarb to chocolate cream. Walker's also makes a mean milk shake, and the diner-like menu includes soups, salads and blue-plate specials featuring a revolving lineup of fried chicken, pork chops, prime rib and other hearty entrees, all at modest prices.

Breakfast/lunch/dinner Tuesday-Sunday; reservations not accepted; DC, D, MC, V.

Won Thai Cuisine

Berkeley: 1459 University Ave. (at Sacramento); 510-848-6483

Thai

Usually you wouldn't think of the restaurant in the local Travel Inn Motel as a location that screams "fine dining experience." Not only is the locale unusual, but the food also inspires questions such as "how can food this good possibly be so cheap?" and "why haven't I ever seen these dishes in other Thai restaurants?" For a special treat, order the tender spareribs simmered in soy sauce, only available on the weekends. Service is friendly, and affable owner Mark Rattapituck surprises return visitors by remembering their names.

Lunch Tuesday-Friday, dinner Tuesday-Sunday; free parking lot; MC, V.

★★★☆
$$$$$

Yoshi's

Oakland: 510 Embarcadero West (between Clay and Washington); 510-238-9200

Japanese

 Sidewalk's choice

 Romantic

 Good for groups

Kid friendly

Yoshi's is better known for its world-class vibes than it is for its sushi, but the restaurant side of this recently relocated, redesigned jazz supper club (now in Jack London Square) has some stellar moments of its own. The 200-seat restaurant across from the swank music lounge offers a first-rate Japanese menu that includes traditional tempura and teriyaki and above-average sushi and sashimi. Portions are generous, and combination plates let you sample a wide range of goodies. Don't leave without trying the dreamy, creamy, melt-in-your-mouth lemon cheesecake.

Lunch/dinner daily; full bar; live entertainment; validated parking; all major credit cards.

★★★☆
$$$$$

Zachary's Chicago Pizza

Berkeley: 1853 Solano Ave. (at The Alameda and Colusa); 510-525-5950
Oakland: 5801 College Ave. (between Claremont and Oak Grove); 510-655-6385

Pizza

 Sidewalk's choice

 Good for groups

 Kid friendly

Zachary's is a prime contender in the Bay Area pizza wars, with its tasty Chicago-style pies featuring a deep-bottom crust packed with a choice of fillings, covered with a thin second crust and topped with tomato sauce. (The bottom crust turns crisp in the oven, while the top one melts into the filling.) Try the gooey spinach, cheese and mushroom or chicken and spinach in a whole-wheat crust. Both outposts are packed with screaming students, plus children and adults with high decibel tolerances. Wise patrons call ahead for their pizza to go.

Lunch/dinner daily; loud; reservations not accepted; cash only.

★★★★
$$$$$

Zatis

Oakland: 4029 Piedmont Ave. (at 40th St.); 510-658-8210

California

 Romantic

Good for groups

Strong wafts of garlic pull you into this unobtrusive neighborhood cafe, featuring a California-Italian daily menu of salads, fish and meat. Past winners included flatbread with roasted garlic and Gorgonzola, smoked mozzarella and vegetable quesadilla, and eggplant with kalamata olives, jalapeños and artichoke hearts. The tiny room gets noisy during lunch, but in the evening, the light is low and the jazz soothing. Think intimate (about 18 tables), and think Valentine's Day (any night of the year). The service is so personal the chef once cooked up a single batch of minestrone for a customer who arrived too late for the soup du jour.

Lunch/dinner Monday-Saturday; AE, MC, V.

Marin County

Reviews and neighborhood maps

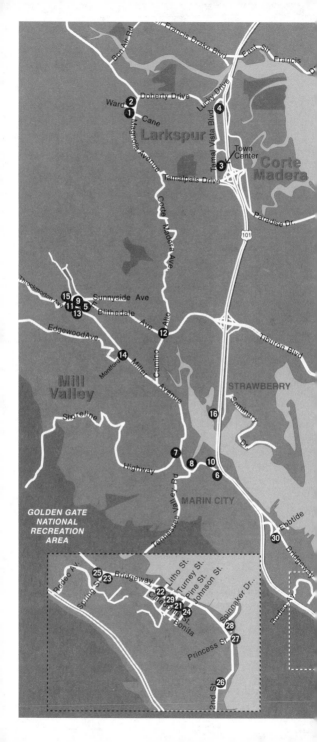

Marin County

Larkspur
1 Fabrizio
2 Left Bank

Corte Madera
3 Il Fornaio
4 Sushi Maru

Mill Valley
5 Avenue Grill
6 Buckeye Roadhouse
7 Chariya Thai Cuisine
8 The Dipsea Cafe
9 El Paseo
10 Frantoio
11 Frog and the Peach
12 Gira Polli
13 Jennie Low
14 Joe's Taco Lounge and Salsaria
15 Piazza D'Angelo
16 Robata Grill & Sushi

Tiburon
17 Guaymas
18 Sam's Anchor Cafe
19 Sushi to Dai For
20 Tutto Mare Restaurant

Sausalito
21 Arawan Thai Restaurant
22 Caledonia Kitchen
23 Fred's Place
24 Gatsby's
25 Guernica Restaurant
26 Mikayla
27 Scoma's of Sausalito
28 The Spinnaker
29 Sushi Ran
30 Tommy's Wok

This area of Sausalito shown enlarged at left

★★☆☆
$$$$$

Arawan Thai Restaurant

Sausalito: 47 Caledonia St. (at Pine); 415-332-0882

Thai

White lace curtains, lush green plants and hand-crafted Thai figurines decorate the dining room of this little restaurant, where the tables are quickly snatched up by neighborhood diners, due to its distinction as Sausalito's only Thai establishment, as well as its consistently good food. Favorite dishes include sizzling spicy calamari and prawns sautéed with hot chilies, onions and sweet basil, and wonderful barbecued short ribs marinated in garlic and Thai herbs. The Pad Four Musketeer, a savory blend of black mushrooms, snow peas and broccoli sautéed in oyster sauce, is a popular vegetarian choice.

Lunch/dinner daily; AE, MC, V, checks.

★★☆☆
$$$$$

Avenue Grill

Mill Valley: 44 E. Blithedale Ave. (at Sunnyside); 415-388-6003

American

Though it gets noisy when the cocktails start flowing, this lively dinner house has been popular with Mill Valley regulars for years. All-American meat loaf served with garlic mashed potatoes and gravy is the restaurant's claim to fame, but the monthly menu also includes more upriver dishes; other crowd-pleasers are the crab cakes and barbecued oysters. Most of the dishes work well, though the kitchen is occasionally sloppy. The mustard-colored walls lined with large mirrors and star-shaped sconces give the room a warm, inviting ambience.

Dinner nightly; loud; AE, MC, V.

★★★★
$$$$$

Buckeye Roadhouse

**Mill Valley: 15 Shoreline Highway
(off 101); 415-331-2600**

American

 Romantic

Good for groups

As with Cindy Pawlcyn's other ventures (Fog City Diner, Bix, and Mustards), the Buckeye tugs at the heartstrings of Americana and gives them a gourmet spin at this popular spot with its rustic, hunting-lodge atmosphere. Start with the thin, sweet onion rings, or tender roasted eggplant and smoky red peppers piled on rosemary toast smothered with melted cheese. Entrees include barbecued baby back ribs, smoked Sonoma duck topped with fresh plum sauce and a tender grilled pork chop with garlic mashed potatoes. Finish with the sinfully rich butterscotch pudding or a slice of s'more pie, a variation on the campfire classic.

Lunch/dinner daily; weekend brunch; ear-shattering; outdoor seating; view; late-night dining; full bar; valet parking; MC, V.

★★★★
$$$$$

Caledonia Kitchen

**Sausalito: 400 Caledonia St. (at Litho);
415-331-0220**

California

This beloved pint-size cafe is home away from home for Sausalito locals, who come for superb salads and hearty sandwiches made with Semifreddi's wonderful bread. Nearly a dozen salads are created daily, such as spinach leaves sprinkled with feta and toasted pine nuts in tangy vinaigrette, Asian noodles dressed with spicy peanut sauce, or rigatoni flavored with chicken, rosemary, caramelized onions and sun-dried tomatoes. Sandwiches range from the turkey roasted with lavender, then layered with mozzarella and roasted red peppers, to a ham and brie spiced with honey mustard. Good coffee and espresso drinks are also available.

Breakfast/lunch/dinner daily; checks.

Chariya Thai Cuisine

Mill Valley: 252 Almonte Boulevard (Shoreline Hwy); 415-389-8759

Thai

Marinites zooming through Tam Junction often pull over here for a good Thai meal in a tranquil atmosphere. As is typical of most Thai restaurants, Chariya's menu is vast and features plenty of made-to-order entrees for meat-eaters and vegetarians alike. The house specialty is a well-prepared *pad kee mao*: stir-fried noodles with fresh prawns, ground chicken, diced tomatoes, and a liberal sprinkling of fresh basil. Be sure to check the daily specials board, which features Thai treats like the tender eggplant stuffed with prawns.

> *Dinner Monday through Saturday; quiet; free parking lot; D, MC, V.*

The Dipsea Cafe

Mill Valley: 200 Shoreline Highway (at Tennessee Valley); 415-381-0298

American

A favorite haunt of bicyclists and runners heading up Mount Tam, the Dipsea is a good stop for fueling up before a day of exercise. In the morning, you'll find hearty *huevos rancheros* and great buttermilk or whole-wheat blueberry flapjacks. Lunch fare ranges from grilled eggplant and Reuben sandwiches to Cobb and spinach salads. Daily specials might include a grilled scallop salad, an Italian sausage sandwich or a portobello mushroom sandwich. Photos of those who have completed the grueling, storied Dipsea Race line the cafe's walls. Bicyclists take note: There are parking spots for two-wheelers.

> *Breakfast/lunch daily; view; outdoor seating; reservations required for large parties; free parking lot; AE, D, MC, V.*

★★★☆
$$$$$

El Paseo

**Mill Valley: 17 Throckmorton Ave.
(near E. Blithedale); 415-388-0741**

French

Romantic

Good
for groups

**For 25 years a well-dressed clientele has come to
this romantic, dimly lit eatery for its classic French
fare, which features delicious plates of escargots,
roasted lamb chops wrapped with minced vegetables,
steak tartare and filet mignon flamed with brandy and
ginger. Though the 50-page wine list is difficult to
navigate, the pricing is excellent. El Paseo's old-
world charm extends from the beautifully restored,
1930s-era brick exterior to a plush Victorian-style
interior overlooking an outdoor patio.**

Dinner nightly; AE, MC, V, checks.

★★★☆
$$$$$

Fabrizio

**Larkspur: 455 Magnolia Avenue (Caine);
415-924-9889**

Italian

**Locals linger over classic Italian entrees at this
small, no-frills restaurant. Numerous specials of the
day are scribbled on a piece of paper: antipasti might
include excellent fried calamari made with Monterey
squid, grilled eggplant sprinkled with feta cheese, or
radicchio and fennel salad. Entrees may include
bowtie pasta with fresh tomatoes, sausage, garlic
and rosemary, gorgonzola and radicchio risotto, and
tender veal piccata. A well-edited wine list, with
about 9 wines served by the glass, complements the
carefully prepared food. The dining room is modestly
decorated and somewhat cramped; in nice weather,
dine on the patio lined with hanging violets.**

*Lunch Monday through Saturday; dinner nightly;
outdoor seating; free parking lot; AE, MC, V.*

Frantoio

★★★★
$$$$$

**Mill Valley: 152 Shoreline Highway
(off Highway 101); 415-289-5777**

Italian

Good
for groups

Kid
friendly

Offering a bird's eye glimpse of the ancient tradition of olive oil-making, Frantoio's high-ceilinged, colorfully tiled room showcases an olive press with 3,600-pound granite wheels and a large open kitchen. The house-made extra-virgin olive oil is put to good use in the contemporary Italian fare, which features excellent Pacific halibut crusted with porcini mushrooms and thyme-scented olive oil, rotisserie chicken with wood-oven-roasted vegetables and crisp, wood-oven-baked pizzas. The one-page wine list's Italian and California selections complement the rustic fare.

*Lunch Monday-Saturday; dinner nightly;
outdoor seating; full bar; free parking lot/valet;
AE, MC, V.*

Fred's Place

★★★★
$$$$$

**Sausalito: 1917 Bridgeway (at Spring);
415-332-4575**

American

Though it's a locals' spot, it's easy enough to fit in at this casual coffeehouse, which has been serving home-style breakfasts to an appreciative clientele since 1966. Fred's French toast (made with to-die-for ice cream batter) is downright addictive, and the steak and eggs with golden hash browns are just like mom used to make. The coffee, appropriately, is diner variety.

Breakfast/lunch daily; free parking lot; cash only.

Frog and the Peach

★★★★
$$$$$

**Mill Valley: 106 Throckmorton Avenue
(Miller); 415-381-3343**

California

Chef Craig Stoll's (previously at Campton Place, Postrio, and Splendido) California cuisine is as intriguing as the name of this stylishly casual restaurant.

Emphasizing farm-fresh ingredients, the small menu offers satisfying starters including a hearts of romaine in a creamy anchovy and oregano vinaigrette, and a soothing lentil soup with smoked ham and cumin. Entrees range from a juicy roast chicken to the ever-popular seared pepper tuna with chive mashed potatoes. The service is professional and attentive, and the wine list, though predictable, is well edited to match the food. Desserts are sinfully good.

Breakfast/lunch Tuesday through Friday; dinner nightly; weekend brunch; full bar; AE, MC, V.

★★★★
$$$$$

Gatsby's

Sausalito: 39 Caledonia St. (between Pine and Johnson); 415-332-4500

California

A favorite since 1940 when it was the only jazz club in Marin, Gatsby's still has a contemporary feel with an airy, pleasant, high-ceilinged dining area. Favorite appetizers include traditional bruschetta, rock shrimp and calamari cakes, chicken quesadillas and deliciously spicy house pizza topped with chicken, jalapeños, mushrooms, yellow squash and mozzarella. Entrees range from a portobello mushroom-topped burger with shoestring potatoes to grilled rockfish with sweet corn risotto, summer squash and fresh basil. The all-California wine list is fairly standard and prices are quite reasonable. Service is prompt and attentive, even when the place gets packed.

Lunch/dinner daily; outdoor seating; smoke-free; full bar; live entertainment; AE, DC, MC, V.

★★★★
$$$$$

Gira Polli

Mill Valley: 590 E Blithedale Avenue; 415-383-6040

Italian

Gira Polli decided to open another branch in Mill Valley when so many commuters were taking their flavorful slow-roasted chickens home from the original North Beach location. While there's a small

selection of salads and pastas to choose from, it's the rosemary-and-lemon-flavored "turning chicken" you'll want, served with a side of slightly browned Palermo potatoes. Order the G.P. Special for $19.95 and you get a meal that easily feeds two: half a chicken, potatoes, salad, veggies, and a roll. It's easier to find a seat here, but if you want to eat quickly, best to order your goodies to go.

Dinner nightly; free parking lot; AE, MC, V, checks.

Guaymas

Tiburon: 5 Main Street (Main/Tiburon); 415-435-6300

Mexican

With its breathtaking location overlooking the bay, Angel Island, and the San Francisco skyline, this is a favorite spot for sipping margaritas and taking in the sights. Chef Francisco Cisneros has a skilled hand with Mexican classics such as pozole, a hearty stew from his native Jalisco; California-inspired variations like the crisp, deep-fried corn shells filled with braised duck, pasilla peppers, onions, and garlic; as well as the spicy tamales and seafood platter. Rainy days can be particularly pleasant here, especially if you sit by the fireplace and sip an aged tequila.

Lunch/dinner daily; view; live entertainment; full bar; AE, CB, DC, MC, V.

Guernica Restaurant

Sausalito: 2009 Bridgeway (at Spring); 415-332-1512

Basque

This simple, popular restaurant has been serving up robust Basque fare since 1974. Carefully tended by chef/owner Roger Minhondo, who was born and bred in the French Basque region, Guernica has a rustic charm with a personable waitstaff who greet regulars by first name, an old-fashioned dining room and an antique, carved-oak sideboard and wood bar. Don't miss Minhondo's famous paella Valenciana; other memorable dishes are baked-onion soup, *pâté de maison*, moist braised lamb shank with beans and grilled chicken napped in a kicky mustard-seed sauce. Minhondo's sinful desserts include a beautiful blackberry tart and a classic crème caramel.

Dinner nightly; full bar; free parking lot; AE, MC, V.

★★☆☆
$$$$$

Il Fornaio

Corte Madera: 223 Corte Madera Town Center; 415-927-4400

Italian

Kid friendly

Good for groups

Unlike its siblings in San Francisco and San Jose, the airy, stylish Corte Madera branch doesn't earn high marks for consistency, but generally offers well-prepared Italian standards, especially those items that come from the rotisserie, and wonderful baked goods. Pizzas and calzones are universally delightful, with a delicate smoky flavor. Interesting pasta choices include spinach and egg linguine tossed with shrimp, garlic and parsley and ravioli stuffed with spinach, Swiss chard and basil. The standard wine list is split between Italian and California wines. Dessert tortes, cakes, and cookies pay tribute to the skills of Il Fornaio's bakers.

Lunch/dinner daily; outdoor seating; fireplace; free parking lot; AE, DC, MC, V.

★★☆☆
$$$$$

Jennie Low

Mill Valley: 38 Miller Ave. (at Sunnyside); 415-388-8868

Chinese

Good for groups

Kid friendly

In 1987, Jennie Low, author of *Chopsticks, Cleaver and Wok*, the '70s bible of Chinese cooking, opened this fine restaurant featuring simple, highly personalized home-style dishes with velvety textures and subtle sauces. For entrees, anything preceded by the word "Jennie's" is a guaranteed winner, as are the wonderfully spicy green beans sautéed in a garlic sauce, or "Snow White chicken" with mushrooms, snow peas and bamboo shoots. Low also offers a few

California-esque dishes and several light creations prepared with no oil. This popular place is always packed but does a fine job of managing the chaos.

Lunch Monday-Saturday; dinner nightly; reservations required; AE, MC, V.

★★★★
$$$$$

Joe's Taco Lounge and Salsaria
Mill Valley: 382 Miller Ave. (at Montford); 415-383-8164

Mexican

Good deal

Kid friendly

Lit up like a Christmas tree at night, it's hard to miss this exuberant little taqueria serving delicious and inexpensive fare. Winning taco choices include grilled Pacific snapper topped with chili habanero mayo and salsa fresca or the breaded prawns with avocado mayo, lime, cilantro and salsa. Though the blending of ingredients is fairly standard, the freshness of each item, right down to the salsa, results in sublime simplicity. Quesadillas, burritos, enchiladas and Mexican pizzas round out the menu, and the "Well-Behaved Kids' menu" offers bargains for small fry not yet 12. Joe's serves up sangria, wine margaritas (no hard liquor) and beer.

Lunch/dinner daily; free parking lot; MC, V.

★★★★
$$$$$

Left Bank
Larkspur: 507 Magnolia Ave. (at Ward); 415-927-3331

French

Good for groups

Roland Passot, chef/owner of La Folie, has transformed the historic Blue Rock Inn into a fun, vibrant restaurant with phenomenal French brasserie-style food. The decor is as inspiring as the menu, with a massive stone fireplace, polished dark-wood bar and an airy dining room. The food is consistently excellent, including Passot's leek and onion tart and roasted duck breast garnished with a sour-cherry sauce. The sleekly chosen wine list features top-notch French and American selections. For the grand finale, indulge in the warm tarte Tatin, topped with caramelized Granny Smith apple slices and vanilla-bean ice cream.

Lunch/dinner daily; weekend brunch; outdoor seating; full bar; live entertainment; fireplace; valet parking; AE, MC, V.

★★★★
$$$$$

Mikayla

Sausalito: 801 Bridgeway (across from Tiffany Park); 415-331-5888

American

 Romantic

The Laurel Burch-designed interior of the Casa Madrona's elegant restaurant is sunny and pleasant, but subtle enough not to overshadow the famous panoramic views. Mikayla's popularity has steadily picked up since the menu has been updated. The menu, which changes daily, might include such memorable dishes as a foie gras "club sandwich" served on brioche with pancetta, frisée and grape salsa, a savory oxtail and potato stew with cilantro pesto, or grilled hamachi with beans and barbecued squid cakes. Traditional California wines spotted with a few French and German selections comprise the small wine list.

Dinner nightly; Sunday brunch; view; valet parking; AE, D, MC, V.

★★★★
$$$$$

Piazza D'Angelo

Mill Valley: 22 Miller Ave. (between Sunnyside and Throckmorton); 415-388-2000

Italian

 Good for groups

The menu at Mill Valley's popular Piazza D'Angelo abounds with good Italian fare, much of it familiar (rotisserie items, a classic *crostini misti*) but some of it more adventurous (wild game, guinea hen). For an unusual starter, try mixed greens with strawberries, corn and balsamic dressing made with Dijon and feta cheese. Of the numerous pasta plates, a favorite is spaghetti with kalamata olives, chiles, baby spinach, onions, sun-dried tomatoes, white wine and pecorino cheese. Calzones come out of the pizza oven puffy and light. The wine list features a selection of California and Italian labels, including several by the glass.

Lunch/dinner daily; weekend brunch; loud; outdoor seating; full bar; AE, MC, V.

Robata Grill & Sushi
Mill Valley: 591 Redwood Highway (Seminary Drive exit off Highway 101); 415-381-8400

Japanese

The fish is impeccably fresh at this casual restaurant, and the sushi is some of the best around. You'll find the usual range, done nigiri-, hosomaki- and futomaki-style, including plenty of vegetarian options: pickled plum, shiitake mushrooms, cucumber, etc. In the tradition of northern Japanese anglers, Robata (meaning "open fire") also grills beef, chicken, seafood and vegetables over a fire.

Lunch weekdays; dinner nightly; AE, DC, MC, V.

Sam's Anchor Cafe
Tiburon: 27 Main St. (at Tiburon Blvd.); 415-435-4527

American

Nothing beats a burger and brew on Sam's vast, sunny deck, particularly if you're one of the many who arrive by bicycle. While the food is not exactly bad, people come mainly for the party atmosphere and smashing view. The daytime menu offers burgers, fries, calamari and steamed clams; dinner features include cioppino, baked free-range chicken breast and New York steak with mashed potatoes, but nothing really distinguishes itself. Service is very casual but Sam's is the kind of place that just begs you to kick off your shoes and stay a while; once the sun sets, hop the ferry back to the city.

Lunch/dinner daily; weekend brunch; loud; view; outdoor seating; full bar; AE, DC, D, MC, V.

Scoma's of Sausalito

Sausalito: 588 Bridgeway (at Princess); 415-332-9551

Seafood

Good for groups

Kid friendly

In its three decades of existence, Scoma's has garnered a national reputation for excellence that seems amply deserved to some and mystifying to others. But this Sausalito landmark in a 19th-century Victorian that once housed a tugboat and ferry service is perpetually packed (mostly with tourists), and when the kitchen is humming, the eating can be mighty fine. The most popular dish is the shellfish sauté, but baby lobster tail, cioppino and simply prepared, grilled fish have their devotees. Scoma's also offers pasta and steak, plus a reasonably priced children's menu. The service is usually efficient, though not always charming, and the views are wonderful.

Lunch Thursday-Monday; dinner nightly; full bar; view; all major credit cards.

The Spinnaker

Sausalito: 100 Spinnaker Drive (at Bridgeway); 415-332-1500

Seafood

Good for groups

Kid friendly

Nearly the size of a department store, and set on the bay with gorgeous views, The Spinnaker occupies one of the choicest pieces of real estate in town. Though the decor and the food is merely nondescript, the restaurant still attracts a stream of tourists and moneyed regulars. The kitchen offers a dish for every palate: from oysters on the half shell and feta wrapped in phyllo to crab quesadillas and Caesar salads. The meat dishes are capably cooked if overly rich, but the pastas get too much time on the burner. The wine list contains mostly California wines, with a hefty markup.

Lunch/dinner daily; weekend brunch; view; full bar; valet parking; AE, DC, D, MC, V.

Sushi Maru

**Corte Madera: 59 Tamal Vista Blvd.;
(at 4th St.); 415-924-7874**

Japanese

Good deal

Good for groups

At this tranquil and attractive Japanese restaurant, Chef Toshi-san's beautifully sculpted sashimi and sushi sail around the circular bar on fish-shaped boats. Despite this gimmick, Sushi Maru is quite elegant, with ornate ceremonial wedding robes artfully displayed on the walls and piped-in Japanese music floating through the air. You can't go wrong with any of the sushi rolls, or the udon-noodle soup served with a choice of seafood, tempura flakes or vegetable toppings.

Lunch Monday-Saturday; dinner nightly; AE, D, MC, V.

Sushi Ran

Sausalito: 107 Caledonia St. (between Pine and Turney); 415-332-3620

Japanese

Good for groups

To the loyal patrons of this culinary landmark, sushi's not just a food, it's a way of life. The sushi here is impeccable, prepared with aplomb and served with a flourish by the amiable sushi chefs, who are truly expert at their art. The kamikaze roll is stuffed with yellowfin tuna, bright flying-fish roe and crunchy green onions; the spider roll enfolds a tempura-fried soft-shell crab. Many kinds of sushi, plus grilled and salted fish, are served here. Rice-wine lovers can choose from 17 sakes, including two from Napa. Weekend nights are particularly packed, so be prepared to wait.

Lunch weekdays; dinner nightly; AE, D, MC, V.

★★★☆
$$$$$

Sushi to Dai For

Tiburon: 1771 Tiburon Blvd. (at Main);
415-789-0919

Japanese

After eight years of successfully serving sushi in his San Rafael restaurant, owner/chef Dai Takeda opened this branch in Tiburon in 1996. It's been a success, judging by the weekend crowds. No fewer than 19 sushi rolls are offered here, including the delicious spider roll with soft-shell crab and dragon roll (tempura shrimp, crab, cucumber, sprouts, eel and avocado). Yakitori, tempura, teriyaki and other Japanese fare are also featured. Service is attentive and casual, and seating is mostly at the sushi bar, though there are a few small tables scattered about the simply decorated room.

Lunch weekdays; dinner nightly; view; outdoor
seating; prix fixe menu; validated parking; AE,
D, MC, V.

★★★☆
$$$$$

Tutto Mare Restaurant

Tiburon: 9 Main St. (at Tiburon Blvd.);
415-435-4747

Italian

 Good for groups

Kid friendly

One can get lost in the ambience of the good life sitting on the upper deck of Tutto Mare, a sibling of the popular Guaymas. Roasted fish, grilled meats, pastas and crisp-crust pizzas are served in both the downstairs taverna and more formal ristorante upstairs. Some standouts include pear and pecorino salad, seafood linguine with clams, mussels and shrimp, and grilled sirloin steak. The respectable wine and beer lists offer plenty of choices. Tutto Mare is extremely popular with locals and tourists, and though the Italian-inspired fare is generally good, it doesn't always live up to the astounding views.

Lunch/dinner daily; view; full bar; live entertain-
ment; AE, D, MC, V.